Dear Reader:

The book you are about to read is the latest bestseller from the St. Martin's True Crime Library, the imprint *The New York Times* calls "the leader in true crime!" The True Crime Library offers you fascinating accounts of the latest, most sensational crimes that have captured the national attention. St. Martin's is the publisher of John Glatt's riveting and horrifying SECRETS IN THE CELLAR, which shines a light on the man who shocked the world when it was revealed that he had kept his daughter locked in his hidden basement for 24 years. In the Edgar-nominated WRITTEN IN BLOOD, Diane Fanning looks at Michael Peterson, a Marine-turned-novelist found guilty of beating his wife to death and pushing her down the stairs of their home—only to reveal another similar death from his past. In the book you now hold, SECRETS OF A MARINE'S WIFE, Shanna Hogan investigates a case of illicit romance gone horribly wrong.

St. Martin's True Crime Library gives you the stories behind the headlines. Our authors take you right to the scene of the crime and into the minds of the most notorious murderers to show you what really makes them tick. St. Martin's True Crime Library paperbacks are better than the most terrifying thriller, because it's all true! The next time you want a crackling good read, make sure it's got the St. Martin's True Crime Library logo on the spine—you'll be up all night!

Charles E. Spicer, Jr.
Executive Editor, St. Martin's True Crime Library

Secrets
of a
Marine's
Wife

A True Story of Marriage,

Obsession, and Murder

Shanna Hogan

St. Martin's Paperbacks

Published in the United States by St. Martin's Paperbacks, an imprint of St. Martin's Publishing Group.

SECRETS OF A MARINE'S WIFE

For information, address St. Martin's Publishing Group, 120 Broadway, New York, NY 10271.

www.stmartins.com

ISBN: 978-1-250-12731-0

Our books may be purchased in bulk for promotional, educational, or business use. Please contact your local bookseller or the Macmillan Corporate and Premium Sales Department at 1-800-221-7945, ext. 5442, or by email at MacmillanSpecialMarkets@macmillan.com.

Printed in the United States of America

St. Martin's Press hardcover edition / February 2019
St. Martin's Paperbacks edition / December 2019

10 9 8 7 6 5 4 3 2 1

*Dedicated to the volunteer cavers from the
San Bernardino County Cave
and Technical Rescue team*

Chapter 1

A festering odor wafted from the derelict mine shaft on the edge of the remote Mojave Desert, just north of California's Joshua Tree National Park.

Stooping to examine the ten-by-ten-foot pit, caver Luca Chiarabini winced. The stench reeked of gasoline mixed with something putrid and indistinguishable. Flashlight in hand, he scanned the darkness, but the yawning chasm was too deep for the beam to illuminate the floor of the mine. Rising to his feet, he wiped the sweat from his forehead and gazed across the vast, endless wasteland. Creosote bushes and gnarled Joshua trees dotted the desolate open desert. Jagged rock formations loomed over the ground pockmarked with abandoned mine shafts—relics of the California gold rush.

Chiarabini, a wiry, shaggy-haired native of Italy, blinked hard and released a deep breath. *Could this be it?* he wondered. *After all this time, have we finally found her?*

For the past seven weeks, Chiarabini and his fellow volunteer cavers from the San Bernardino County Cave and Technical Rescue team had been on a mission most macabre. Teaming up with California homicide detectives, they were searching for the remains of a missing nineteen-year-old girl named Erin Corwin, the wife of a Marine.

On the morning of June 28, 2014, Erin Corwin had left her apartment at the Marine Corps Air Ground Combat Center in Twentynine Palms, California. Her husband, Marine corporal Jon Corwin, had told detectives she was headed to Joshua Tree National Park to scout scenic spots for an upcoming visit with her mother. But Erin never returned.

She was three weeks pregnant.

Evidence pointed to foul play. Detectives believed Erin had been murdered and discarded in one of the more than one thousand mines and horizontal passages—known as adits—that fall within the Dale, Eagle Mountain, and Brooklyn mining districts, a cluster of shuttered gold mines fifteen miles east of Twentynine Palms.

The original search area had covered approximately two thousand square miles, including Joshua Tree National Park, the Twentynine Palms Marine base, and the unincorporated community of Amboy, a ghost town off historic Route 66. Detectives had tapped a professional local caver to draft a map of the mines in the region, highlighting the ones most likely to conceal a dead body. Using forensics and electronic evidence, detectives had narrowed the search to the mining districts just outside of the park, about a two-hour drive from downtown Twentynine Palms. Aerial searches had identified more than a hundred potential burial sites.

Searchers worked in teams, breaking into crews of two and three to check and clear each of the mines. Days began as early as 3:00 a.m. as summer temperatures soared past 115 degrees. To guard themselves from the fragile state of the abandoned mines, the rescuers wore long-sleeve shirts, helmets, and protective gear.

By the seventh week, hundreds of mines had been thoroughly searched and cleared from the lists. But there was no sign of Erin. As the expansive and costly search stretched on, hope had begun to fade and resources were dwindling. The San Bernardino County Sheriff's Department decided that this was it: Saturday, August 16, would be the last day they would officially look for Erin.

"We felt like we had one more shot at it," recalled San Bernardino County Sheriff's detective Daniel Hanke, one of the lead investigators on the case.

The sun was still high in the sky at about 4:30 p.m., when Chiarabini and his team headed to the very last location on their list—a 140-foot deep hole in the shadows of a sheer cliff. Approaching the pit, a glimmer of light caught the attention of one of the cavers on Chiarabini's team. Near the collar of the mine, a spent brass bullet casing twinkled in the sunlight. The rescuer picked up the shell casing with a gloved hand and placed it in a plastic evidence bag. Kneeling beside the mine, Chiarabini peered into the darkness. Then he reached for the radio on his belt.

A few miles east, John Norman, coordinator for the rescue team, was clearing a different mine with his team when Chiarabini's voice crackled on the radio.

"We found something. We're at site 108," Chiarabini said. "Could you come over and help set up the bucket cam?"

To expedite the search, Norman had created a device to record video from inside the mine using a one-gallon bucket, a generic GoPro camera, a floodlight, and model airplane batteries he borrowed from a neighbor. Dubbed the "bucket cam," the device could be dropped down the shaft and record footage of the bottom of a mine, making it much easier for the team to evaluate prospective open graves.

At forty, Norman was lean with closely cropped dark blond hair that contrasted with his tan complexion. Gathering their supplies, Norman and his crew piled into the truck. After a half hour of crawling over the rocky and sandy terrain, he and his two teammates arrived at the site, joining half a dozen rescuers and sheriff's deputies already huddled around the mine.

At first glance, the mine appeared to be little more than an anonymous hole in the ground—no different from the dozens of other mines they had searched. But immediately, Norman was struck by the smell. The rescuers had inadvertently stirred up the air inside the mine, and a noxious scent was now billowing to the surface.

"It was awful. Everyone on the surface could smell this really bad decay sort of smell," Norman recalled. "It was like gasoline and possibly some sort of human decomposition."

The vertical chute sloped gradually to one side, making it impossible to simply lower the bucket cam from the mouth of the mine. Instead, someone would need to descend into the hole, pass the gradient, dangle partway down the shaft, and lower the camera down to fish around the debris.

"Any volunteers?" Norman asked, imploring the other searchers.

Glancing to his left and right, Chiarabini saw no other volunteers, so he stepped forward.

"I'll go down," he said. "I have a mask."

A software engineer by day, Chiarabini joined the rescue team in 2010 and spent weekends volunteering on caving rescue-and-recovery missions. An intrepid adventurer, Chiarabini was typically the first to volunteer for a challenge. He retrieved from his backpack a face mask that covered his nose and mouth as the other cavers fashioned their equipment into an intricate rapelling system. A large tripod was situated above the mine. The cavers weaved a climbing rope through the tripod, latching it onto a truck. The rigging would allow Chiarabini to drop down the center of the mine and avoid touching the walls.

Belaying the rope to his harness, Chiarabini stepped backward into the hole, slowly descending into the darkness. A few feet underground, the air was dank and cooler. The clatters of crumbling rocks echoed off the walls as they tumbled to the mine's floor.

When he got about twenty feet down, a gas detector on his belt alerted Chiarabini that the air was toxic and lacked oxygen. Because he was breathing oxygen through the face mask, he was safe. But the fumes stung his eyes, causing them to water.

"The smell of the gas was so intense," Chiarabini remembered. "When I went thirty or forty feet down, it was just unbearable."

Once he passed the slope, Chiarabini fed the rope through his gloved hands, lowering the bucket. The light attached to the base of the bucket illumined the shaft. Squinting, he could almost make out the outline of a body coiled on the floor.

"I couldn't quite distinguish what it was," he recalled. "From where I was at, it looked almost like she was headless."

Just then, the voice of one of the detectives rang out from above, resonating off the rock walls. "Can you go any lower?"

Chiarabini mumbled quickly, "I'm almost suffocating here." When he tipped back the mask to talk, his lungs burned.

After about fifteen minutes underground, Chiarabini

was hauled back to the surface. He stepped away from the shaft, pulled back his mask, and started wildly coughing. The sticky scent clung to his clothes and hair and even adhered to his skin. Later, he would have to throw away his clothes because the smell would not dissipate, even after several washes.

Meanwhile, Norman took the memory card from the GoPro camera and inserted it into his personal laptop. He and Detective Jonathan Woods reviewed the footage. The video was dark and difficult to decipher. In the center of a pile of debris was a narrow object that appeared vaguely like the remains of a human being.

"It could be a body," Norman told detectives. "It's hard to tell."

Crumbling rocks covered the floor of the mine, along with a discarded tire and what looked like a propane tank, which seemed to be venting toxic fumes into the shaft. Remarkably, Woods told the crew that a propane tank and tire actually aligned with the evidence in the case. It was decided Chiarabini would descend into the mine again and lower the camera farther to gather better footage. By then, the camera's memory card was nearly full, so Norman took the SIM card from his personal cell phone and inserted it in the camera.

On the second run, Chiarabini tried to get as close to the bottom as possible, letting the camera hover over the floor and swing for several minutes before once again being towed to the surface. Norman reviewed the footage.

"This time it looked very strongly like a person," Norman recalled. "You could see what seemed to be feet, and maybe something like a face or a head."

Conferring privately, the detectives considered their next move. It was essential to prove it was Erin's body at the bottom of the mine, and they needed to capture a close-up image of her corpse on video. After a brief discussion, it was decided another volunteer would enter the mine and drop as low to the bottom as possible. Because he had a full-faced respirator with him that would protect him from the fumes, searcher Justin Wheaton, thirty years old, volunteered to descend farther than Chiarabini. Dressed in a set of coveralls and harness, he clipped onto the climbing rope.

An inch at a time, Wheaton descended below the surface. When he was just feet from the bottom, he called out on his radio, "Stop." Hanging above the dirt floor, Wheaton focused the beam of light from his bucket cam on the ground. Then he saw her.

The obscenely broken body bore no resemblance to the pretty young brunette Wheaton had seen on missing persons flyers posted around the Marine base. Curled facedown, her knees were bent, arms splayed. Her body was in the late stages of decomposition, her skin withered and blackened. She was still clothed in the tattered remains of a pink shirt and jean shorts.

Gawking at the body, it was almost impossible for Wheaton to imagine the ghastly cadaver was once a beautiful, living person. Suspended inside the mine, just a few feet from the corpse, he called over the radio, "It's her."

Above ground, a somber silence fell over the rescue team.

"Everything stopped. It was definitely a powerful moment," Norman recalled. "The seven weeks plus of searching had reached its conclusion. We were no longer in the search phase. We know she's there; we know she's deceased. There's no one to save, unfortunately. At that point, our mission changes to recovery."

The searchers and homicide detectives gathered to discuss options. The detectives wanted to retrieve Erin as soon as possible and suggested sending down another caver with a respirator. But the crew had concerns.

"I don't think we can do this ourselves," Norman told a detective. "This is more of a hazmat situation. It's better to call the fire department or someone who does this every day."

As the sun sank behind the mountain peaks, the search was called off for the day. Sheriff's deputies were stationed at the site overnight to guard the crime scene. After packing up their gear, three of the searchers drove to the San Bernardino County Sheriff's Department to surrender all contaminated equipment that might be considered evidence.

Meanwhile, the detectives made arrangements to bring in a crew of firefighters the following day. A helicopter would also be stationed near the mine, and a forensic dentist would be brought to the coroner's office to identify the body once it was recovered. Recovery efforts would commence in the morning.

Erin Corwin would spend one more night on the floor of the filthy hole that had served as her tomb for nearly two months.

A massive search effort that had once spread across thousands of miles of desert was now focused on a single ten-by-ten-foot hole. The recovery began that Sunday at sunrise, as sheriff's detectives, deputies, volunteer rescuers, and five firefighters from the elite San Bernardino County Fire Department's Urban Search and Rescue team, plus three additional county firefighters, made their way to the Mojave. The firefighters, who specialized in mine searches, had all been trained to work in tight spaces with sophisticated breathing gear. At the entrance to Joshua Tree National Park, the fire trucks parked—they were too massive to traverse the treacherous hillsides. The firefighters transferred their equipment to the sheriff's department's SUVs and trucks.

By noon, more than a dozen public safety workers surrounded the mine. Most of the crew stayed huddled under a shaded red tent. The caving crew handled the rigging, spending the morning positioning the tripod above the hole and stringing together a maze of rope.

At about 3:00 p.m., when temperatures simmered at around 106 degrees, firefighter Brenton Baum entered the mine shaft. Lanky with cropped brown hair, Baum was admittedly claustrophobic. But his job consistently required him to push his personal boundaries. Wearing yellow coveralls and an orange helmet with a mask that covered his entire face, Baum was lowered into the mine until he was just feet from the corpse.

"It was eerie," Baum recalled at being more than a hundred feet underground. "It was deeper than I had ever been."

While suspended above the grisly scene, Baum used a camera to snap photos, which would later be used as evidence. Erin's body was partially concealed by rocks and debris. An empty, translucent green Sprite bottle sat on the side of the mine shaft. A length of blue climbing rope was tied around a white propane tank smeared with blood and muck. Two dusty water jugs, etched with the words *Property of the U.S. Government,* were lying near Erin's head.

Methodically documenting and collecting evidence, Baum delivered each item back to the surface. In addition to the rope and water tanks, he retrieved zip ties, pieces of black plastic, and about six to eight inches of black electrical tape. After nearly forty-five minutes underground, he was drenched in sweat and feeling fatigued. The fire captain decided to rotate

Baum with another firefighter. When Baum emerged onto the surface and removed his respirator, he fell to his knees.

"When I took my mask off, I was hit with this smell all the sudden," he remembered. "I smelt it in the top side because it was all saturated in my clothes. I started dry heaving."

Changing places with Baum was Paul Anastasia, a burly veteran firefighter with coifed dark brown hair graying around the temples. Anastasia clipped the rope to his harness and narrowed the beam of his flashlight on the floor of the mine. But once he reached the bottom, he recognized that retrieving the body was going to be more difficult than expected.

"I realized that that was a false bottom," Anastasia explained. "I had no idea how deep that shaft was."

A wooden platform had been wedged into the shaft, cutting off access to lower sections of the mine. The floor was likely rotted and could easily collapse. If it fell through, Erin might be buried so deep she could never be recovered.

Suspended in midair, Anastasia gently examined the body. Erin's head was thrown forward, her brown hair matted and darkened with soot. Looped around her neck was a braided nylon cord tied to two pieces of rebar. Later, Anastasia would learn the device was a crude, homemade garrote—a weapon used to strangle the life out of a human being.

Once the body shifted, Anastasia noticed something else. In the corner of the mine was a flat wooden stick with some sort of green cloth wrapped around the top and knotted with white twine. It appeared to be some sort of unburned homemade torch. Along with the propane tank and gasoline smell, it became clear that someone had tried to incinerate the body and the contents of the mine. Suddenly, Anastasia realized how combustible the situation truly was. If not for the lack of oxygen, the mine would have burst into flames.

Gently, Anastasia placed Erin's frail corpse into two body bags, cradled both under his arms, and carried her to the surface. When he emerged, the sun had just slipped into the desert.

Erin's body was flown by helicopter to the morgue, where a coroner and forensic dentist conducted an autopsy. She was so decomposed and disfigured she had to be identified using dental records. But by 9:30 p.m., the body was confirmed to be that of Erin Corwin.

"I felt it was a small miracle. I get emotional just thinking about that day," Detective Hanke recalled. "All these hours we had worked and just thinking deep down inside she's got to be somewhere in one of these last caves. She just has to be. And actually having that confirmed, it was just overwhelming emotion."

The eight-week investigation was one of the most prolonged and technically difficult searches in the history of San Bernardino County. On the day they'd determined to be the last, Erin Corwin had been found.

The disappearance of a pregnant young wife in the summer of 2014 had astonished the military town of Twentynine Palms and cast suspicion on her Marine husband. But the discovery of Erin Corwin's mummified corpse at the bottom of the mine shaft would expose an insidious tale of devious deception, lurid betrayal, and venomous hatred. Unbeknownst to the teenager, she was being pursued by a predator skulking behind a uniform at the world's largest Marine base.

Erin's brutal murder would unearth a mystery much deeper and darker than any mine shaft in the Mojave.

Chapter 2

A few minutes before midnight, a shrill screech roused Bill and Lore Heavilin from a fitful sleep in the master bedroom of their home in Oak Ridge, Tennessee.

The moment her cell phone rang, Lore knew it was bad. Over the past eight weeks, as California detectives searched for her missing daughter, Lore had set her phone on a specific, obnoxious ringtone so she would be sure not to miss their call. Glancing at her cell phone screen, she confirmed it was Detective Jonathan Woods calling. Releasing a deep breath, Lore answered the phone.

"We think we found Erin," the detective told her.

The blood drained from Lore's face; her stomach sank. Lore Heavilin would never again see her compassionate, trusting teenage daughter—the shy, gentle girl who connected passionately with animals. The sweet soul who trained her cat to do tricks, taught a rabbit to walk on a leash, and tamed a thousand-pound quarter horse. Erin Renae Corwin died just shy of her twentieth birthday. Yet in her short nineteen years of life, she had touched countless lives, leaving an enduring impact.

Born on July 15, 1994, in a hospital in Chattanooga, Tennessee, Erin was just two weeks old when her birth mother, Debra, made the difficult decision to give her up. By that time, Debra had already proven herself ill equipped to raise a child. Her three sons had all either been adopted or were being raised by their fathers or paternal grandparents. Just days after Debra gave birth to Erin, Debra's own parents realized their daughter was incapable of caring for her newborn. They issued an ultimatum: Debra could temporarily place the baby in the Tennessee Baptist Children's Home while she prepared to raise her properly or they would call Department of Children's Services and report her as an unfit parent. Debra chose the first option and placed her newborn in foster care.

What was a burden for her birth mother would become a blessing for Tennessee foster parents Bill and Lore Heavilin.

Bill and Lore both grew up in Indiana and met at a Catholic youth retreat when they were in high school. Then sixteen, Lore was the oldest of three girls. She was born in Indiana; her sisters were born in New Mexico. Her father worked for the government, and the family moved around to Hawaii, Connecticut, and New Mexico before returning to Indiana. Throughout her childhood, Lore's parents fostered numerous children, which would have a meaningful and lasting impact on her life.

Born and raised in Indiana, Bill was the second oldest of ten children. Six of his siblings had the last name *Heavilin,* while the other four were from his mother's second marriage. His father worked for the post office.

Four years after meeting, Bill and Lore were married. Lore, who turned twenty just five days before the wedding, wore a long-sleeved white gown and a floppy hat encircled with ribbon covering her short, dark hair. Sporting a mustache and oversized glasses, Bill dressed in a tuxedo with a ruffled shirt and black bow tie. The young couple appeared happy and in love.

"We were high school sweethearts," Lore remarked. "I think we just always knew we were going to get married."

The Heavilins settled in Kouts, Indiana, a small former farming town with a population of 1,600. Like his father, Bill got a job working for the post office, a career he would stay with for decades. In 1978, when Lore was twenty-two, she gave birth to the couple's first daughter, Kristy. Two years later, they had a son, Keith.

While Keith was a fussy baby, childhood was idyllic for both the kids. Lore was a very dedicated mother and highly involved in her children's after-school activities. Family vacations were spent in Texas or visiting relatives in Tennessee. Sundays were spent in church. Each evening, Lore, who loved to cook and bake, prepared a meal and the family gathered at the dining room table to talk about their day. It was a tradition—no matter how many people were there, they always ate dinner at the table together.

The Heavilins possessed a strong relationship with God. In Indiana, they were active in their small Baptist church, where everybody in the town seemed to congregate. In the mideighties, Lore and Bill believe they received a message from the Lord. Kristy was then in second grade and Keith was in kindergarten when God led them to their calling: fostering newborns and babies who needed a safe, temporary home.

"We didn't decide. God convinced us that we were to foster," Lore remembered. "At first, I kind of fought it."

Having grown up in a home with foster children, Lore knew how difficult it could be to care for a baby that she'd later have to give up. While contemplating foster care, the Heavilins spoke with an employee at the Baptist Children's Home. For several weeks, the worker was supposed to bring the Heavilins an application to start the foster care process, but he kept forgetting. A part of Lore, already apprehensive about becoming a foster parent, was relieved by the delay.

Then, one day in 1985, while saying her devotions to God, she asked the Lord a question about being a foster parent. "Why do I want to mess up what I already know?"

That's when she heard a message from above.

"God just said to me, 'With me, you made it through your son's infancy. I will be with you with whatever child I place in your home,'" Lore recalled.

The next day, Lore drove directly to the Baptist Children's Home and picked up an application to be a foster parent. She spent the afternoon grocery shopping and running errands, and when she returned home, the phone was ringing. It was a friend named Becky, who was in charge of the foster parent program.

"I heard you picked up an application to be a foster parent today," Becky said, explaining they had a new baby in foster care who needed a home.

At first, Lore was hesitant. "I thought we would have months before we had to really make that decision," Lore remembered.

Although Lore no longer had the baby essentials, Becky offered a crib and car seat; other foster moms donated clothes and purchased bottles. Becky had also already consulted the Heavilins' pastor as a reference. The required home study ended up being a formality, since everyone at the church already knew the Heavilin family. That same afternoon Lore picked up the foster parent application, the family received baby Matthew.

For the next ten months, they cared for Matthew as if he were their own, before a loving family adopted him.

"When he was adopted, we mourned him as if he died," Lore recalled. "It was rough."

A month after Matthew left the home, the Heavilins decided to relocate to Oak Ridge, Tennessee, to be closer to Lore's family. In 1986, Bill got approval to transfer post offices, and the Heavilins relocated.

In eastern Tennessee, about twenty-five miles west of Knoxville, Oak Ridge has a storied history. The town didn't exist before December 7, 1941, when the Japanese bombed Pearl Harbor during World War II. In response, the city sprang up as the national administrative headquarters for the Manhattan Project, a top-secret operation resulting in the development of the atom bomb. As the production site for the Manhattan Project, the city population ballooned to seventy-five thousand.

Nicknamed the "Secret City" and the "Atomic City," power plants were established throughout Oak Ridge to manufacture materials used for war, including the K-25 uranium-separating facility, which was the largest building in the world in 1945. All plant employees wore badges, with the buildings surrounded by fencing and guard towers, creating an ominous atmosphere.

"We joke that everybody who lives in Oak Ridge glows in the dark," Lore remarked with a laugh.

After the war ended, the population dwindled to about thirty-one thousand people, but Oak Ridge remains one of the world's leading centers for scientific research and development. While the federal government has since reduced the size of the projects, they continue to be the city's biggest employer and main source of revenue.

At first, the Heavilins lived in an apartment in Oak Ridge. Within months, they purchased a quaint, 1,100-square-foot house originally built in the 1950s. About five years after they bought the house, Lore's parents rented a property across the street.

In Oak Ridge, the family became active in the local Southern Baptist church. Through the pastor, they also began fostering children through the Tennessee Baptist Children's Home.

For the next several years, the Heavilins mainly fostered newborn babies during the interim period when parents still had a chance to change their minds before signing their rights away. The children would stay in the family's care for about four weeks before they were either placed with a permanent adopted family or returned to their birth parents. While it was rewarding to care for newborns, it was also emotionally taxing.

"You definitely bond with each of them," Lore explained. "And a piece of your heart goes with every one of them."

In 1989, the family took in a seventeen-month-old boy named Alex, who suffered from learning disabilities and was eventually diagnosed with fetal alcohol syndrome. The family grew to love Alex, and Bill expressed interest in adopting him permanently into the family.

Alex was the youngest of four biological children. Two of his older siblings had been adopted by different families. His brother, then nine-year-old Jon, was living in a group home. Like Alex, Jon had special needs, having been diagnosed with attention deficit hyperactivity disorder and other behavioral problems.

Officials from the Baptist Children's Home asked the Heavilins if they would be willing to take in Jon as well. The Heavilins agreed and made room in the house for both boys. Two years later, in 1992, when Jon was eleven and Alex was five, the Heavilins officially adopted their new sons. Because of Alex's disability, Bill and Lore became his conservators, and he would remain in their custody throughout his adult life.

A couple of years later, the Heavilins took in a fifteen-year-old girl named Taylor with the intention of adopting her. That adoption was made official in the spring of 1995, when Taylor became the newest member of the Heavilin family.

As the family grew, so did their house. They constructed a second story and increased the square footage to 2,500, with five bedrooms and three bathrooms.

By 1994, Lore's oldest children were enrolled in Oak Ridge High School, while the boys were in middle school. Kristy and Keith were both active in the school band, and as a parent-volunteer, Lore sewed the band's uniforms and attended nearly every event practice.

That summer, as Lore was preparing to go to band camp for the weekend with her oldest children, the family received a call from the Baptist Children's Home: a newborn baby girl needed a home.

Chapter 3

Weighing just five pounds, three ounces, the scrawny newborn peered up from her crib through doe-like blue eyes. Gurgling with laughter, she curled her tiny fingers around Lore Heavilin's pinkie. The three week-old baby would be named Erin Renae.

The Monday after the family returned from band camp, the Heavilins took Erin in as a foster child. But when Lore held the newborn for the first time, something told her the baby was where she was meant to be.

"The day she came, I knew she was not leaving," Lore remembered. "Her birth mom sent everything she had for her, including a size two dress. That said something to me. I just felt like the birth mom wasn't going to do what she needed to do to get her back."

The family quickly fell in love with Erin. When she joined the family, the older children were all teenagers, and Alex was six.

"I often said that she was a breath of fresh air amongst our normal chaotic life," Lore recalled. "We were blessed to be chosen to be her family."

Both Kristy and Taylor were sixteen and adored their new baby sister, carrying her around like a little doll.

"We thought she was the sweetest little thing," Lore remembered. "They loved her."

A quiet baby, Erin slept late and loved being held. She became a regular at Oak Ridge High School football games, which Lore attended to support the school band. Tucked inside a front-facing carrier, the baby would snuggle against Lore's chest. A friend of Lore's even made a tiny sweatshirt, denoting Erin the "band baby."

When Erin was three years old, her adoption became official: She was a Heavilin.

Around this time, the Heavilins began to feel that the local Baptist church was not a good fit for the family. They separated from the Baptist faith and joined a small nondenominational church. They continued to foster children through Tennessee's Department of Children's Services and Bethany Christian Services.

Because of Alex's learning disabilities, he struggled in school. When he was in fourth grade and Erin was in preschool, Bill and Lore decided to homeschool Alex out of the dining room of their home. A year and a half later, when Erin was starting first grade, they began homeschooling her as well.

"I was never going to homeschool, but when God tells you to homeschool, you don't argue with Him," Lore explained.

To homeschool the children, Lore needed to remake her home. By 1999, the four older siblings had all graduated from high school and moved out of the Heavilins' house, and Lore converted one of the spare rooms into the classroom for Alex and Erin. Taught by her mother, Erin excelled in math, science, and history. She tolerated English and hated writing, although she was a remarkable storyteller.

Over the years, the Heavilins owned dozens of animals, including dogs, cats, guinea pigs, rabbits, and fish. Surrounded by pets, Erin grew up with a special fondness for animals. There was something about her peaceful demeanor that animals gravitated toward. Sister Taylor jokingly called her Elly May Clampett, the animal-addicted daughter on the 1960s show *The Beverly Hillbillies*.

"Erin was very calm, very patient," Lore recalled. "She was loving and nurturing from a very young age."

Lore would take Erin to the pond to feed the ducks. Family photos capture the girl sitting with her legs crossed, ducks flocking around her, pecking bread crumbs from her hand. When Erin was a toddler, the family had a pet rabbit named Kendall. Lore often let the rabbit out to hop around the fenced backyard. But when it was time to return the rabbit to its hutch, Kendall would be difficult to catch. One day, Lore turned to her daughter and asked, "Would you catch Kendall for me?" Chasing after the bunny, Erin crouched down, and the creature leaped easily into her arms. When Erin got a little older, she even taught the rabbit to walk down the sidewalk on a leash. On another occasion, the family was watching Keith's pet cat when it escaped. It was missing for three days before Erin finally said, "Why don't you let me catch him?"

"A few minutes later, she walks in with the cat," Lore remembered.

Erin was even able to train her own cat. In a cell phone video, she demonstrated her cat performing tricks typically executed by trained dogs.

"Shake," Erin says as the cat stretches out his paw and lays it on her palm. "Good boy." The cat's tail waves back and forth as Erin points to the floor and adds, "Lie down." The cat curls its feet under its body and sits, staring at Erin.

"She was like the animal whisperer," recalled one of her best friends. "She could train any animal to do whatever she wanted."

Erin grew up knowing she was adopted. The Heavilins permitted all their adopted children to keep in contact with members of their birth families. While Erin's birth mom was seldom in her life, Debra's parents remained close with the girl.

"She had an incredible relationship with her maternal birth grandparents," Lore explained. "We were open to her birth mom having contact with her, but she never really took advantage of that."

In 1999, Erin turned five. That October, the Heavilins brought home another baby girl. Bill and Lore first met baby Trisha in the neonatal intensive care unit in a hospital in Tennessee. The baby had been born with multiple birth defects, including spina bifida, a condition in which the backbone and membranes don't close completely around the spinal cord.

When Trisha joined the Heavilin family, the girl was just five months old and had spent most of her life in the hospital's infant intensive care unit, where seventeen different doctors treated her.

Before Trisha could leave the hospital, Lore spent a week working with medical professionals, learning how to care for the baby's unique disabilities. At home, Lore situated Trisha in the living room, where she was attached to an oxygen tank, a Sleep Apnea Monitor, a Pulse Oximeter, and a feeding tube.

"We thought if she was in the living room, she could interact with people better than if she was in a bedroom," Lore recalled. "We wanted her to be a part of the family."

The entire family doted on Trisha. Thrilled to be a

big sister, Erin loved to play with the baby and make her smile. For the first six months of Trisha's life, on doctors' orders, she was not permitted to leave the house aside from medical appointments. During this time, Lore's mother helped provide childcare for the other kids, as the Heavilins learned to adjust to Trisha's needs.

"It was pretty overwhelming when she joined our family," remembered Lore. "But it got to the point where we could do it in our sleep."

Because of the spina bifida, Trisha's nerve endings didn't function, and she needed a catheter to urinate. This caused frequent kidney infections, and doctors later operated on her bladder.

Much of the first few years of Trisha's life were spent in the hospital. In January 2001, when she was just twenty-one months old, the Heavilins officially adopted her. The same day the adoption was finalized, Trisha was in the pediatric intensive care unit, having had her tonsils and adenoids removed two days prior. Her breathing was so compromised following the surgery that Trisha had to be monitored closely for days.

Then tragedy struck. When Trisha was just three, she contracted an infection that spread to her bloodstream. Trisha became septic and died from blood poisoning on April 29, 2003. The entire family was shattered.

"It was really hard on Erin," Lore recalled. "Because she always wanted to be a big sister. She cried a lot."

After Trisha's death, the family continued to foster newborns but would never adopt another child.

Because Erin and Alex were both homeschooled, the Heavilins joined the New Life Baptist Church, a bigger church with a more active youth group. When they were still in grade school, both kids also attended the Smoky Mountain Christian Camp, a nature program and retreat in the small rural town of Tellico Plains, Tennessee.

Erin was close with all of her siblings, but because Alex was the closest in age, they participated in many of the same activities.

"When they were young, they were best of buds," Lore recalled.

When Erin was ten, she joined the 4-H club, a youth organization with 6.5 million members in fifty countries around the world. The name of the organization represents four personal development areas of focus: head, heart, hands, and health.

Erin was drawn to the 4-H equestrian program. While she adored all animals, through 4-H she discovered a true passion for horses. Eager for any opportunity to be around a horse, Erin became a fixture at the East Tennessee Riding Club and barn, a peaceful horse farm about four miles from the Heavilins' house. She quickly ingratiated herself among the horse owners.

"For a period of time, she offered to help people when they were on vacation, take their horses out when they weren't here," remembered friend Victoria Alphen. "People thought she was a great helper for that."

Linda Comly, an Oak Ridge native in her seventies, housed a horse at the East Tennessee Riding Club.

"Erin grew up at that barn," Linda recalled. "I told her that one day. I said, 'Erin, you've got a way with horses.'"

The two became unlikely friends, with Erin visiting Linda for "grandma talk."

Erin would end up meeting many of her friends at the barn. When she was in fifth grade, she was introduced to a boy at the barn who changed her life forever. Jonathan Wayne Corwin didn't much care for horses, but his younger sister did and kept a horse at the same barn as Erin. The two girls became friends, and Erin occasionally hung out at the Corwins' house.

At the time, Jon saw Erin as his little sister's friend. But as Erin blossomed from a skinny, shy ten-year-old to a beautiful and bubbly teenager, Jon Corwin would be one of the first to take notice.

When Erin was twelve, a family friend gave her an Arabian rescue horse named Autumn. Owning a horse is a substantial responsibility, which Erin took on with dedication and enthusiasm. Twice a day, Lore took her youngest kids to the barn, where Erin was charged with feeding, exercising, bathing, and caring for the horse.

Erin spent countless hours at the barn training and riding Autumn, and she became fascinated with the sport of barrel racing, a rodeo event popular with female riders. In barrel racing, the horse and rider compete to navigate around three large barrels in the quickest amount of time. The sport combines the athletic ability of a horse with the skills of a rider.

As she practiced the sport, Erin would regularly show off her skills performing at the barn. In addition, she trained for showmanship, trail, hunter, and hunter jumper competitions.

In 2008, Erin's horse suffered a splint fracture. Unable to perform jumps or tricks, the Heavilins decided to donate Autumn to a family friend. Because Erin had been responsible with Autumn, her parents decided to buy her a two-year-old brown quarter horse named Rye Leigh.

As Erin trained Rye Leigh, a special bond formed. She rode the horse nearly every day, before brushing her down, cleaning her hooves, and preparing her feed.

The horse grew so comfortable with her that Erin was able to ride bareback.

"They were a pair," Lore remembered. "Erin loved that horse."

While Rye Leigh was well behaved with Erin, the horse was temperamental around strangers. After suffering a minor leg injury, Rye Leigh was stalled for a couple of days to recover. Around that time, the horse developed a mean streak. When strangers touched her, the horse would kick and bite. Rye Leigh hated being in a trailer and would knock herself into the walls, threatening severe injury. The only person who Rye Leigh would allow to ride her was Erin.

Erin wrote about her struggle with Rye Leigh on her Facebook page.

"Problem is: she is momma's girl and she doesn't want anyone else touching her," Erin wrote. "I do everything with her. Riding, showing, trail riding, and working with her in the round pen. And she does great."

After another incident when Rye Leigh acted out while being treated by a veterinarian, the horse developed a reputation around the barn for having behavioral problems. Frustrated, Erin defended her horse online.

"I'm so tired of hearing people talk bad about me and my horse," Erin wrote. "My horse has come a long way, and I have brought her a long way, and will take her a lot farther. There's no such thing as a bad horse, just a good horse with a bad attitude."

For a while, it seemed like every horse owner at the barn wanted to provide Erin with unsolicited advice on how to train Rye Leigh. Exasperated, she turned to her friend and fellow horse owner Linda Comly.

"I told Erin, 'It's your horse, you do what you want

to do with this horse. It's nobody's horse but yours,'" Linda explained. "I said, 'You've got something that the good Lord has given you. You stay with it and you don't listen to all these other people.'"

Erin seemed to take Linda's words to heart, spending hours training Rye Leigh. Slowly, with lots of work, the horse's behavior improved. Eventually, the Heavilins transferred Rye Leigh to a different barn with forty acres of open space. By then, the horse had become friendly, well behaved, and lovable.

"She had a way with Rye Leigh," Linda remembered. "The important thing with horses: they have to have confidence in their owner. And Erin mastered that."

Being around horses also turned out to be a positive transition for Alex. A family friend from the barn let Alex care for their horse in exchange for the boy being able to ride whenever he wanted.

"Really one of the best things that happened to Alex is that horse," Lore recalled. "People there at the barn accepted Alex for who he was. That brought out a maturity in him I didn't think I'd ever see."

Soon, the Heavilins purchased Alex a black walking horse named Prince.

Erin helped train her brother's horse. One day as Alex and Erin were riding, Prince began bucking and rearing his head, trying to knock Alex from his back. Erin asked Alex if he wanted her to work with his horse, and he readily agreed. When Erin mounted Prince, the horse tried to buck her off as well. But she wasn't having any of it.

"Erin jumped down off of him, grabbed ahold of his reins, got in front of him, and just started shaking his reins, yelling, 'Back up, back up, back up,'" Lore remembered. "Here is this little bitty thing with the big old horse. As much as Erin loved animals, she knew the horse had to know that you're the alpha."

In the spring and summer of 2010, Erin was preparing to compete in the Eastern Region Horse Show at the Roane State Arena in Harriman, a small city in Tennessee near Knoxville. It was the second-biggest horse show of the year, and if Erin did well, she could potentially go to state. She spent an entire day cleaning tack, washing her riding clothes, bathing her horse, and trimming and brushing Rye Leigh's mane and tail.

But when she tried to load Rye Leigh in the back of the trailer, the thousand-pound horse tried to escape, bucking against the trailer. Both Erin and Lore tried multiple times to load the horse in the trailer, but Rye Leigh resisted. Erin realized she wouldn't be able to attend the horse show for which she had been training.

"Can't go to regionals tomorrow 'cause the horse won't stop trying to kill herself in the trailer!" she vented on Facebook.

Instead of being discouraged, Erin only became more motivated and determined to retrain Rye Leigh. Erin's friends were amazed and impressed to see her transform into a knowledgeable and capable horse handler. At times, it seemed like she was better with horses than with humans.

"When I think of Erin with horses, she is very confident and knew exactly what she was going to do," recalled her friend Abby Gouge. "But with people, she was much meeker, much quieter."

Chapter 4

As Erin entered her teens, she transformed into a pretty young woman with an alabaster complexion, striking blue eyes, and a demure smile. At five foot two inches and about 120 pounds, she was petite. Her thick, light brown hair was cut shoulder length, and she occasionally wore wire-rimmed glasses.

While Erin was comfortable outdoors and at the barn, she was also quite girly. Her favorite colors were pink and purple, and she enjoyed styling her hair, wearing makeup, and shopping. She had a closetful of clothes, although she was quite thrifty and knew how to find a bargain. Weekends were often spent going to yard sales with Lore and Alex.

"She was a great yard saler," Lore remembered. "She was even better than me."

Like many teens, Erin was thrilled when she got her first cell phone, excitedly posting online, "Getting a phone with texting!!!!!"

Once Erin had a cell phone, she rarely let it out of her sight. She always seemed to be texting her friends or snapping photos.

Through church and the barn, Erin had developed a large network of girlfriends who regularly got together for movies, for lunches, or just to hang out and gossip. They also stayed overnight at each other's homes for regular sleepovers. The girls would stock up on candy and soda and stay up all night talking and laughing. While Erin could be shy and quiet around strangers, she was talkative with friends.

"Erin was shy until she got to know you," Lore remarked. "She could immediately connect with people. If she knew you, she wouldn't stop talking."

Erin always seemed to be a beacon of positivity and compassion, willing to do anything to help a friend. Whenever a friend was sad, Erin would be the person trying to cheer him or her up.

"She just always had this way about her—she was always happy and excited about life," friend Jeanne Cardinal recalled. "She was just happy to be wherever she was and do whatever she was doing."

Like many teens, Erin hated cleaning her room and enjoyed sleeping late. But she rarely got in any trouble and never rebelled.

"She was an incredible teenager," Lore recalled. "You couldn't ask for a better teenager."

At fourteen, Erin got a part-time job at a veterinarian's office. But as much as she adored animals, the job helped her conclude she could never be a veterinarian because it would break her tender heart to have to euthanize any pets.

Because her adopted children had issues with parents who abused drugs and alcohol, Lore never imbibed in front of the kids when they were young. But when Erin was in her teens, Lore purchased a six-pack of Smirnoff wine coolers, a drink she had previously tried on a trip with her oldest daughter. The bottles sat in the refrigerator for a couple of weeks, with Lore having just one or two. Still, Erin gave her mother teenage attitude for drinking the wine coolers.

Around this time, Erin saw her family pediatrician,

Dr. Katy Stephens, for a regular checkup. Dr. Stephens was a family friend of the Heavilins. Knowing that many teens experience peer pressure, the doctor asked Erin if she had tried alcohol or drugs.

"I can't tell your mom anything you tell me," the doctor told Erin. "That's the law."

Erin had a quick response. "No. But I think you need to talk to my mom."

Reaching in her purse, Erin grabbed her cell phone and dialed her mother. When Lore answered the phone, instead of her daughter, she heard Dr. Stephens.

"Lore, I think Erin thinks I should talk to you about something," the doctor said.

Immediately, Lore knew what the call was about and explained to the doctor that she had fewer than two wine coolers in two weeks. Hearing that, Dr. Stephens explained to Erin that it was way under the recommended guidelines for alcohol consumption and that recent studies had actually shown a glass or two of wine could be good for blood pressure. In the doctor's office, Erin made a dismissive gesture, and the doctor laughed. "I don't think that's what Erin wanted me to say," Dr. Stephens said.

It was one of those moments that made Lore realize that Erin had a lot of maturing left to do.

"That's how naïve and innocent Erin was," Lore remembered. "She was very naïve and extremely trusting. She saw the good in people. She very seldom said anything bad about anyone."

When Erin was fifteen, her parents let her join Facebook. She logged on for the first time on January 1, 2010, posting: "Happy New Year, everybody!!!"

Erin used Facebook to communicate with friends and post pictures. She enjoyed photography and was always snapping pictures, especially of her pets. On

Facebook, she posted numerous pictures of herself with Rye Leigh. In one, Erin is wearing a red plaid shirt, jeans, and a black cowboy hat as she holds on to Rye Leigh's reins. In another, she wears full riding gear with her hair swept into a ponytail under a helmet. In a different shot, Erin is grinning as Rye Leigh rests her head on her shoulder.

Her posts also included funny animal videos, inspirational quotes, selfies, and pictures of friends. She shared stories of her horses and links to animal rescues, and she played the game FarmVille. On occasion, she posted song lyrics from her favorite artists, including Kelly Clarkson, Jordin Sparks, and Bruno Mars. Many of her posts were Bible passages and inspirational quotes.

"Go ahead and write down your plans . . . But do it in pencil, and be sure to give God the eraser," she wrote in 2010.

On Facebook, Erin amassed several hundred friends and family members. Soon after posting her first selfie, her old friend from the barn, Jonathan Wayne Corwin, added her as a friend and sent her a private message. Erin quickly wrote back, and the two started talking online.

Born and raised in Oak Ridge, Jon was a year older than Erin and a junior at Oak Ridge High School. His parents, Tommy Corwin and Sheila Braden, had divorced when Jon was young and had both since remarried. Tommy and his new wife, Patricia, lived in Sevierville, a small city about fifty miles from Oak Ridge. Jon, his older brother, Zachary, and younger sister lived in Oak Ridge with their mother and stepfather, Michael Braden. Years later, Michael would be diagnosed with amyotrophic lateral sclerosis, or ALS, a rare, incurable neurological disease that affects the nerves responsible for controlling muscle movement.

Short and slight, Jon had closely cropped hair and a boyish face. Like Erin, he was quiet, reserved, and earnest. He described himself as stoic and sometimes detached.

"I don't show emotions at all," Jon explained.

An outdoorsman, Jon liked to shoot guns and go four-wheeling. He spoke often of his plans to join the Marines after graduating from high school.

Soon after Jon and Erin started talking, a spark ignited. At the time, Erin had limited dating experience. Her longest relationship had lasted five months. She first met Lee Abbott, a junior at Oak Ridge High School, when she was fourteen. In the spring of 2009, Lee asked her to be his date to the prom. Although her parents didn't allow unsupervised dates before the age of sixteen, the Heavilins permitted Erin to attend the dance because it was a group activity with two other couples and the church's music minister chaperoned them. But they insisted if she attended the dance that she pay for her own prom dress as a way to instill responsibility in Erin.

For months, Erin saved money working at the veterinarian's office, and she purchased a purple satin halter dress that was cut short in the front and long in the back, so it wouldn't require any alteration.

Erin's brief relationship with Lee had fizzled out shortly before she met Jon at the barn. Because of the Heavilins' no-unchaperoned-dating rule, for several months Jon and Erin only chatted online and saw each other occasionally at the barn. On Erin's sixteenth birthday, July 15, 2010, Jon approached Lore at the barn and asked permission to ask Erin on a date. For

Jon, it was important to gain parental consent as a sign of respect.

"That was the way I was raised: get the parents' permission for everything," Jon explained.

While the Heavilins didn't know much about Jon, he seemed like a polite, well-behaved young man from a respected family, and they approved.

"He appeared to be a good guy. We didn't get to know him very much," Lore recalled. "He's very quiet."

When Jon asked her out, Erin was interested, but before she said yes, she also got permission from her parents. On July 20, five days after her sixteenth birthday, Jon and Erin went on their first date to the movie theater to see the animated film *Despicable Me*. Erin's friend Jeanne Cardinal accompanied the pair. The next day, Erin posted about it on Facebook. "Had a great night last night at the movies with Jon . . . and Jeanne," she wrote.

A week later, Jon and Erin went on their second date. And by the end of August 2010, they were officially a couple.

"They were pretty much instantly a couple," Lore explained. "She definitely was very smitten."

While both Erin and Jon were shy, quiet people, they connected with each other. Jon was attentive and protective of Erin.

"I was always able to talk to her and know what she was feeling," Jon remarked.

Erin's friends thought the couple seemed like a compatible, well-suited match.

"She talked about Jon a lot," remembered one of her best friends. "She was always so giggly and bubbly when she brought him up."

Jon took Erin to dinners, movies, and picnics, and

to the lake to shoot guns. Although Jon didn't care much for horses, he accompanied Erin on a trail ride on a few occasions. On Facebook, Erin posted several photos of her with her new boyfriend. In one, Jon's holding the camera, arm outstretched. Erin is peeking over his shoulder and grinning. At sixteen, Erin was very much a teenage girl in love. "I'm not lucky, I'm blessed," she wrote on Facebook.

Online she posted a poem she wrote for Jon titled, "Take My Hand and Never Let Go." In it, Erin gushed about her enthusiastic commitment to Jon and vowed he'd be the only love in her life. The last line is both sentimental and haunting.

> *Not everyone is lucky enough to find "the one."*
> *But somehow I found my little piece of heaven*
>   *in this crazy world.*
> *My best friend, soul mate, and everything in*
>   *between.*
> *Jonathan Wayne Corwin. That's where my*
>   *story began,*
> *And that's where it ends.*

When it came time for Jon's senior prom, he asked Erin to be his date, and she said yes. Because she was frugal, Erin decided to wear the same purple halter dress she had worn the year prior with Lee Abbott. But she bought new heels because the old ones had hurt her feet.

On prom night, as Erin descended the staircase in her purple gown, her hair piled on top of her head, Jon reached out and grabbed her hand. To coordinate with Erin's dress, Jon wore a dark suit and purple tie. He had purchased her a pink corsage, which he nervously pinned to her dress.

As Lore snapped pictures of the couple, shy Erin turned away from the camera and shielded her face.

"Getting prom pictures was torture for her. She would rather be behind the camera than in front of it," Lore recalled. "She did not like to be the center of attention. She tried to be a wallflower."

When Jon saw Erin on prom night, he was in awe. It was the first time he had ever seen her all dressed up, and there was just something special about the way she looked that night.

Jon Corwin had fallen in love.

Chapter 5

A squat, sprawling warehouse off the main turn-pike in Oak Ridge houses a chain store called Tractor Supply Company. With aisles of agricultural and livestock supplies, the locale is a popular hub for Oak Ridge residents. Horse owners and breeders frequent the warehouse for feed and equestrian supplies. Farmers from the surrounding communities make the trek into town for tractors, backhoes, and heavy machinery.

In early 2011, when she was sixteen, Erin was hired at Tractor Supply as a cashier. As one of the youngest employees at the time, she was well loved among the tight-knit group of employees.

"Erin was like the little sister of the group," recalled one former coworker. "She grew up on us, and she blossomed into a beautiful young woman. She went from the ditzy little girl to this independent woman in front of our eyes."

For an animal lover like Erin, the job came with extra benefits. Because the store hosted regular veterinary clinics for pets and livestock, it was typical for pigs, donkeys, and calves to be roaming the aisles among the hardware and home décor. Each spring, the store sold baby chicks out of a pen set up under a heat lamp. In Oak Ridge, residents could own up to six hens for personal use. Farmers from surrounding communities would also come to the store to grow their flock. While most of the other employees at Tractor Supply Company grew sick of the birds after a few days, Erin was always the first to volunteer to clean their cages and feed them.

"She was the only person I knew that could love chickens even after dealing with them for the entire length of our chick days," remarked a former coworker.

It was through Tractor Supply that Erin met the woman who would become her best friend. A Tennessee native with a thick Southern accent and dirty blond hair that framed her round, pale face, Jessica "Jessie" Trentham was two years older than Erin and lived in a rural community on the outskirts of Oak Ridge.

Months after Erin started working at Tractor Supply, Jessie was hired as a cashier. But when Jessie was promoted to team leader, she and Erin began hanging out more frequently.

"The more we got to hang out during and after work, the more our friendship blossomed," Jessie recalled. "Our personalities just clicked. She was so bubbly and innocent, and sometimes very gullible."

After their shifts, the two girls would stop for sodas and french fries at the nearby Sonic drive-in or head across town to the Waffle House for breakfast food. Because there weren't a lot of options for entertainment in Oak Ridge, sometimes they would just drive around and gossip.

"I always knew I could call her if I just needed someone to talk to," Jessie remembered. "She was never one to judge and was always such a supportive friend. I could call her on my way home from work just to talk about nothing to make my thirty-minute drive home a little better."

Erin and Jessie spoke about their pets, friends, and future goals. Mostly, however, they talked about boys. Although she hadn't had much dating experience, Jessie says Erin was remarkably good at relationship advice and helped coach her through a couple of heartbreaks.

When Erin first started dating Jon, many of their conversations revolved around her new relationship.

"I remember one time we caught her cleaning the counters off at the register at work and she was doodling Jon's name on the counter," Jessie recalled.

By 2011, Jon and Erin's relationship had grown serious. They professed their love for each other and began talking about marriage. Jon's parents welcomed Erin into the family, and she began referring to the Bradens and Corwins as her in-laws.

That May, when Jon graduated from Oak Ridge High School, Erin was there, posing next to her boyfriend in his cranberry-colored cap and gown. It was a bittersweet moment for the couple. Jon had signed up for the Marines and would soon leave for boot camp. That summer, between her job and friends, Erin spent much of her spare time with Jon. And as his departure date approached, Jon promised they would stay together long distance.

In June, the night before he left for basic training, Jon's family got together for dinner at an upscale restaurant. When the meal was served, Erin found a surprise on her plate—a small, silver band with six gemstones that formed a flower.

The next day, she excitedly showed off the promise ring on Facebook: "Look what I found in my french fries last night," Erin wrote.

On June 12, Jon boarded the bus for a ten-hour ride to the Marine Corps Recruit Depot at Parris Island in South Carolina. For the next thirteen weeks, Erin wouldn't be able to see or speak to Jon. As she watched the bus disappear around the corner, she burst into tears.

"Said good-bye to my boyfriend," Erin wrote on Facebook. "Miss him tons already. It was probably the hardest thing I've done so far and this is just the beginning."

Meanwhile, the Heavilins were a bit relieved. Erin was so young, and the relationship was becoming so serious so fast. Lore thought some distance would allow them to truly get to know each other.

"I kind of felt like it was a good thing because they could develop that friendship before other stuff got in the way," Lore remarked.

During basic training, new military recruits are not permitted to make or receive phone calls for weeks. So Jon and Erin communicated through handwritten letters. For thirteen weeks, Erin wrote Jon a new letter every single day. Her first was five pages long. Jon wrote back quickly, and Erin was thrilled when she received her first letter.

"Just got a letter from Jonathan Wayne Corwin," Erin wrote on Facebook. "Made me cry happy tears!"

In his letter, Jon told Erin that her messages made him happy and gave him something to look forward to as he trained.

"He told me one time that thinking of me and our future helped him push through the day, and that I was the best thing that ever happened to him," Erin shared on Facebook.

On July 15, Erin celebrated her seventeenth birthday and her first anniversary with Jon. Anxious for him to return, she created an online countdown on her Facebook page marking the date of Jon's graduation from basic training.

"Cannot wait to hear from my baby! I miss him so much!" Erin wrote. "It will be gone before we all know it! Time flies by faster than you can feel it."

While Jon was in boot camp, the Corwins and Bradens rallied around Erin like she was their daughter. Throughout the summer of 2011, Erin spent much of her time at Sheila Braden's home. One Saturday in June, she stayed up all night watching movies like *Die Hard* with Jon's cousin and brother.

"Had an awesome weekend with Jon's family," Erin wrote on Facebook. "Almost fell asleep in church the next morning though!"

Erin was proud to be dating a future Marine and became increasingly patriotic as Jon absorbed himself in all things military. On July 4, she posted on Facebook about Independence Day.

"A day to remember our troops who've fought for our freedom," Erin wrote. "My boyfriend is training right now to be a part of those troops. We owe a big thanks and much more to our troops, our heroes. I love you Jon, my hero."

To her friends, Erin never missed the opportunity to brag about Jon.

"She was tickled to death that he was in the Marines," recalled barn friend Linda Comly. "She talked all the time about how proud she was of her boyfriend."

By August, Jon was permitted to make phone calls from South Carolina. Whenever Erin spoke with her boyfriend on the phone or through a video call, she was elated. But although she missed Jon, she didn't sulk. Instead, Erin focused on family, friends, her horse, and her job.

"Some girls when their boyfriends are gone, they mope. We didn't deal with that at all," Lore remembered. "She was just her normal self."

On September 8, Jon successfully completed boot camp, and Erin rode with Jon's family to Parris Island to join him for graduation. Jon had been anticipating her visit for weeks and surprised her with an assortment of gifts.

"He's the sweetest person on planet Earth!" Erin later wrote on Facebook. "He also asked me if I needed anything while he was away and he would find a way to get me taken care of."

While on Parris Island, Erin snapped dozens of photos. In one picture, Jon is in full Marine regalia. Erin is wearing glasses and a vintage-style black-and-white dress. As she locks arms with Jon, she stands tall and appears bursting with pride.

"Was so happy to see my boy today! It's been too long!" Erin wrote in Facebook. "I'm so happy . . . I was so tired but it was cool to get to see the place. So pretty!"

Once Jon had completed boot camp, he was sent to Fort Sill, a military post about eighty-five miles southwest of Oklahoma City, Oklahoma. There, he and Erin could speak regularly by phone, text, and Skype. On December 16, 2011, Jon completed training.

"Today Jon Corwin graduates from Fort Sill," Erin wrote on Facebook. "Congratulations! I'm proud of you!"

That Christmas, Jon was unable to return to Tennessee for the holiday. Instead, he mailed Erin a gift: a new Canon EOS Rebel T3 camera with a pink strap. Erin would use the camera to document her life.

"Best present ever," she wrote. "I love you."

Soon after, Jon was stationed at the Marine Corps Air Ground Combat Center in Twentynine Palms in southern San Bernardino County, California.

In the spring of 2012, during her senior year of homeschool, Erin had senior portraits taken with her horse. When Erin couldn't find Rye Leigh a harness in her favorite color, pink, she purchased one in purple and got a matching purple plaid shirt for herself. In one picture, Erin poses beside Rye Leigh, holding her reins. Her hair is pulled partially back, displaying dangly earrings.

As things grew more serious with Jon, Erin began planning her future around him. She didn't consider attending college or pursuing a career. Instead, she wanted nothing more than to marry Jon and join him in Twentynine Palms.

The Heavilins worried about their daughter, and Lore tried to tell Erin what a sacrifice she would be making.

"Erin and I had many conversations of what to expect living that kind of lifestyle," Lore recalled. "How hard it would be to be that far from all of us for so long. Her young self would assure me that she knew. She did not know."

Life as a military wife can be lonely and tough, Lore told Erin. A deployment would take Jon away for months at a time. And the Marines required him to be in the field for training ops at least five days each month. Lore was also concerned about Erin moving two thousand miles across the country to California.

Erin was a homebody who had never lived anywhere but Oak Ridge. But Erin was very much in love and determined to be with Jon.

In early 2012, Jon first approached Bill and Lore to ask for permission to propose to Erin. At first, the Heavilins requested the pair slow down.

"We had asked the both of them to consider waiting two years," Lore remembered. "That didn't happen. They wanted to be together."

Realizing they couldn't convince the couple to wait, the Heavilins reluctantly gave their permission. That summer, Jon returned to Oak Ridge to ask Erin to be his bride. On July 4, Jon took Erin to a family picnic to watch fireworks. Erin was drinking one of her favorite drinks: Sprite. When Erin stepped away, Jon slipped a solitaire diamond ring around the straw, resting it on the lid.

"My hands are clammy and everything. I'm nervous as heck," Jon recalled. "I go grab the Sprite and I put the ring on top of it and asked her to marry me."

At first, Erin didn't notice the ring.

"Hey, look at your drink," Jon told her with a nervous smile.

Erin glanced down and looked back up at Jon with tears in her eyes. She squealed, "Yes."

"She was crying tears of joy, just ecstatic and screaming, 'Yes, yes, yes, I would love to,'" Jon remembered.

Erin was just seventeen when she and Jon got engaged. Eleven days later, she turned eighteen. Because Jon was about to be deployed to Japan, the couple decided that Erin would remain in Tennessee until the next year.

Although the Heavilins were worried about Erin, they supported her decision. Bill and Lore had saved money for each of their children to contribute to their weddings, and Erin began planning a Christmas wedding in Oak Ridge. But those plans came to an abrupt halt when Jon was unable to secure leave from the Marines that December.

Jon wasn't sure when he'd have time for the wedding, but he and Erin didn't want to wait to be husband and wife. As a married Marine, Jon would also earn more money and nicer housing options on base. So he and Erin decided to elope. That November, Erin flew to Las Vegas to attend the military's annual ball celebrating the anniversary the Marines were established. For the ball, Erin dressed in an elegant navy blue strapless gown, which she accessorized with a rhinestone necklace and earrings. Jon wore his dress blue uniform. They posed for a picture together in front of the United States flag. In one photograph, he stands behind her, affectionately touching her arm.

Late on the night of November 10, still dressed in their formal attire, Jon and Erin drove to Las Vegas Boulevard and found a wedding chapel on the strip: the Chapel of the Bells, one of the oldest and most famous wedding chapels in Las Vegas. Outside, a neon sign reading *World Famous Chapel of the Bells Weddings* hangs on the white façade of the building. Inside, rows of white chairs face a grand piano and a podium surrounded by flowers. For an extra fee, an Elvis impersonator will even officiate the ceremony.

Jon and Erin recited the traditional vows and exchanged rings. Although it wasn't the wedding she had dreamed about as a girl, Erin was so infatuated with Jon that at the time she didn't seem to care.

"We were young. It was Vegas," Jon remarked. "We honestly didn't plan a lot of things. It was a spur-of-the-moment type deal, and that's how we lived."

A photographer at the chapel snapped wedding photos. In one picture, Jon and Erin pose in front of a piano. They are facing each other with her right arm draped around his shoulders. Her smile is soft and subdued.

Jon Corwin excelled in the Marines, rising from the rank of private to corporal. He was a dutiful and brave soldier, waking each morning at sunrise for personal training before reporting for duty. Like most Marines, Jon was trained to fire a sniper rifle with expert precision and became a skilled shooter. In the field, he followed orders and was well respected by his fellow Marines and commanding officers.

Throughout his four years in the military, Jon would receive many commendations, including the Marine Corps Good Conduct Medal, Sea Service Deployment Ribbon, Korean Defense Service Medal, Global War on Terrorism Service Medal, and National Defense Service Medal. During this time, Jon transformed from a scrawny, baby-faced boy to a strong, mature young man.

For the first year of his marriage, as Jon became immersed in Marine life, he and Erin lived very separate lives. In the spring of 2013, Jon was deployed to Okinawa, Japan, so Erin and her parents decided it was best for her to remain in Oak Ridge until he returned to Twentynine Palms. But now that Erin was married, it was important for Bill and Lore to prepare their daughter for adult responsibilities.

"I know you're an adult," Lore told Erin. "But I'm afraid my heart will take over and I'll still try to parent you if you live at home."

Keith offered to let his little sister live at a condo

he owned, about a mile from the Heavilins' home. It seemed the perfect place for Erin to transition into living on her own.

"We thought it was good to prepare her as much as possible," Lore explained.

Living on her own for the first time in her life, Erin matured and developed her own sense of responsibility. She continued working at Tractor Supply, saved her money, created a budget, and paid her bills on time. She brought her cat, Alfons, whom she'd had for nearly ten years. Soon after moving in, she also acquired a second cat named Izzy, and a brown-white-and-tan guinea pig she called S'mores.

Although Erin no longer lived with her parents, she spent much of her spare time at the Heavilins' home. After her shift at work, Erin often picked up S'mores from the condo and went to her parents' to watch her favorite shows, *America's Got Talent* and *The Voice,* with Lore and Alex.

By 2013, the house in Oak Ridge had emptied out. The four older kids had long since moved out, with Kristy and Keith both earning full-ride academic scholarships to college. After getting an accounting degree from the University of Tennessee, Kristy took a job at an engineering company. In her twenties, she met a man from church. They married and had two daughters.

Keith attended college for two years before dropping out to try his hand at entrepreneurship. He had always been smart with money and skilled at investments. At nineteen, he had purchased his first home. After managing and selling a liquor store, Keith got a job as a general manager at a car dealership, where he found success. He also met a beautiful blonde named

DeeAnna. On July 4, 2012—the same day Jon and Erin got engaged—Keith asked DeeAnna to marry him. Three months later, they were married. They went on to have two children, a boy and a girl, and moved to Corpus Christi, Texas, where Keith continued to work in the car business.

Taylor married and had a son, but later divorced. She eventually settled in Knoxville, and remained close with her adopted family.

Jon Heavilin moved outside Nashville, but he rarely saw his adopted parents or Alex.

By 2013, Alex was twenty-five years old and the last remaining child living in the Heavilins' home. He had grown into a tall, strapping young man with a round face, short buzzed hair, and thick-framed glasses. Because of his developmental disabilities, he remained in the Heavilins' custody.

When Bill Heavilin retired from the post office in 2013, he and Alex ministered to the neighbors from church and volunteered to help with construction projects and yard work. People knew Alex as a sweet young man who loved helping people.

"He's got a heart of gold," Lore remarked. "He will do anything for anybody."

By 2013, Lore Heavilin was in her early sixties, with a youthful face framed by short gray hair and glasses. She and Bill relished their roles as grandparents. When each of her grandchildren was born, Lore quilted them a blanket with their name, date, weight, length, and time of birth on them. By the time Bill retired, his shock of black hair was graying around the temples. He and Lore spent vacations visiting their children and grandchildren.

Erin was a very involved aunt. Whenever she spent time with her nieces or nephews, she would play games and bake treats. Her oldest nephew always requested her chocolate chip cookies because they were so tasty.

In the summer of 2013, Erin prepared to move to Twentynine Palms. Because she knew she couldn't take Rye Leigh with her, she decided to sell her beloved horse. Knowing it would be sad to say good-bye, Erin asked her mother to accompany her as she met with potential buyers at the barn. The first few people to respond to the ad were adult women. When the ladies tried to approach Rye Leigh, the horse was standoffish. Then, a twelve-year-old girl came to see the horse with her mom. When Rye Leigh responded warmly to the girl, Erin knew it was the right match.

"Erin didn't even cry because she knew that was where she was supposed to be," Lore remembered.

While living in the condo, Erin had saved some money. Because she and Jon had eloped, the Heavilins also gave her the money they had saved for the wedding to help the newlyweds start their new lives. Still, Lore worried that Erin was just too young and didn't understand what she was getting into.

"It was scary for me," Lore recalled. "I knew it was going to be harder than she ever dreamt."

One day that fall, Jessie came over to help Erin pack up her condo. Although she was sad that Erin was leaving, Jessie was also happy for her best friend, who seemed anxious to begin her new adventure.

"She was nervous about moving to California but extremely excited to be back with Jon," Jessie remembered.

When it came to organizing the trip across the country, Erin seemed a little lost about how to proceed. Lore spoke with her daughter, knowing that figuring things out on her own would give her the confidence boost she needed to start her new life.

"Erin, you're married now," Lore told her. "If you're old enough to be married, you're old enough to take care of yourself."

With her mother's prodding, Erin hired a moving company and booked a flight to California. On September 25, Lore brought her daughter to the airport to see her off. Lore knew Erin often got confused when it came to directions. Because the flight had two layovers on the way to California, Lore was nervous Erin would get lost, even in the confines of an airport.

"When you get off that plane, you ask someone where you need to go," Lore told her. "And you let me know as soon as you get there."

Embracing her daughter, Lore gave her a kiss and watched as she disappeared into a sea of people. Lore took some solace knowing that Erin and Jon planned to live on the military base, surrounded by upstanding Marines.

"Because her husband was out in the field so often, we felt like base housing would be safer for her," Lore recalled. "We figured she'd be protected."

Tragically, the real danger would be much closer to home.

Chapter 6

Twentynine Palms is a uniquely isolated military town about 142 miles east of Los Angeles in Southern California.

It is the last main on Highway 62, a 151-mile route that runs through the Mojave Desert from the Coachella Valley to the Arizona border. The city serves as a gateway to desert wilderness preserves and one of the main entrances to Joshua Tree National Park.

Traveling northeast to Twentynine Palms, drivers pass the more developed city of Yucca Valley and then the tiny town of Joshua Tree, as Highway 62 shrinks from a four-lane expressway to a two-lane path. Just north of Highway 62, the Marine Corps Air Ground Combat Center is surrounded by steep mountains and flat valleys on 998 square miles of harsh terrain. The base accounts for more than half of the city's population of about twenty-seven thousand.

Commissioned in 1952 in response to the Korean War, the combat center warehouses a vast supply of artillery and weapons in a cluster of beige, brown, and gray buildings at the center of the base. Encircling the combat center, Marines and their families live in the barracks or one of the fifteen housing areas dispersed across the base. Hundreds of military families also live about thirty minutes downhill in Yucca Valley, which features big-city commodities like Walmart, Home Depot, Walgreens, and Starbucks.

The desert attracts an eclectic type of folk who plant roots in the area. For many of the civilian locals, Twentynine Palms provides a chance for rebirth, to escape their pasts and reinvent themselves. The residents rely on the Marines as a primary source of revenue and express great reverence for the military.

Many of the Marines, like Jon, grew up with ambitions to join the ranks of more than 185,000 active-duty members. But for others, the base is something of a way station along the highway of life—a checkpoint on their route to adulthood. The Marines recruit many men and women who can't afford or don't want to go to college. Teenagers and young adults just starting out their lives, taking on adult responsibilities. Most are young, with nearly 70 percent of the base's residents between the ages of eighteen and twenty-four.

There's one more reason people come to this lonely desert town. Chasing after the Marines are the military wives who, like Erin Corwin, go to Twentynine Palms for love.

On September 25, 2013, Erin Corwin became the newest resident of Twentynine Palms.

When married or single Marines report for duty at the base, they receive their housing assignment at the Family Housing Office. Single Marines typically live free of cost in the barracks. Married Marines have the option of living in one of the apartments and houses on the base or getting a stipend to rent or buy a place off base in one of the surrounding cities, like Yucca Valley.

After he and Erin were married, Jon Corwin filed papers with the Family Housing Office and was assigned an apartment on the southeast corner of the Marine base. When Erin first arrived, Jon was still on deployment in Okinawa. Picking up a set of keys, she moved her belongings into unit F on the second floor of a two-story tan stucco building at 6650 Jasmine Drive.

The L-shaped complex consisted of six units, most occupied by young military families. Each apartment included two bedrooms, one bathroom, a small kitchen, and a living room.

A few days after Erin arrived, Jon returned to Twentynine Palms.

It had been months since Erin had seen her new husband—so she was quietly disappointed when his mom, Sheila, also arrived in California to spend a week with the couple.

Once Sheila left, the newlyweds were able to settle into the apartment and their new lives together. Because Erin missed her animals, she and Jon adopted two rescue dogs, Max and Grace, and later a cat. They used some of Erin's savings to buy her a blue 2013 Corolla. Jon also purchased a used truck. In the beginning, Erin was a little homesick, but whenever she spoke with her mom, she seemed cheerful and happy.

Erin also remained close with Jessie Trentham, her friend from Tennessee. As she adjusted to life on the base, her friendship with Jessie became increasingly important to her. When life got tough for Erin, it would be understanding and nonjudgmental Jessie who was always available to lend a sympathetic ear. In Jessie, Erin would confide her deepest and darkest secrets.

Shortly after moving in, Jon and Erin met their neighbors in the complex. The residents of units A, B, and C kept mostly to themselves and didn't associate much with the others. But two of the other couples in the complex were already close friends.

Downstairs in Unit E lived Conor and Aisling Malakie. Conor was lean and lanky with thick black hair and bushy eyebrows. At six foot one, Aisling was tall and pretty with pale skin and long sandy blond hair. When Erin first moved in, Aisling was pregnant with her first child. Aisling noticed Erin for the first time when she was carrying her large husky, Max, up the stairs to the second floor.

"I asked if she needed help," Aisling remembered. "She insisted she didn't need help, that she could do it all on her own, and that she had to get used to it."

Aisling was having a difficult pregnancy and visiting the doctor twice a week. When Erin heard about the complications, she expressed concern for both Aisling's health and the health of her unborn son.

"Do you need anything?" Erin texted Aisling soon after first meeting. "Is there anything I can do to help?"

Aisling was impressed with Erin, who seemed much older and maturer than a typical teenager.

"She was always wondering what she could do for others," Aisling recalled. "I'd never met anyone so sweet and innocent before—she was just so genuinely caring."

After her son, Brian, was born in November 2013, Aisling and Erin began hanging out frequently at each other's apartments to watch movies and talk. Their favorite thing to do together was to go out to eat. The friends often went out for fast food, including Erin's favorites, Jack in the Box and Del Taco.

"I was amazed and still shocked at the amount of food that girl could eat because she was so tiny," Aisling recalled. "I joked that she had the appetite of a man."

The Malakies were already friends with the couple upstairs, Marine corporal Chris Lee and his wife, Nichole. The Lees and their six-year-old daughter, Liberty, lived directly next door to the Corwins—their kitchens shared a wall. Originally from Anchorage, Alaska, the Lees had been married since 2009.

Erin briefly met Chris when she first moved in, while Jon was still in Japan. The two chatted briefly, making small talk about the building before parting ways. When the Corwins later hosted a welcome-home party at their new apartment to introduce Erin to Jon's Marine buddies, both the Malakies and the Lees attended.

Living and working so close together, many young military families in Twentynine Palms are tight-knit and frequently socialize. Marines, especially those who deploy overseas, often bond for life. Military wives, who understand the stresses of Marine life, regularly lean on one another for support.

Jon and Erin Corwin were no different. When Jon returned home, he and Erin bonded with both the Lees and Malakies.

"Jon would come down to have drinks with Chris and Conor, and then Erin started coming around and hanging out," Aisling remembered. "Slowly everyone started clicking together and got more comfortable and settled."

During the weekdays while their husbands were on duty, Erin, Aisling, and Nichole would stop by each other's apartments for snacks and gossip. When Jon, Conor, and Chris were home, the couples barbecued on the grill outside their complex or watched movies and TV shows at each other's apartments. On weekends, the men often went to Joshua Tree National Park to shoot guns, race off-road vehicles, and hike.

At first glance, it appeared like three young, wholesome families beginning their lives together in the shadows of the military. But their connection was cursed.

The ubiquitous beige apartment complex on Jasmine Drive would become the stage for bitter betrayal. Over the next few months, a clandestine bond would form between two of the people living in the apartments—a connection that would have dire consequences on Erin's life.

Chapter 7

Chris Lee was tall and brawny with a wide nose, full cheeks, and deep-set brown eyes. His thick black hair was buzzed around the sides and slightly longer on top in a traditional "high and tight" Marine buzz cut. At twenty-four, Chris was older and more experienced than many of the other Marines in the apartment complex. He had already served two tours of duty in Afghanistan.

When Erin first met Chris, he seemed friendly and nice, but she didn't think much about him. Over the next few months, however, Chris would make a big impression on his new neighbor.

Born on September 12, 1989, Christopher Brandon Lee had grown up in Anchorage—Alaska's most populous city with around 226,000 residents at that time. Located on the south-central part of the state on the Cook Inlet, Anchorage is an entryway to a vast Alaskan wilderness, where bears roam the snowy banks and eagles soar in the skies. Petroleum, tourism, and the military posts make up the local economy.

Chris's father, Robert Dennis Lee, who went by Dennis, was a native Hawaiian, born and raised in Oahu. Like his son, Dennis first migrated to Anchorage for the military. In 1975, after graduating from Hawaii's elite private Kamehameha Schools, Dennis went on to attend Purdue University on a football scholarship, where he played as a running back during his freshman year. After an injury ended his football career, Dennis joined the air force, where he was stationed in Alaska and served as a firefighter in the Air National Guard.

Dennis loved Alaska so much that he settled in Anchorage, where he would later meet his wife, Karen. Originally from Colorado, Karen was visiting Alaska on a family vacation when she crossed paths with Dennis. An attraction formed, the two started dating, and Karen eventually relocated to Anchorage to be with Dennis.

The couple married and had four children. In 1987, they had their first child, Robert Jr., who went by Bobby. Christopher was the second born. His sister, Malie, came two years later. The youngest, Steven, arrived in 1996.

Meanwhile, Dennis got his pilot's license and launched a successful career as the fire chief at Anchorage International Airport. In his spare time, Dennis built an airplane in his garage and often flew in formation with his friend, who owned a similar plane. Each summer, Dennis performed in air shows across Alaska. Karen was a stay-at-home mom, raising the kids in a working-class neighborhood in Anchorage.

By all accounts, the Lees were a happy, close family. They lived a comfortable lifestyle and took frequent vacations, visiting Hawaii more than half a dozen times throughout Chris's childhood. Living in the Alaskan wilderness, Chris was an outdoorsman who camped, fished, and hunted at a young age. As a boy, he developed a fascination with swords and weapons, assembling a large collection that included Japanese throwing stars.

In high school, Chris was a jock who played football as a center and middle linebacker. He could be aggressive on the field and suffered a few minor concussions, which he would later claim caused memory issues. When it came to academics, Chris wasn't particularly bright and received average grades, although he enjoyed math. Outgoing and funny, Chris was a popular student with an immature, rebellious streak. He had a twisted sense of humor some would later describe as disconcerting.

During his junior year of high school, Chris met Nichole. One year younger than Chris, Nichole was a pretty, curvaceous blonde with light blue eyes, a slightly bulbous nose, and dimpled cheeks. Originally from Kodiak Island on the south coast of Alaska, her family moved to Anchorage when she was still in elementary school. In school, Nichole was well liked and shrewd, although a little lazy and directionless. She adored animals, especially dogs and horses, and was close with her family, especially her younger brother.

There was an instant attraction between Chris and Nichole. Nichole was a football fanatic, and the two bonded over their love of the sport. On their second official date, he took her sledding. But the romantic excursion took a dreadful turn when Nichole fell and broke her ankle. Chris accompanied her to the hospital, where pins were inserted to secure the bone. The accident brought them closer, and the two became high school sweethearts.

Their relationship was passionate, and unbeknownst to their parents, the teens were sleeping together. When Nichole was seventeen, she found out she was pregnant, and the young couple decided to keep the baby. Although the pregnancy was unexpected,

Chris and Nichole had fallen in love and wanted to be together. Both their families were supportive of the pregnancy.

In February 2008, Nichole gave birth to a baby girl they named Liberty. As they raised Liberty, Chris and Nichole leaned heavily on their parents, relying on them for childcare. At just eighteen, Chris was forced to mature quickly and became an attentive and involved father. Friends remembered him as a polite young man who clearly loved his daughter.

"He was devoted to them," friend Michele Herring recalled. "He would have done anything for them. He wasn't an angry person; he was just a nice guy. Chris and Nichole were best friends as well as being a couple; the way they interacted was so good. They just got along so well."

To support his new family, Chris decided to follow in his father's footsteps and join the military. On July 7, 2008, he enlisted in the Marines under a six-year, delayed-entry program. Traditionally, military members sign four-year active-duty contracts that include another four years of inactive reserves. Through the six-year contract, Chris spent a year preparing for boot camp, while shaving time off his inactive reserve commitment. At the end of his four years of active duty, he would only have to complete one year in the Individual Ready Reserve.

Because his admittance was delayed, Chris was able to spend much of the first year of Liberty's life with her before being shipped to boot camp. When he learned he would be stationed at Twentynine Palms, he worked out in the sauna to prepare for the dramatic climate change. But nothing could truly prepare him for summers in the desert.

Though separated by thousands of miles, Chris and

Nichole remained strong in their relationship. The first few months he lived in California, Nichole and Liberty bounced back and forth between her home and Chris's parents'. Chris called home often, and Nichole regularly sent photos and videos of their daughter.

"They were very much in love, very close," remembered Michele. "They were together since they were teenagers, so they had this connection. A lot of people grow apart after high school, but Chris and Nichole never seemed to lose that closeness."

During Chris's first leave block, he returned to Anchorage, where he and Nichole got married in June 2009. Nichole and Liberty moved to Twentynine Palms soon after. When Nichole first relocated, she hated the desert and the secluded Marine town. Although it was more expensive, she insisted they rent an apartment off base in Yucca Valley, where she would have access to bigger accommodations like Walmart.

Chris and Nichole were just teenagers, raising a baby girl and facing adult responsibilities, and real life began to take its toll. Neither one was very domestic, and their apartment was often unkempt. Chris wasn't the type of guy to do chores or clean. Similarly, Nichole liked to sleep late and could be slothful, according to former friends. As a result, they often fought about the household chores.

"They were a very weird family," recalled Marine wife Jessica Wilkerson, who knew the couple. "They weren't the type of people you could leave your kid with. Their place would always be dirty. It was just crazy."

Money was always tight. Chris wasn't responsible with his cash and tended to buy whatever he wanted, especially weapons and guns. Nichole, on the other hand, was sensible and keen at pinching pennies. She served as her husband's treasurer and secretary, keeping track of both the money and his appointments. She considered taking a part-time job to earn extra cash, but instead decided it would be too difficult while raising Liberty. Often, Nichole hired babysitters whenever she needed a break. When she couldn't afford to hire anyone to watch Liberty, Nichole would leave the girl with friends.

Despite conflict over chores and money, the Lees had a passionate marriage.

"We've always had a pretty physical relationship," Chris remarked. "We always had a very good sex life. It was pretty frequent."

As they settled into life on the base, they adopted two dogs and purchased matching Jeep Cherokees: Chris's 1997 model in black; Nichole's in maroon. They also scraped together enough cash to afford matching off-brand Acer laptops. Nichole also had an iPad and iPhone. Chris didn't like Apple products but owned a smartphone, a Samsung Galaxy S. Unlike some young men his age, Chris was not at all interested in social media and did not use Facebook or Twitter.

Over the years, Chris had built an impressive collection of weapons, which he kept secured at his apartment. That included a .22 Winchester bolt-action rifle with a 3×9 standard scope, a .357 Ruger revolver, a .325 Winchester Short Magnum, a pellet gun, and a BB gun. He also bought and sold knives frequently and owned a blowgun and machete.

"I'm a really big knife person," Chris explained.

Chris was assigned to the Second Battalion, Seventh Marines, which conducts mechanized, armed operations to support contingency operations. When ordered, active-duty Marines were expected to deploy in as few as forty-eight hours.

At first, Chris appeared well suited for the uniform. He followed orders well, promptly completed duties, and seemed to possess the Marine traits of valor and patriotism. But other Marines noticed he often seemed preoccupied with weapons. At least once, he was reprimanded by a commanding officer for using the rifles and rocket launchers like they were toys. Over time, Chris gained a reputation for being rash and reckless.

"He was definitely the type that liked to build weapons and blow things up," recalled Aisling Malakie.

Still, while it was a very different lifestyle from Alaska, Chris fit in well in Twentynine Palms. Affable and witty, he was well liked among his fellow Marines. One of his closest friends was a Marine from his unit, Skyler Dent, who was also from Alaska and lived in the barracks. The two men bonded, sharing jokes about Alaska the other Marines didn't seem to understand.

When he wasn't working, Chris made the surrounding desert his personal playground. He went off-roading in his Jeep, traversing the rocky dirt paths that cut through the desert. Whenever it rained, he sought out muddy parking lots to go "mudding," spinning in circles in his Jeep until it was dripping with sludge. He frequently took weekend trips in the desert to shoot guns, blow things up, and set bonfires.

In Twentynine Palms, there are two main gates in and out of the combat center: the Ocotillo Gate in the front and the Condor Gate in the back. A few miles outside the back Condor Gate, Chris discovered a dirt path running parallel to the main road. Treating the trail like a racetrack, he would speed off in his Jeep, kicking up a cloud of dust.

"I liked to see how fast I could drive my Jeep there down that dirt road without crashing," Chris remarked. "I would do that a couple of times a week."

In 2010, during the housing market crisis, Chris and Nichole learned the owner of their apartment building in Yucca Valley wasn't paying the mortgage, and the bank foreclosed on the property. For two months, they stayed in the apartment, paying rent directly to the bank at a monthly rate. But just before Chris's first deployment overseas, the Lees were told to vacate the premises.

To save money while Chris was deployed, Nichole and Liberty moved in temporarily with their Marine friends Tiffany and David Peterson. While the Petersons liked Nichole, they felt there was something off about Chris, according to mutual friend Jessica Wilkerson. The Wilkersons were originally from Kansas and had two kids before moving to Twentynine Palms when Jake joined the Marines. Living off base near Yucca Valley, the Wilkersons were close friends with their neighbors, the Petersons.

"Chris had a lot of anger issues," Jessica remembered. "[The Petersons] didn't like him. They didn't like the way his personality was. He was always sketchy around them."

That fall, soon after Nichole and Liberty moved into the Petersons' small house at the end of a cul-de-sac, tension formed. Tiffany found Nichole to be lazy and rude. Nichole complained constantly and seemed to play the victim. The friendship between them began to fall apart.

"Nichole always just wanted pity. She wanted everyone to feel sorry for her," Jessica remarked. "I guess because Chris wouldn't help out. He would take off with the guys a lot. She played that 'poor, pitiful me' card."

Nichole ate the Petersons' food without asking, leaving trash and wrappers all over the house. When Nichole left the house to run an errand, she often expected Tiffany to babysit her daughter without even asking. One weekend when the Petersons had an out-of-town obligation, Nichole whined, "Who's going to take care of me?"

On another occasion, Tiffany returned home to find the house a mess, with Nichole napping on the couch. Frustrated, Tiffany confronted Liberty.

"Liberty, did you do this?" Tiffany asked.

Bolting off the couch, Nichole was red-faced and angry. "Don't yell at my daughter!" she shouted.

"I wasn't yelling at your daughter," Tiffany shot back. "I was just asking if she did this."

"It doesn't matter if she did or didn't," Nichole said defiantly. "She's my daughter. You don't yell at her."

"Well, it's my house!" Tiffany responded.

Soon after, Tiffany asked her friend to leave. By the time Nichole moved out, she and Tiffany were no longer speaking.

"It started becoming where she was starting to take advantage of them," Jessica explained.

Seething at the perceived betrayal, Nichole told Chris how the Petersons had wronged her and left her in a dire position. When Chris returned from deployment, he was furious.

"I can't believe they just kicked out my wife and daughter like that!" Chris told other Marines.

Around this time, strange things started happening to the Petersons. One night, Jessica and her children were at the Petersons' apartment. All the kids were playing in the front yard except the Petersons' youngest child, Bailey. Suddenly, Jessica and Tiffany heard a scream from the girl's room. They rushed into the room and found Bailey wailing and in a panic.

"There's a man!" The little girl pointed at the window. "There's a man in the backyard!"

One of the husbands grabbed his gun and raced to the backyard, where he got a quick glimpse of a shadowy figure, who spun around and fled. When the Marine described the intruder and his black Jeep to the Petersons, Tiffany's face went pale. "Oh my God!" she said. "That's Chris."

The Petersons believed Chris was stalking them. More than once, they spotted that same black Jeep parked behind their house. Though they never had any concrete proof it was Chris, the Petersons believed he held a grudge against them.

"He was watching us. He would drive by our cul-de-sac real slow," Jessica explained. "We were all freaking out. It got really weird. It was just craziness."

After a few months, the sightings stopped, and the Petersons never interacted with the Lees again. But privately, they were convinced: There was something wrong with Chris.

In 2012, Chris, Nichole, and Liberty moved into apartment D on the second floor of the complex on Jasmine Drive. Shortly after, they were introduced to their downstairs neighbors Conor and Aisling Malakie. Chris and Conor quickly bonded and became the best of friends, frequenting the pubs and bars along Highway 62.

"We would go out drinking pretty heavily," Chris

recalled. "We were just hanging out a lot doing guy things."

Off an empty desert road a few miles behind the back Condor Gate, near where Chris raced his Jeep, he recruited Conor to regularly practice shooting pellet guns. Periodically, the pair would go off-roading in his Jeep or four-wheeling with other Marines in the nearby Joshua Tree National Park. Chris also purchased a potato launcher, a homemade cannon that shoots pieces of potato and other small objects, which he regularly used to fling potatoes into the desert. He stored the gadget in an outdoor garage adjacent to the apartment complex.

By 2012, Chris had also started taking regular weekend trips to the desert around Joshua Tree National Park to hunt coyotes and rattlesnakes, and Conor Malakie occasionally joined him. Because coyotes are nocturnal, the two men started early. They would leave their apartments at around 3:00 a.m., dressed in camouflage fatigues, and drive to the desert with rifles. Later, as hunting season approached, Chris and Conor attempted to obtain hunting licenses to kill bigger game, but were unsuccessful.

After the first few trips, they got lazy and started hunting in plainclothes with pistols in the late mornings and afternoons. The trips instead became about beer and male bonding.

"We never got very good at it," Chris admitted.

While Conor quickly bonded with Chris, Aisling was less fond of the Lees. Their apartment was often dirty, with dishes piled up in the sink and children's toys tossed around the floor. Nichole was blunt, rude, and "in your face," bombarding Aisling with nosy questions.

Like the Petersons, Aisling was also tasked with baby-sitting, often for free.

"I had to babysit Liberty all the time without being asked," Aisling remembered. "Because they would just come down the stairs and leave her."

Aisling's biggest concern, however, was Chris's influence on Conor.

"Chris always wanted Conor to go out drinking with him," Aisling recalled. "He had a very immature personality."

Aisling was also disturbed by how frequently he talked about death.

"Joking about killing people was just his sense of humor," Aisling remembered. "He was just so nonchalant about it, like it was the most natural thought in the world. I think that was one of the things that turned me off of the friendship."

Still, because of Conor's friendship with Chris, Aisling often found herself socializing with Nichole.

"If Nichole came around, I was nice to her," Aisling explained. "I was never the type of person who wasn't friends with someone."

Chris Lee—the native Alaskan—had grown to love the Mojave Desert. And he seemed to prove himself a dedicated and loyal Marine. On July 7, 2011, he was awarded the Marine Corps Good Conduct Medal. He went on to receive a Navy and Marine Corps Achievement Medal, a Global War on Terrorism Service Medal, and the National Defense Service Medal.

In 2012—a decade into the indecisive war in Afghanistan and a year after Al Queda founder Osama bin Laden was killed by Navy SEAL Team Six—the United States deployed one hundred thousand troops to the area. President Barack Obama's administration had escalated efforts in the regions, resulting in the massive troop surge. Major Taliban leaders had been killed, leaving behind a motley unorganized crew of angst-filled teenagers and poor Afghan farmers.

In November, Chris discovered he was being deployed to Afghanistan to fight in support of Operation Enduring Freedom. After years of training, Chris actually looked forward to seeing some action. When military service members deploy into combat zones, they receive a temporary salary increase, and he and Nichole anticipated the extra money.

Chris had just over a week to make preparations before his unit left, right before Thanksgiving. As a rifleman for the Second Battalion, Seventh Marines, he was in the primary infantry of the Marines. His duties were to scout protected areas of Afghanistan, armed with service rifles, grenade launchers, automatic weapons, and rockets.

The area where Chris was stationed was protected and generally safe. In fact, he was assigned a rifle that he wasn't ever expected to fire. Chris's routine was regimented, but he never saw any combat or even had to aim his weapon at an enemy.

"When I went to Afghanistan, I took a weapon that was supposed to be thrown away," Chris explained. "They were like, 'Don't worry. You won't need to use it.'"

While Chris was overseas, he and Nichole kept in regular communication through phone calls, emails, and video chats. Shortly after Chris deployed, Nichole learned she was pregnant again. The couple had always planned on having more kids eventually. But with her husband in Afghanistan, Nichole worried about his safety.

Since childhood, Nichole had suffered from asthma, a condition often exacerbated by her anxiety. Despite Chris's assurances that his work was safe and routine, Nichole lived in fear, which triggered several asthma attacks that she told Chris about. Then, two months after Chris left, Nichole was devastated to discover she had miscarried.

While the miscarriage left Nichole distressed, it would be Chris who would return from Afghanistan troubled. At first, the changes in Chris would be almost imperceptible. Soon, Nichole would feel she was living with a stranger.

Chapter 8

A white wooden fence borders a seventeen-acre ranch on the outskirts of Yucca Valley. Perched beside a large white boulder near the gate, a mosaic handmade sign reads, *White Rock Horse Rescue*.

The ranch, located about forty-five minutes from the Marine base, houses more than fifty rescue horses at a time and features several stables, a barn, and a riding area. Isabel Megli, a lifelong horse lover in her late sixties with darkly tanned skin and curly brown hair she often wore under a cowboy hat, had founded the nonprofit organization in 2004. She carved the ranch out of acres of undeveloped desert to create a habitat for horses in Southern California.

At the center of the property is a beige, stucco single-family home with brown trim and dark shingle roof where Isabel lives. On the west side of the dirt trail, a guesthouse is painted rose with a half-moon window on the white front door.

By 2013, the rescue had taken in more than four hundred unwanted horses, nearly three hundred of which had been adopted by new custodians. For a hundred dollars a month, volunteers can sponsor a horse and help care for it at the ranch. A child can also sponsor a horse by putting in ten hours of work per month at the ranch. About forty regular volunteers assist Isabel and about six ranch hands live on the property, help-ing care for around fifty horses at a time.

"They visit it, love it, bathe it, ride it. They get the horse what it needs, and they get a relationship with it," Isabel explained. "Volunteers are really the core of White Rock."

One of the volunteers, thirteen-year-old Jaelynn Watson, first came to the rescue for her birthday and fell in love with horses. Helping out after school sev-eral times a week, Jaelynn was a regular at the ranch and called Isabel "Grandma."

Because the rescue is only about a half-hour drive from the Marine base, it's a popular haven for military wives.

"The spouses come to the ranch when their hus-bands or their fiancés or their boyfriends are out in the field," Isabel remarked. "They have nothing to do. Most of them don't work, and they get very lonely. Loneliness is probably the biggest problem that they have."

As Nichole coped with the loss of her unborn baby alone in Twentynine Palms, she found sanctuary at the White Rock Horse Rescue.

In April 2013, Chris returned from his deployment to the apartment on Jasmine Drive. For his service, he was also awarded the NATO Medal—ISAF Afghani-stan. While he never saw any combat, those six months in Afghanistan affected him greatly. While on deploy-ment, he missed his wife and daughter, but once he was back on base, everything seemed wrong. Things that used to bring him joy now seemed trivial and meaningless. As his world slowly tilted, Chris grew apathetic and nihilistic. Over the next six months, he drifted and isolated himself from his family. He became a reclusive, brooding, short-tempered man who drank too much and started slipping at work.

"I was having a really hard time adjusting back at home," Chris explained. "My emotional state was like, 'I don't give a fuck about anything.' I was just kind of falling apart mentally."

Following a lengthy deployment, reintegrating into family life is often one of the most difficult transitions for a military couple. Marines are forced to abruptly shift from a war mentality to family life. For the spouses left behind, raising kids and maintaining the home alone can breed resentment. For the six months Chris was gone, Nichole had managed to get by on her own. Now that he was home, it was challenging to function as a couple.

"You come back and it's a lot of pressure," Chris remarked. "I started going downhill. It started when I first got back, and it got worse."

For a while after returning from deployment, Chris thought his depression was a temporary side effect of the transition. But months passed and Chris didn't snap back. He started drinking more and gained weight. His mental state took a toll on his marriage.

"You get so used to being away from each other that it's actually hard to be together sometimes," Chris described. "So we just weren't communicating, and I was in my own world."

When Nichole tried to talk to Chris, he would insist nothing was wrong.

"You're different. What's up? What happened?" Nichole confronted her husband on multiple occasions.

Repeatedly, she urged Chris to see a counselor, but he refused. Over the next few months, Nichole persisted, pleading with Chris to seek help. When he only grew more reclusive, Nichole became angry. Tension simmered between the once happy couple, and they fought frequently. Feeling pestered during their fights, Chris threatened to seek out another deployment in Afghanistan. More than once, he said he'd prefer to be in a war zone than with his wife.

"I wanted to go back to Afghanistan because it's easier there," Chris explained. "All I had to do is wake up and go on patrol. Real simple stuff. You don't have to have real-life responsibilities. It was just easier over there."

To help him battle his depression, Nichole brought Chris to the ranch and introduced him to Isabel Megli.

Over the next few months, Chris would become progressively interested in horses, and he and his wife decided to sponsor two horses. The first horse Chris was working with had to be put down because she was old and suffering chronic pain in her knees. Nichole also had a horse that had to be euthanized when it cut its leg. After that, Chris and Nichole adopted two new rescue horses: Humorous and Mack. Chris's horse was an offtrack Thoroughbred.

The couple also became close to the ranch owner. Chris had a lot of respect for Isabel and considered her a "strong lady." He helped her hang fences, mend broken stalls, and scoop manure.

"I was just starting to get into horses at that time," Chris remarked. "Mostly, I would go around and fix things on the ranch, being helpful when I could."

Isabel appreciated the help and grew fond of the Lees and their daughter, Liberty.

"Chris was wonderful. He was very good to me, and he did a lot of nice things for the ranch," Isabel remembered. "He was incredible with the horses."

The ranch was constantly bustling with Marines,

local volunteers, and petty criminals serving out their community service. Witty and boisterous, Chris always seemed to be the center of attention at the barn—a far cry from the depressed, angry figure he'd become at home.

"At the ranch, Chris was very funny," Isabel recalled. "He was a real soft individual when he talked about his daughter, his wife, or his family. But he also had the ability to be very stern."

But Isabel also sensed something off about Chris. She knew he had a difficult time in Afghanistan and that he didn't like to discuss his time there.

"There was something that you just stayed away from that subject," she remarked.

Still, Chris seemed fascinated by his fellow Marines' battle stories. Unlike some veterans, Chris didn't have gallant tales of fighting terrorists. During both his deployments, he said he had served as a glorified security guard. If given the opportunity, however, Chris said he wouldn't hesitate to kill.

"Chris would sit around at my table at night with other Marines and talk about death," Isabel remembered. "And it was very graphic. Killing was nothing. He said that's something you have to do. And I was always so shocked."

By 2013, Liberty Lee was five years old and in kindergarten at Onaga Elementary in the Morongo Unified School District in Yucca Valley. She was a bright young girl and had already learned to read simple books. Her teacher recommended she join an enrichment program when she started the first grade.

"She's pretty advanced," Chris commented proudly.

With Liberty, Chris was an involved father. Chris and Nichole would regularly bring their daughter to the ranch, where she would play with some of the other volunteers' children.

In a series of photos taken at the ranch, Chris sits with Liberty on his lap. She is dressed in a cowgirl costume, holding a toy gun. In another, Chris is leading a pony around a paddock, while Liberty sits in the saddle.

"Chris adores that little girl, and Liberty loves her daddy, too," his friend Michele recalled. "He's a very gentle and patient father."

Nichole was a loving mother, but she was not the most attentive.

During the day, Nichole frequently left her daughter outside alone to play with her toy ponies. Although Nichole didn't work, she relied heavily on her neighbors to watch Liberty.

"Everyone in the apartment complex knew and loved Liberty," Aisling remembered. "She was the sweetest little girl."

A huge football fan, Nichole had a rule on Sundays that she would not answer her phone, respond to texts, or be bothered by anyone. This policy even applied to her daughter, who was told, "Don't ask Mom for anything."

"Shh! Don't talk to me," Nichole would tell Liberty. "The game's on."

"I had to do absolutely everything for Liberty on Sundays because Nichole did not leave that couch," Aisling recalled. "She sat and watched TV. That's all she did."

One weekend, Chris and Nichole dropped Liberty off at the Malakies' apartment for what was supposed to be just the night. Instead, the Lees spent the weekend in Las Vegas, ignoring Aisling's repeated phone calls.

On another occasion, Aisling heard a knock on the front door around midnight. When she opened it, Liberty was standing by herself on the porch.

"I don't know where my mom and dad are," she told Aisling.

Shocked, Aisling walked the girl upstairs to the Lees' apartment. The front door was open, and it was pitch-black inside.

"Hello! Anyone home? It's Aisling," she called out. "Liberty was just downstairs in my apartment."

Nichole hollered from the bedroom but refused to get out of bed.

"Oh my God, Liberty!" Nichole bellowed. "Go to bed!"

"Does someone want to lock the door?" Aisling yelled back. "Because your daughter is sneaking out at night."

"It's OK," Nichole replied. "She's fine. She'll go back to bed."

During his annual leave from the Marines, Chris and his family regularly returned to Anchorage to visit. By then, Chris's father, Dennis, had retired after twenty years as the fire chief for the Anchorage airport. He went on to teach firefighter rescue and confined-space rescue, as well as continued to perform in air shows. Chris's oldest brother, Robert Jr., was working at Bass Pro Shops. His sister, Malie, had just completed school and gotten a job as a medical technician. Like her father, Malie also earned her pilot's license. In 2013, Chris's brother Steven was still in high school.

Dennis and Karen were proud of Chris, both for his service as a Marine and for his responsibility as a father. But after his second deployment, they noticed he seemed detached and uncommunicative.

There was no way for them to know about the darkness swirling in their son's head. No one could know how truly disturbed Chris had become.

Chapter 9

For a shy, small-town teenage girl from Tennessee, Erin fit in well in Twentynine Palms. Though neighbors Aisling and Nichole were older than Erin and had children, they both took an early liking to Erin and befriended the teen.

Soon after they first met, Nichole and Erin bonded over their mutual love of horses. One weekend, Chris and Nichole brought Erin with them to White Rock. Missing her horse Rye Leigh, Erin was instantly enamored by the rescue.

On Erin's first day there, Isabel Megli showed her thirty available horses to sponsor. Erin selected an eight-year-old quarter horse named Cassy.

"Are you sure?" Isabel asked. "Cassy is pretty skittish."

The horse had been rescued from an abusive household run by a hoarder and wouldn't let anyone touch her. When Cassy was first brought to the rescue, the horse was "skin and bones," Isabel recalled.

To Isabel's surprise, Erin walked right into her pen, caught Cassy, and rode her bareback without a bit. The bond between Erin and the horse was instant and profound.

"She picked a horse that I would have never chosen for her," Isabel remarked. "The horse was standoffish. It didn't like anybody. And it liked her. This horse was so bonded to her. We couldn't believe it."

With Erin's help and dedication, the horse gained three hundred pounds and thrived at the ranch.

"Erin came here to find a horse, to volunteer, and to enjoy herself with horse riding," Isabel explained. "It offered her someplace to go, peace of mind."

By then an experienced rider, Erin also became a role model among some of the younger equestrians at the rescue. On one occasion, Erin noticed a younger girl being bullied by a group of teenagers who were making fun of her cheap boots. Erin marched over to them and knelt so she was eye level with the girl.

"Your boots aren't going to make a difference on how you ride," Erin told her. "Let's go and do what we know you can do."

Soon, Erin began tagging along with the Lees several times a week to the rescue. Jon, however, never shared his wife's passion for horses and rarely accompanied her. Isabel could only recall one occasion when Jon and Erin came together.

"One time when they came out here, they chased Cassy for a half an hour," Isabel remembered. "They worked together and caught her."

Because of Jon's disinterest, Erin either went to the rescue with the Lees or by herself. When Erin told her mom about the horse rescue, Lore, back in Tennessee, was comforted.

"I was excited when Erin and Nichole met because Nichole was into horses and I knew that Erin needed the horses," Lore remarked. "I knew that would be so healthy for her."

Often after visiting the ranch, the Lees and Corwins would get dinner together. Because both couples had two dogs, they also frequented the nearby animal park. At least once, Chris accompanied the Corwins to the local Mexican restaurant, Santana's, for dinner. On another occasion, they were all at the dog park when Chris decided to get fast food from Carl's Jr. Because Erin was hungry, Chris gave her his number so she could text him her order. Erin saved the number in her phone.

Like many of the young Marine families, the neighbors helped each other, running errands, picking up food, or watching each other's children. If Chris went to the grocery store or gas station, he often asked Jon or Erin if they needed anything. A few times when Nichole was busy with Liberty, Erin offered to pick up Chris when he was coming back from a field ops training exercise. Like Aisling, Erin was also a frequent babysitter for Liberty and often watched the girl for free without being asked. But Erin never seemed to mind. She loved children and quickly grew to adore Liberty.

Jon and Chris also became close friends on their own. On several occasions, the Lees and Corwins went to the desert to go shooting. After, Chris and Jon would drop Erin and Nichole off at the rescue and go off-roading or take a dune buggy ride. Whenever it rained, Chris took Jon, Erin, and Conor mudding. Nichole, who wasn't fond of driving around in the dirt, stayed behind. For about an hour, Chris drove in circles in a muddy parking lot, covering his car in muck. He and Jon laughed while Erin nervously braced herself in the back seat.

After three months in California, it seemed Erin had found her place surrounded by new friends and horses.

When Erin first moved to Twentynine Palms, Lore

had encouraged her daughter to join a military wives' support group or attend church. But Jon didn't want to go to church, and Erin didn't want to go alone. Now it seemed like Erin didn't need that type of support—she had a group of supportive friends. Still, something told Lore that perhaps she wasn't hearing about everything in Twentynine Palms.

"I'm sure she was lonely. But we discussed so much ahead of time what to expect and everything like that," Lore recalled. "I don't know, maybe she didn't want to admit how lonely she was."

In December 2013, Jon and Erin returned to Oak Ridge for Christmas. It had been several months since Lore had last seen Erin, and she was thrilled her daughter seemed to be thriving. During the trip, Jon and Erin stayed at the Heavilins' home, sleeping in Alex's bed while Alex slept on the couch.

As was tradition with the Heavilins, the Christmas Eve celebration included a big dinner with Lore's sisters and their families. Each family member brought a dish for a potluck. After dinner, the family played Dirty Santa, a gift exchange in which participants can steal each other's presents.

After spending a few days visiting both of Jon's parents, the couple returned to the Heavilins' for New Year's Eve, playing board games late into the night. When they left the next morning, Lore hugged Erin and told her how much she loved her.

She had no way of knowing it would be the last holiday she would ever spend with her daughter.

Chapter 10

As Chris sank further into his misery, his marriage fragmented. While he seemed affable and friendly when hanging out with the Malakies and Corwins, alone with his family, he was a different person. By January 2014, his arguments with Nichole became increasingly heated and were often escalated by alcohol.

"I was, like, indifferent about life—I didn't like the way it was going," Chris remarked. "I was like, 'I'm alive, but I don't really care.'"

During one particularly bad night, Chris and Nichole got into a fight over dinner. Chris was drunk and erupted in anger, terrifying his wife. The next morning, she confronted him, pleading with him once again to talk to a counselor. At the time, Chris balked at the suggestion. Later, reflecting back on the fight, he admitted he knew something was wrong with him.

"I just felt like I didn't need help," Chris admitted. "I didn't listen to her when [Nichole] said I needed to talk to somebody. I was not all there."

Instead, Chris further withdrew and stopped talking to his wife. Nichole was scared for her husband.

"She kept trying to get me to open up, and I just kept shutting her out," Chris remembered. "I got to the point where I was shutting everybody out. I wasn't talking to my parents anymore. It was bad."

At work, however, Chris managed to mostly conceal his deteriorating mental state. He was promoted from the rifle range and put in charge of a platoon of Marine lieutenants. But soon Chris complained that he was overwhelmed by his new duties.

"I was swamped with responsibility over my level," Chris explained.

The promotion gave Chris more freedom on base and control of his morning routine. Every weekday in Twentynine Palms, Marines are expected to report at 6:00 a.m. for personal training. But because Chris was now in a leadership role, he wasn't required to participate. Over time, he started skipping the workout. Instead, he'd arrive on base for work at 8:00 a.m. and spend a few hours filling out rosters. Each day around 11:30 a.m., he returned to the apartment to have lunch with Nichole before heading back to work. At the end of the workday, Chris changed out of his fatigues and ate dinner. But he'd often stay up past midnight playing video games and drinking beer and hard alcohol.

"I wasn't sleeping a lot at the time," Chris remembered.

For a newly married couple just starting out their life together, money was tight for Jon and Erin Corwin.

The couple lived off Jon's salary: a private first class's basic pay of $1,793 per month and free housing. After paying the bills, there wasn't much money left.

"The pay's not that great," Jon commented. "We had food on the table; we just didn't have money for extracurriculars."

Erin had spent a big portion of the money her parents had saved for her wedding to relocate to Twentynine Palms. And over the last several months, the couple had purchased vehicles, furniture for the apartment, clothing, and other necessities. Soon, they had blown through much of the money Erin's parents had given them and were racking up credit card debt. Erin spoke to her mother about their finances.

"I said, 'I know it looks like you have quite a bit of money, but if you keep this up, pretty soon you're not going to have anything,'" Lore recalled. "They just kept buying things, and then all of the sudden, that huge chunk of money was not there."

In early January 2014, Erin got a retail sales job at a Tractor Supply Company located in Yucca Valley. Although Erin was excited to be back at Tractor Supply, the forty-five-minute commute was draining. Erin was never good with directions and hated driving. Around this time, she contracted a severe upper-respiratory infection and ended up in the emergency room. Her medical issues, coupled with her dislike of driving, caused her to quit the job after a few weeks, citing personal reasons.

"As much as she loved Tractor Supply, she hated driving even more," Lore explained.

To contribute to the bills, Erin found work babysitting some of the couples' children on base. At the same time, as Chris's mental state deteriorated, Nichole also grew increasingly dependent on Erin's help as a babysitter for Liberty. The arrangement seemed to work. But while Erin was happy to help out with Liberty, she often found Nichole abrasive.

Still, for the Corwins, their money never seemed to go far enough. Erin and Jon started to blame each other for their money woes. He claimed she was spending too much on groceries, clothes, and personal things. She accused him of lying about where he spent the money and wasting their extra cash on unessential "toys." One contentious issue was a sand rail Jon purchased—a lightweight, off-road vehicle specifically designed for traveling on sandy terrain. Jon thought it would be a fun activity, off-roading through the desert with his Marine buddies. Erin went out with him once but hated it and told Jon she had had enough—she was no daredevil. As she and Jon argued more frequently, Erin confided in her friends about her frustration.

"I know they were having money problems—that's the main thing they would fight about," best friend Jessie Trentham explained. "When she moved away, she would tell me about their fights and troubles when married life got the best of them . . . I don't think she was as prepared for it as she thought she was."

Things between Erin and Jon were only going to get more difficult.

In early January, soon after she got the job at Tractor Supply, Erin found out she was pregnant. While she and Jon had not been trying to have a baby, Erin always dreamed of being a mom. One of her first calls to share the news was to her mom in Oak Ridge.

"She was really, really excited. And I was excited for her," Lore remembered. "We talked about how much it's going to change her life."

Erin also shared the news with her friends at the apartment complex. Soon after finding out, Erin went downstairs to talk to Aisling, her closest friend in Twentynine Palms. As they were chatting, Erin rubbed her stomach and asked, "Do you notice anything different?"

Aisling looked at Erin's flat tummy. Erin wasn't yet showing, but Aisling got the hint. "Oh my God! Are you pregnant?"

"Then she started squealing and freaking out about how excited she was," Aisling recalled. "All she wanted was to be a mom. She was just so excited to have kids.

When she found out she was pregnant, it was the greatest thing in the world for her."

Erin posted an announcement on Facebook: a blue-and-pink image that read, "I'm pregnant." She even started perusing baby clothes online and thinking of baby names.

But Erin's excitement was short-lived. A few weeks after discovering she was pregnant, Erin suffered severe cramps. Jon was in the field for training and couldn't be reached, so she texted Aisling, who rushed her to the hospital.

The doctors performed an ultrasound and determined Erin had suffered a miscarriage. Erin was shattered.

"Her miscarriage was just awful," Aisling remembered. "I entered the room, and she's staring at me with this blank face. And she asked me, 'What am I supposed to do now?'"

When the doctor returned to the examination room, Erin started blaming herself.

"I did everything I was told," Erin told the doctor. "What did I do wrong? Did I stress too much?"

That afternoon, Aisling took Erin to lunch and hung out with her inside her apartment, watching movies. Erin held Aisling's son, Brian, much more that day.

Later, Erin phoned her mom in tears.

"I was brokenhearted for her," Lore recalled. "I knew how much she wanted to be a mom."

A sudden sadness overtook Erin. The bubbly, joyful girl from Tennessee seemed to fade away. Feeling empty and alone, Erin stopped going out and grew emotionally distant from her husband. Jon didn't know how to comfort his wife.

"It was heartbreaking, and Erin had trouble coping," Jon remembered. "She became very closed off and depressed."

While Erin cried and talked about her pain, Jon internalized his emotions. Outwardly, he didn't seem to be grieving. To Erin, it seemed like her husband was not affected by the loss.

"She felt like I didn't care. I did. It actually hurt me a whole lot," Jon explained. "It actually took a toll on our relationship."

Though she was struggling, Erin kept up a brave face when she talked to her mom.

"She sounded fine on the phone," Lore remembered. "We talked about it, and it was almost like she turned it off."

Still, Lore wanted to be there for her daughter. She considered flying to California.

"I wanted to go out there. If she would have asked, I would have done it in a heartbeat," Lore remarked. "But I also didn't want to overstep my bounds. They needed that time to work together to get through it."

During this time, Erin leaned more heavily on Jessie Trentham. Erin phoned Jessie frequently, often to complain about Jon and her marriage. Jessie noticed sorrow devour her best friend.

"After she had the miscarriage, they just weren't as close anymore," Jessie remembered. "I guess they didn't have the time to grieve together like they should have, and it just drove the wedge further between them."

As she mourned, shopping became like a coping mechanism for Erin. She continued to accumulate credit card debt, which only worsened the Corwins' money woes. Jon feared they were digging themselves into a financial hole.

"It was hard," Jon remembered. "We ended up racking up debt, and I ended up taking away her cards."

Without access to any money, Erin felt trapped in the apartment. She grew increasingly resentful toward Jon, and she confided in her friend Jessie.

"He would try to cut her off even though he would be spending more money than he should on unimportant things," Jessie explained.

Chris had been observing Erin when they hung out together and noticed a sorrow in her face that mirrored his own sadness. To Chris, Erin seemed broken, and he thought he could fix her. He started spending more time with her without Nichole around.

"You could tell [Erin and Jon] were having marital problems," Chris remarked. "They would yell at each other. I caught her crying and stuff like that."

A friendship between Chris and Erin formed, based partially on their mutual struggle with depression. The more time they spent alone together, the further their bond cemented.

But by early February, others had begun to observe that Erin and Chris seemed a little too friendly.

One afternoon, Erin and Aisling were taking a walk when Chris approached them. As he was talking, he seemed to be standing closer to Erin.

"I just picked up on the fact she was giggling at everything he said," Aisling recalled. "And the two of them were looking at each other. Something didn't feel right."

After he walked away, Aisling asked Erin about it. "What's up with you two?"

Erin confessed she thought he was good-looking, while reassuring Aisling that the attraction was harmless.

At the horse rescue, Isabel Megli also witnessed Erin and Chris hanging out alone. One afternoon, they were seated together in front of the computer in the main property on the ranch. Chris had one hand on Erin's arm; she was leaning close to him, blushing.

"They were laughing and carrying on about something on the computer," Isabel remembered. "She was giggly. I never saw her act like that. I wasn't used to it; it stuck out."

It was very obvious to Isabel that Chris was attracted to Erin. She found the encounter so alarming that the next time Nichole was at the rescue, Isabel pulled her aside.

"Nichole, something's wrong," Isabel began. "The way they're acting . . ."

"No, no, no." Nichole shook her head. "They are just friends. They just connect."

Nichole explained how Chris had struggled with depression once he returned from Afghanistan. Having recently suffered a miscarriage, Erin seemed to relate to Chris. Because Nichole had suffered her own miscarriage, she felt sympathetic toward Erin and at first didn't object to their friendship.

"She said Chris was sad. When he came back from the service, he was a different person. He just wasn't himself," Isabel recalled. "And Erin could understand depression."

At first, Nichole was actually relieved about Chris's new friendship with Erin. By then, she had grown exasperated by Chris's depression and heavy drinking. When Chris formed a friendship with Erin, his mood seemed to improve.

Soon, Nichole would feel much differently about the relationship between her husband and their teenage neighbor.

Chapter 11

It began one Sunday night in early February 2014. The Lees, Malakies, and Corwins regularly got together to watch the AMC zombie apocalypse show *The Walking Dead*. Repulsed by the show's graphic violence, Erin was the sole exception and rarely watched the program, choosing instead to hang out alone in her bedroom.

That particular night, the Malakies were unavailable because they had family in town. The Lees went next door to the Corwins' apartment to watch the show. Chris said he had missed a few episodes and intended to catch up later online. He joined Erin in the bedroom and suggested they play the first-person-shooter military-themed video game *Halo* on Xbox. Meanwhile, Nichole and Jon watched the show in the living room with another couple.

In the bedroom, Chris and Erin were alone, seated on the floor beside each other, playing the game. Suddenly, one of them paused the game, and Erin glanced in his direction.

"We're playing Xbox, and we kind of looked over," Chris recalled. "And then we just started kissing."

It only lasted a few seconds. But that one kiss changed everything. Later, once the Lees had returned to their apartment, Chris sent Erin a text, and they started talking about the kiss.

"And we were like, 'It wasn't that weird, you know,'" Chris described. "We were both kind of, like, surprised that it happened, but OK with it at the same time."

A few nights later, Chris was up late when he received a text message from Erin, who said she'd had a fight with Jon and couldn't sleep.

"I can't believe this is happening," Erin texted Chris. "This isn't what it was supposed to be like."

Chris had been aware his neighbors were having problems. Now, Erin revealed how the tension between her and Jon was only getting worse.

"Why don't you come outside and we can talk about it," he texted back.

It was already late, and Nichole was getting ready for bed when Chris told his wife he was leaving the apartment.

"Erin's having a really hard time," Chris told his wife. "I'm going to talk to her."

While Nichole was annoyed, she didn't protest. "Just don't be long."

There was a playground behind the apartment complex where Chris told Erin to meet him. Leashing her two dogs, Erin took them for a walk. When Chris arrived at the playground, Erin was swaying on the swing, holding her dogs' leashes and weeping.

"That's the first night we talked for a really long time by ourselves," Chris remembered.

At one point, Chris wiped a tear from Erin's cheek, grabbed her by the waist, and kissed her again. The two stayed at the playground for hours, talking and kissing. It was nearly 2:00 a.m. before Chris returned home. By then, Nichole was fuming. "Why were you out there for so long?"

Chris lied to his wife and said he was simply trying to comfort Erin.

"Nichole was really mad at me that night," Chris admitted. "I was just feeding her some bullshit."

Eventually, Nichole calmed down, and she and Chris both went to bed. The next morning, Nichole slept late, as she had a tendency to do. Chris woke up early and waited for Jon to leave his apartment for personal training. Then, Chris snuck over to the Corwins' apartment, where they kissed again.

From there, an affair quickly blossomed.

"We were texting a lot back and forth. A couple of times an hour, every day," Chris explained. "When I was at work, when I was home. Anytime I got the chance, really."

They regularly exchanged pictures, shared random thoughts, and complimented each other.

"You look really great today in that dress," Chris wrote.

"That shirt looks nice on you," Erin responded. "I like it when you wear that shirt with your cowboy hat."

Both Chris and Erin were infatuated with the excitement of the new relationship.

"There was just, like, a real strong emotional bond there," Chris explained. "I'm not really sure how it happened. We just sort of meshed somehow."

The new relationship ignited something in Chris and gave him something to look forward to each day. Erin became his escape from his mundane, unhappy life.

"It was just a change from what I thought was wrong," he remarked.

After just a few short weeks, Chris thought he was in love.

"I'm glad we're seeing each other," Chris texted Erin. "I love you."

Unaware of the affair, Nichole found Chris to be

colder and more distant than usual. Whenever she and Chris had even a minor disagreement, he would rudely ignore her, blow her off, and then go and have a drink and text. Nichole didn't know exactly what was wrong, but she suspected her husband was straying. Meanwhile, Chris was so focused on Erin, he didn't care about his wife. Still, while Erin was a distraction from his problems, he continued to battle depression and anxiety at home and work.

"I was under a lot of duress, a lot of strain. Nichole kept trying to talk about things, and I just kept shutting her out," Chris remembered. "Because in my mind, I was like, 'Why do I need to talk to her? I'll talk to Erin.'"

In the military, adultery is against the law. However, punishment is rare. When Marines are charged with adultery, it's normally in combination with another offense. Instead of being prosecuted, the most common reprimand Marines receive is counseling and orders to stop from their superiors.

Affairs are fairly common in the military. At Twentynine Palms, many of the young couples got married because they had kids or joined the military.

"It can be isolating, especially when the husbands are on deployment," explained Marine wife Jessica Wilkerson, a former acquaintance of the Lees. "Some of the women seek comfort with another Marine. Or they go out one night and hook up with a guy. A lot of wives do."

The depression that had plagued Erin vanished around the time she and Chris started their affair in February. Suddenly, Erin was her happy, giddy self again. Because she told her best friend everything, Erin confessed to Jessie about her new relationship with her neighbor. By then, Jessie had seen how unhappy Erin had become. While Jessie didn't typically support adultery, she encouraged her friend to pursue what made her happy. In phone calls, Erin went from complaining about Jon to gushing about Chris. Erin even sent photos of Chris to Jessie, with comments about how cute he was.

"I saw a spark in her again," Jessie explained. "She told me that the closer she got with Chris, the further she got from Jon."

But because Erin knew the affair was wrong, she didn't tell anyone else in her life about Chris at first, especially her mother.

Both Chris and Jon worked the same morning schedule with weekends off, which didn't afford Erin much private time with Chris. Most of their rendezvous took place early in the morning after Jon left for personal training, around 5:30 a.m. or 6:00 a.m. Chris used those few hours before Nichole awoke to be with Erin. Once Jon left the apartment, Erin would send a text. "Do you want to come over and give me a kiss?" To fool his wife, Chris pretended to go for personal training, but instead crept next door.

Snuggling and kissing on the Corwins' living room couch, Chris and Erin would talk about their day and what was happening in their lives. Before Jon returned home from his morning workout, Chris returned to his apartment, pretending he was just finishing his own training.

At night, the Corwins and Lees would often still get together for cookouts, movies, and video games. When the rest of the group was together, Chris avoided standing too close to Erin or speaking with her privately.

"I wasn't trying to attract a lot of attention in case

anyone was out and about," Chris explained. "I'd see her in the morning. We'd sit outside and talk or just hang out. Over time, we started getting closer and having longer conversations. If I went over there at night, it was either to see Jon or because me and Nichole went over there together."

At home, Nichole noticed an odd shift in her husband's behavior. Suddenly, it seemed like Chris was texting constantly. He also added multiple passwords and downloaded security apps to his phone. Previously, he had never been so secretive with his cell phone. Knowing her husband didn't use Twitter or Facebook, a suspicious Nichole asked Chris who he was chatting with online. But Chris always had a ready response: It was either his sister, Conor, or his friend Skyler.

"I talked to Erin around Nichole a lot," Chris admitted. "Sometimes I told her I was texting Erin when the conversation was casual. But sometimes I told her I was texting someone else."

Chris Lee thought he was "playing smart," he'd later admit. But Chris would soon learn he was not nearly as clever as he thought he was.

Chapter 12

Throughout their affair, Chris and Erin confided in each other about the difficulties in their respective marriages. Chris grumbled that his wife was a nag who just didn't understand him. Erin resented Jon for their money problems and for cutting her off from the credit cards.

"She would tell me they were in a super amount of debt and Jon was spending all the money," Chris recalled. "She kept telling me she had her own money when she was living by herself and had plenty, but that she used it all to move here to be with him."

Erin also identified her recent miscarriage as what led to the deterioration of her marriage. While Erin loved children and wanted to be a mom, she ultimately made peace with losing the baby. Seeking meaning in the miscarriage, Erin decided the timing must have been bad and that perhaps it was better that she didn't stay trapped in an unhappy marriage.

"She said she wasn't upset by it, because she didn't want to have Jon's baby and she was scared she'd get tied down," Chris remarked.

Erin seemed filled with regret. Although it was difficult to admit to herself, she now seemed to acknowledge that her parents had been right when they'd said she was too young to marry. While Erin had been happy to marry Jon at the time, she now complained to Chris that she hadn't gotten a traditional wedding ceremony and lamented ever coming to Twentynine Palms. She longed to return to Tennessee but said money was so tight she couldn't go back home. Erin claimed Jon wouldn't give her the money for a plane ticket to return to Oak Ridge. And Erin was too embarrassed to call her parents for money, according to Chris.

"Mostly it was her telling me how she was unhappy and that Jon scared her," Chris claimed. "She thought about leaving him all the time; the big thing was she didn't have any money to get home."

Chris's confessions to Erin were much darker. With Erin, he admitted for the first time the extent of his depression. In recent months, it had gotten to a point where he didn't care if he lived or died. With his platoon, he'd take them and do "crazy stuff" like fire rockets at nothing, he told Erin. Around the base, he raced his Jeep and nearly crashed several times.

"I just wanted to feel something. I was really numb to the world," Chris described. "Anything to get a rush or distraction from the feeling of nothing or emptiness."

He even confessed to Erin that he had attempted suicide. One morning, Chris had loaded a single bullet into the chamber of his .357 Ruger revolver, spun the chamber, and clicked it into place. He put the muzzle to his temple and pulled the trigger. It didn't fire. The next morning, he tried again.

"I confided in her that I was feeling suicidal," Chris remembered. "I was playing Russian roulette three or four times a week, like every morning. Not caring about anything. And she was like, 'You can't be doing that stuff.'"

Compassionate and sympathetic, Erin wanted to

help Chris. As he slowly opened up to her about his mental issues and suicidal urges, Erin pacified his pain. Erin became Chris's counselor and confidante, and he'd later say Erin helped save his life. Because no one else knew about the relationship, he felt he could talk to Erin.

"She was someone to talk to about stuff I didn't want to talk about with my wife," Chris explained. "Problems that I didn't think I needed to fix."

On the evening of Valentine's Day 2014, just weeks into Chris and Erin's rapid romance, Aisling and Conor Malakie invited the Lees and Corwins over to their apartment downstairs to watch movies. By midnight, everyone dispersed and went back to their own apartments, aside from Chris and Erin, who remained in the Malakies' living room watching the 2001 jukebox musical *Moulin Rouge!*

At the beginning of the movie, Erin was on the love seat and Chris was on the couch. But as the film progressed, Chris had scooted the love seat closer to the couch so they were touching. The lights were dimmed, and they were alone. Leaning over Erin, Chris kissed her tenderly.

The Malakies' son, Brian, cried out from his bedroom. Aisling groggily rose from her bed and got up to feed him a bottle. Stepping into the living room with her son on her hip, Aisling saw Chris bent over Erin, kissing her. Stunned, Aisling blinked hard, turned, and walked away toward the kitchen, not knowing what to say.

"I just stood there for a few minutes kind of hoping my son would make a noise, but he didn't," Aisling remembered. "So I just went in the kitchen and started opening cabinets and messing around with the bottles."

From the kitchen, Aisling could hear Erin and Chris whispering in the living room. Suddenly, out of the corner of her eye, she saw Chris rush past her, through the front door, and up the stairs back to his apartment. When Aisling returned to the living room, Erin had her eyes closed like she was sleeping.

"I stood in the living room for a second, and Brian made a noise," Aisling remarked. "Erin opened her eyes and looked at me and tried to pretend that she was sleeping."

Glowering at her friend, Aisling asked. "Hey, what are you still doing here?"

Erin said she'd had a fight with Jon about staying out too late and decided to sleep over on the couch. But Aisling knew her friend was lying.

"Whatever you say." Aisling rolled her eyes, turned, and walked to the master bedroom.

"I just went to bed," Aisling recalled. "I was more disappointed that she was lying to me."

Back in her bedroom, Aisling texted Chris. "What were you just doing?"

Chris replied quickly. "We were just telling each other secrets. I was whispering in her ear."

"OK. Well, Erin just told me a completely different story," Aisling responded. "Do you want to get your story straight or keep lying to me?"

After some coaxing, Chris admitted the truth.

"At first, he told me they were just whispering," Aisling recalled. "Then he admitted they were kissing."

Later, Aisling confronted Chris, who admitted that he and Erin had been secretly dating. He begged Aisling not to tell anyone. Aisling wasn't one to gossip and didn't want to get involved. Chris was her husband's best friend, and she adored Erin. She agreed to keep the kiss confidential but issued Chris a warning:

"You're going to ruin your life. You need to end it before Nichole finds out. Infidelity doesn't fly in the military."

In a separate conversation with Erin, Aisling told her friend she knew about her involvement with Chris and urged her to call it off.

"I know you are hurting because of the miscarriage," Aisling told her. "I won't judge you for needing support, but be honest with me."

Both Chris and Erin seemed to agree with Aisling and told her they were ending the affair. Still, the ordeal put a chill on the friendship between the three couples.

"When I found out about everything, I was like, 'I don't want to be a part of it. I don't want to keep that a secret,'" Aisling remembered. "It was completely awkward being around Jon and Nichole and everybody and having to keep that to myself."

While she didn't reveal the affair to Nichole, Aisling didn't keep secrets from her husband and told Conor about witnessing the kiss. When Conor confronted Chris about his intentions with his neighbor, Chris told Conor the relationship wasn't serious. He divulged that he planned on ending it in a few months when he completed his Marine contract in July, after which he'd return to Anchorage. Chris also bragged about fooling his wife with a secret messaging phone app.

Conversely, when Chris spoke to Erin, he romanticized their relationship, and they talked often of divorcing their spouses. They even discussed how Nichole and Jon would react to the divorces, custody arrangements with Liberty, and how Erin would shine as the girl's future stepmother. At one point, Chris texted Erin, "Why don't we just stay with each other?" Erin replied, "OK."

"We thought we were, like, perfect together. We were happy because it was a new relationship," Chris described. "Nothing could go wrong. We didn't fight at all."

In phone conversations and texts with Jessie Trentham in Tennessee, Erin made it known she was in love with Chris. She spoke about divorcing Jon and moving to Anchorage to be with Chris, even researching the city online.

Later, Chris would claim he fell in love with Erin but was reluctant to leave his wife because of Liberty. Chris loved his daughter, and it was important to him that Liberty grew up with both parents in one household. He feared Nichole would get primary custody in a divorce and that he would only get limited visitation.

By then, Erin had been babysitting Liberty regularly for months and had grown attached to the girl. Erin imagined one day marrying Chris and possibly being Liberty's stepmom.

Depending on his mood and who he was talking to, Chris would waffle on whether or not to divorce Nichole. He'd later say he subconsciously knew he would never leave because of Liberty. But he never told Erin that.

Chapter 13

Nichole Lee no longer trusted her husband. She had known Chris for nearly ten years and knew there was something very wrong.

"She was starting to get suspicious," Chris admitted.

Nichole had quietly observed as Chris befriended and progressively became infatuated with their teenage next-door neighbor. She didn't say anything when he became possessive over his phone. For a while, she just watched and waited.

Chris was a heavy sleeper, and one night after he'd had a few drinks, Nichole snatched his cell phone from the nightstand. Unable to unlock it without the password, Nichole pulled the SIM card out of the phone and plugged it into her laptop. That way, she was able to bypass the phone's passwords and access his text messages.

Scanning hundreds of texts, Nichole's face grew flush. Finally, there was the proof her husband was cheating. He wrote to Erin, "You're so gorgeous," and "I think I'm falling for you."

With tears in her eyes, Nichole stormed into the bedroom. Enraged, she woke Chris, and they got into an intense fight. Nichole screamed at him until sunrise.

"She lost her mind," Chris remembered. "We

had a huge argument. She got really upset and was crying."

Nichole demanded to know exactly what had happened between Chris and Erin.

"Did you have sex with her?" Nichole demanded.

"No," Chris replied quickly. "We just kissed a couple of times."

Hearing that, Nichole dissolved into a flood of tears. She was never a touchy-feely person, and for her, kissing was a big deal. Demanding to know how many times they kissed, Chris capped his interactions with Erin at about four—which was another lie.

Chris blamed his depression for the affair and admitted he had been suicidal. While Nichole knew Chris had not been himself, it was the first time he'd admitted his mental issues had spiraled beyond his control. His brief affair with Erin had simply been a distraction from his despair and apathy, Chris told Nichole. While he had momentarily gotten lost in his secret fantasy life, he would never leave her, he said. Begging for a second chance, he told Nichole he didn't want to lose her or Liberty.

Confronted with losing his daughter, Chris was suddenly willing to get help for his depression and go to counseling. While Nichole was incensed about the affair, she still loved Chris and didn't want her marriage to end.

"You're going to have to work to earn back my trust," Nichole told Chris. "Prove yourself to be a good husband if you want to stay in this marriage."

During the fight, Chris also confessed that Aisling Malakie had caught him kissing Erin but said nothing. Hearing that, Nichole was furious. The next morning, she texted Aisling.

"I am so hurt and I am so disgusted that you as my friend didn't tell me my husband was having an affair with Erin," Nichole wrote. "I can't believe you didn't tell me. You said nothing. And you hid it from me."

Aisling was taken aback. She didn't even consider Nichole a close friend.

"Listen, Nichole: I was in such a shitty position it was not even funny," Aisling replied. "They are adults. I said my two cents. I thought they ended it and apparently they didn't."

For a while at the apartment complex, Chris and Nichole kept to themselves and seemed to be working on their marriage. But when Nichole saw Aisling, she confessed how much she hated Erin and blamed the teen for seducing her husband.

"Even after everything came out, it was always Erin's fault. It was 100 percent Erin's fault," Aisling recalled. "Nothing was on Chris."

For the next several weeks, Nichole closely monitored Chris. After confiscating his phone, she deleted Erin's number.

"Nichole took my phone for a while and was holding on to it," Chris remembered. "So me and Erin just stopped talking."

One day, Nichole even recruited Aisling to monitor Chris.

"I need to go somewhere. Can you watch Chris for me?" Nichole asked Aisling. "Because he needs to be watched. Can you just keep track of him and see if he's texting?"

Astonished, Aisling reluctantly agreed.

A few minutes later, Chris came downstairs and plopped down on Aisling's couch in the living room. Aisling ended up going into the bedroom.

"When Nichole left, I walked over and was like, 'Look, Chris, don't be stupid. I'm not going to be reading over your shoulder,'" Aisling explained. "I was thinking, *I don't need to be babysitting Nichole's husband. I have my own child.*"

In April, Chris followed through on his promise and started going to marriage counseling with Nichole. Slowly, they began to repair the cracks in their marriage.

Nichole and Chris had always had a passionate physical connection. Even when she was mad at her husband, they never stopped having sex because Nichole viewed it as a stress reliever. But she was deeply troubled by her husband's affair.

"We stopped having sex for a while after she found out. She was really mad at me, and she didn't trust me," Chris recalled. "She didn't want to have me touch her because I kissed another girl. It was a really big deal for her."

Without his phone, the affair appeared to abruptly end.

One night in April, the Corwins, Lees, and Malakies planned a cookout. It was the first time all three couples would be together since Nichole discovered her husband's affair. Early that evening, Nichole came downstairs holding a glass of hard liquor in her hand.

"I need some liquid courage," Nichole said to Aisling. She was nervous because she had decided to finally tell Jon about the affair. She wanted Erin to be held responsible for the pain she'd caused. "I need you to make sure I don't go after Erin."

Soon, Jon came down to the apartment with a bag of meat he had purchased from the store. Nichole,

Aisling, Conor, and Conor's brother, Devin, also a Marine, were in the kitchen. Jon was standing at the sink washing off the meat. Aisling glanced over at Nichole, who was trembling.

"Jon." Nichole tapped him on the shoulder. "I have something to tell you."

Jon paused what he was doing but didn't turn around. Suddenly, Nichole blurted out, "Erin has been having an affair with Chris."

"She starts telling him everything she knows, everything she has seen," Aisling remembered. "He turns around and looks at her for a second. And he's like, 'OK.' You could see he was trying to process it."

In front of his friends, Jon learned for the first time that his wife had been unfaithful.

"It was a bombshell," Jon recalled. "It was earth-shattering."

As Nichole was talking, Jon turned to Aisling. "Can you go upstairs and get Erin?"

"Sure," Aisling said. "But I really don't want to."

Stepping closer to Aisling, Jon said more quietly, "I need you to go upstairs and get her right now."

Agreeing reluctantly, Aisling climbed the stairs to the second story and knocked on Erin's door. Erin opened it a crack and peeked out. "What?"

"I need you to come downstairs," Aisling said.

"For what?" Erin asked. "Why?"

"Nichole just told Jon about the affair," Aisling told her. "Everybody knows."

Opening the door wide, Erin burst into tears. "Oh my God. Jon is going to hate me. He's going to leave me!"

"She starts hyperventilating, holding her throat like, 'Oh my God. I'm going to die,'" Aisling remembered. "She was completely freaking out. There was a part of me that wanted to hold her and tell her everything was going to be fine. But the other part of me was just so angry with her. I was like, 'You did this to yourself. Let's go downstairs and face what you did.'"

After a few minutes, Aisling walked Erin downstairs. Inside the Malakies' apartment, Erin stood down the hall, feet from Nichole. Jon tried to talk to his wife as Nichole ranted. The argument became heated, and Erin threw her hands in the air. "I'm not doing this right now," she said. Erin locked eyes with her husband. "Jon, I'll be upstairs if you want to talk."

As Erin turned to leave, Nichole stormed after her, eyes flashing with anger. She shoved her finger in Erin's face.

"If you ever have anything else to do with my husband, I'll kill you myself!" Nichole screamed.

Aisling chased after Nichole, grabbed her by the shoulder, and spun her around. "That's enough!"

By then, Erin had already booked it up the stairs and was inside her apartment. Nichole returned to Aisling's kitchen and downed a gulp of liquor.

Looking over at Aisling, Jon said, "I'm going upstairs to talk to her. Can you come with me? You're the only one who knows the truth. I don't want her to lie to me."

For nearly two hours, Aisling served as mediator inside the apartment while Jon interrogated his wife. Erin confessed that she and Chris had kissed, but said he was the one who initiated it.

At one point, Erin asked Jon, "Do you want me to leave? Do you want to try and make this work? What do you want to do?"

"I want to be with you!" Jon said.

While Jon was angry and had been deceived, he still loved his wife and didn't want to divorce.

"I tried my hardest to make it work," Jon recalled. "You should always try and fix something instead of replacing it. And I was trying everything I could to fix it."

That night when Chris returned from field ops, Nichole gave her husband a few details of the skirmish, claiming she knew Erin had been lying about Jon. While it was true the Corwins were having marital problems, Nichole claimed that Erin had been inflating the extent of their issues in a bid for sympathy from Chris.

For a while, there was tremendous tension between the neighbors at the apartment complex on Jasmine Drive. Aisling and Conor still spoke to both couples and tried not to pick sides. Conor didn't want to get involved, and Aisling was exhausted by being thrust in the middle.

"We all just kind of stayed quiet for a little bit and let everybody sort it out," Aisling recalled.

However, the affair abruptly terminated the friendship between the Corwins and the Lees. Jon never addressed it with Chris, but the two former friends stopped speaking.

"He was having an affair with my wife, and all contact and friendship stopped," Jon explained.

It was awkward with the couples living so close. For his part, Chris tried to prevent running into the Corwins.

"I was trying to avoid the conversation as much as I could," Chris admitted. "Whenever they were out, I went back inside because I was trying to avoid him. I just didn't want to talk to any of them."

For a while, Erin and Jon considered moving away

from the apartment complex and renting a house off base with the Malakies. However, Aisling and Conor didn't want to be involved in the relationship drama and ultimately decided not to relocate.

In Tennessee, Lore knew nothing about Erin's affair, but she was aware the couple was having problems. Erin briefly told her mom about plans to move out of the apartment complex. Then, it seemed, her daughter abruptly changed her mind.

"She talked to me about it quite a bit, and then it just stopped," Lore recalled. "It didn't happen. And that just kind of seemed odd to me."

Instead, Erin and Jon created a new plan. Although Jon had always intended to make a career in the Marines, he now decided he wanted to find a new job, and Jon and Erin discussed moving back to Oak Ridge in 2015 when his military contract was complete. When she spoke to her mom, Erin explained she was considering moving back home but never clarified her reason for the change of heart.

"I don't know exactly why he wanted to get out of the Marines," Lore remembered. "Maybe he realized it was harder on Erin than what he thought it was going to be . . . I don't know."

But even talk of returning to Tennessee caused issues with the Corwins. Shelia Braden wanted her son and Erin to move into the family home with Jon's brother, Zachary. Erin, however, didn't like that idea at all.

Meanwhile, Isabel Megli noticed Erin had stopped coming to the ranch with the Lees. Instead, she would visit the ranch on the weekends, while Nichole hung out there during the week.

"I would say to Nichole, 'Where's Erin?'" Isabel

explained. "And Nichole would say, 'I don't know.' She never said another word."

After her affair with Chris ended, Erin felt even more empty and alone. On phone calls with Jessie, Erin complained that Chris was ignoring her.

"Chris became distant, and he wouldn't really talk to her," Jessie explained. "They were just getting close when Jon and Nichole found out."

The infidelity furthered the divide between Erin and Jon. While Jon said he wanted to work on his problems, he continued to be cold toward his wife. Erin told Jessie her marriage was over and Jon didn't seem to care.

"She didn't feel like she was loved in the relationship anymore," Jessie recalled. "She was pretty much by herself out there."

The couple's money issues worsened. When Jon's truck broke down, they couldn't afford to have it fixed. To report for work, he used Erin's blue Corolla, leaving her marooned in her apartment. At the ranch, Erin started having trouble keeping up the hundred-dollar monthly payment to sponsor her horse, Cassy. Soon, she told Isabel she could no longer support Cassy.

To improve their finances, both Jon and Erin became more frugal. While Nichole no longer permitted her neighbor to watch Liberty, Erin continued to earn extra money babysitting children around the base. Jon also listed the sand rail online for sale for $3,000, but sold it for just $1,500.

Jon had previously taken away Erin's credit cards, and her only access to money was the checking account. Once, she bought too many groceries using the debit card, which caused another fight.

By then, there was such animosity between Erin and Jon that even trivial things caused vicious arguments. One night, Erin was charging her laptop in bed and Jon got angry because the power cord was in his way. The fight grew heated, and cruel words were exchanged.

"She ended up sleeping on the couch because he started a fight over her laptop cord. It was something that stupid," Jessie described. "She didn't want to deal with him."

The next morning, Jon was still angry. As he stomped out of the apartment, he made a flippant comment. "I'll bring the divorce papers home today."

By the end of the workday, his temper had cooled. When he got home, Jon apologized and tried to be a bit kinder to Erin that night. Still, when she spoke to Jessie, Erin seemed resigned that her marriage was heading to divorce.

"Basically, she knew it was ending," Jessie explained.

By May, the awkwardness began to fade around the Jasmine Drive apartment complex. As inexplicable as it seemed, the Lees and Corwins seemed to put the affair behind them.

Jon was the first to try to repair the friendship. "It wasn't the same as it was before, but you always give someone a second chance," Jon remembered.

One night, he was barbecuing in the common area outside the apartment complex when Chris arrived home. Instead of ignoring him, Jon offered his old friend a drink. Chris, however, maintained his distance.

"Jon wanted to move past it, I think," Chris explained. "He'd offer me a drink or offer me a shot. And it just seemed weird to me."

Whenever the three couples were together, however, it continued to be chilly, especially between Nichole and Erin.

"Everyone was hanging out again," Aisling remembered. "But Nichole still wasn't talking to Erin. There was no communication there."

Meanwhile, Chris was making plans for his life back in Alaska. After five years in the Marines, his contract was ending on July 7, 2014.

"I started trying to focus on moving forward, getting ready to leave, moving past all that," Chris remembered.

While Chris loved the desert and was nostalgic about leaving, his affair with Erin had only furthered Nichole's desire to return to Alaska. The couple planned to live temporarily with Nichole's brother in the Anchorage community of Jewel Lake.

During his career in the Marines, Chris hadn't put much thought into furthering his education. Now at twenty-four, he wanted to use funds from his GI bill to go to college. Taking a college placement test, he learned that his reading and writing comprehension were acceptable, but he would have to work toward college-level math.

After researching universities, Chris settled on the University of Alaska–Anchorage and planned to pursue a degree in chemical engineering. His ultimate goal was to land a job in northern Alaska working at one of the numerous oil refineries in the area. With a degree, engineers can earn six-figure salaries at an oil company.

Once settled, Nichole would continue to be a stay-at-home mom and expressed desires to have another baby.

The Lees also planned on bringing their horses, Humorous and Mack, with them. That meant the Lees would drive across the country, through Canada, and up to Alaska, hauling the horses in a trailer.

Chris spent most of June making preparations. Because he still had annual leave time available, Chris took time off from duty from June 9 to June 29. He planned to use the time to complete a few final projects at Isabel's barn, pack up the apartment, and hang out with his Marine buddies. Chris's sister, Malie, had also booked a visit to the base.

During most of the leave, however, Chris and Nichole ended up confined to their apartment. Chris's black Jeep Cherokee had broken down and was in the shop having the transmission rebuilt. Chris picked up his newly repaired Jeep in mid-June, just days before Malie's visit. That week, Chris showed his sister around the base and took her to the desert.

There was something about her visit that would rattle Malie. On one of the last days of her trip, the siblings went off-roading in Chris's Jeep. As they were stopped at a light, heading west toward Palm Springs, the vehicle lurched forward and crawled to a dead stop. It was towed back to the shop, where Chris would discover the transfer case had blown. To make her return flight, Malie had to rent a car and drive alone to San Diego.

When the Jeep broke down, Chris erupted in a burst of anger his sister had never seen before. It would be years before Malie Lee would understand exactly what was troubling Chris.

Chapter 14

Splashes of red, yellow, and purple painted the muted landscape of Joshua Tree National Park as the desert wildflowers that bloom each spring wilted in the summer heat. The contorted Joshua tree that gave the park its name cast gnarled shadows on the desert floor. Towering over the terrain, rugged, sharply perpendicular mountain ranges lurched skyward.

Spanning nearly 800,000 acres comprised mainly of the Mojave Desert, the tranquil Joshua Tree National Park juxtaposes the bustling Marine base. Parallel to the combat center, on the south side of Highway 62, the park is a popular destination for hikers and adventurers, as well as the Marines and their families.

The sand, rocks, and creosote bushes of the Mojave form a vast scape of tortured beauty—an oasis of oblivion. This sandy stage would be the unlikely setting for a grisly act of murder.

On the morning of June 22, 2014, Chris was passing through the park in his newly repaired Jeep with his civilian friend Joseph Hollifield. Throughout his five years in Twentynine Palms, Chris had often frequented the park to go off-roading, explore the desert, and to hunt coyotes and snakes. In fact, the two men had previously hunted coyotes together at least twice. Chris first met Joseph in 2009, when Chris hired him to fix his Jeep, and the two became friends, hanging out once or twice a month. Joseph, who had lived in Yucca Valley since 1989, was a few years older than Chris and had deeply tanned complexion and dark hair.

It was midmorning, and temperatures were climbing toward one hundred degrees by the time Chris and Joseph reached their destination—a remote area just north of the park. Armed with his .22-caliber rifle, Chris got out of his Jeep and wandered around the desert. At one point, he encountered a rattlesnake, which he shot and killed.

Joseph pulled out his cell phone and snapped a picture of the dead snake. Aiming the camera toward the Coxcomb Mountains, he snapped another picture of the sheer mountains. In one shot, Chris is holding his hunting rifle and standing beside his Jeep, his back to the camera. Hiking through the desert, the two men climbed up a hillock and discovered a cluster of abandoned gold mines.

Joseph captured an image of a dilapidated brick cabin that had once been painted yellow. In another picture, a broken-down water tower rusts in the sun. Approaching one of the vertical mine shafts, Joseph peered down into the pit and caught an image of an eerie, deep hole.

Later that afternoon at the horse rescue, Chris talked animatedly about his desert trip. He told Isabel Megli he found so many "interesting things," but he seemed particularly enthralled with the abandoned mines.

"There was a mine shaft so remote that no one would ever find it," Chris told Isabel.

That same morning, June 22, Erin awoke feeling queasy. The nausea got so bad, she asked Jon to take her to the emergency room. Once there, the doctor ran a urine test, which revealed the source of her nausea: Erin was about three weeks pregnant.

Jon was somewhat surprised. They hadn't been planning the pregnancy, and it had been a while since the two had even been intimate. But Jon also felt like the baby could provide a chance to repair his marriage. He called his father in Tennessee and told him he was going to be a grandfather.

But there was something strange about Erin with this pregnancy. She seemed stressed out, distant, and oddly distracted. Jon wasn't quite sure what was troubling his wife.

Unlike with her first pregnancy, Erin didn't post about it on Facebook or even call to tell her mom. She did, however, tell her best friend, Jessie Trentham.

For Erin's twentieth birthday, Lore had been planning a visit to Twentynine Palms. Erin wanted to show her mom the base and take her to explore the local landmarks, including Joshua Tree National Park. As her birthday gift, Lore also planned to take Erin to San Diego, about three hours south of Twentynine Palms, to go to the San Diego Zoo and SeaWorld.

On June 25, Erin told Jessie that she was cleaning the apartment to get ready for the visit.

"I got to focus on getting the house in perfect condition," Erin texted. "My mother comes in a week. I'm excited!"

A few minutes later, Jessie responded, asking about the pregnancy. "Are you going to tell her?"

Erin replied that she was waiting to do it in person. The next day, Thursday, June 26, Erin called her mom in Oak Ridge.

"She and I had talked about all the things we were

going to do when I got out there," Lore recalled. "We weren't necessarily going to hike, but just walk around and try to find places that would be pretty to look at."

Around this time, Jon had been talking more and more about leaving the military. His latest plan was to go to school to be trained as an auto mechanic. Researching online, he found an auto mechanic school with campuses in California and Tennessee. Jon was considering checking out the California location while Lore was in town. Because they only had one working car at the time, Erin and Lore discussed accompanying him.

Toward the end of the conversation, Erin mentioned how much she missed her mom's cooking. Lore promised to cook her daughter's favorite dishes and listed for Erin all the items she would need to prepare her cheddar chowder and cheesy enchiladas.

"That's probably the last part of our conversation, talking about all the things she wanted me to cook and making sure she made the grocery list right," Lore remembered. "To make sure she would have all the ingredients."

As she was hanging up, Erin told her mother what she always said when they spoke: "I love you, Mom."

"I love you, too," Lore replied.

It was the last time Lore Heavilin would ever hear her daughter's voice.

It was a warm morning on Friday, June 27, and Chris and his family spent the day at the horse rescue. Chris worked with his Thoroughbred, training her to go up and down hills. Nichole fitted her mare for new horseshoes while Liberty played with some of the other volunteers' children.

As he was preparing to leave, Chris noticed a white Blue Rhino propane tank in one of the toolsheds.

"Could I borrow that?" Chris asked Isabel.

"Sure, take it," Isabel said. She planned on seeing the couple the following morning at the ranch. "Plan on barbecuing?"

"No," Chris said with a wry smile. "I'm going to use it to play games."

Isabel wasn't quite sure what he meant by that, and she didn't ask.

The Lees left the ranch at about 9:00 p.m. and headed to a Stater Bros. grocery store near the base. Unsure if they would receive Chris's final paycheck because of all the leave time he'd taken, money had been tight. Nichole gathered spare change and went inside the store to buy a loaf of bread.

Liberty had fallen asleep in the back seat of the car, so Chris stayed by the vehicle while his wife shopped. As he waited, he texted his Marine buddy Skyler Dent. Earlier in the week, Chris had invited Skyler to go on one last coyote-hunting trip in the desert. But Skyler recently had surgery on his shoulder and told Chris he didn't think he could go.

Because Skyler wasn't far from the grocery store, he drove to meet Chris in the parking lot, arriving at about 9:30 p.m. Chris repeatedly urged Skyler to join him the next morning.

"It will be our last trip," he pleaded.

"I can't, man," Skyler replied. "My shoulder's been killing me. It hurts even riding in the car."

They spoke for about ten minutes before Nichole returned to the Jeep, and they all headed back to the Lees' apartment, Skyler trailing behind in his own vehicle.

As they passed the stairwell to the second floor,

Chris noticed Conor in his own apartment, drinking with his buddies. Chris mentioned he was going hunting the next day and invited Conor to come with him.

"I can probably go," Conor said. "I'll let you know for sure in the morning."

Skyler joined Chris and Nichole upstairs in their apartment, where he stayed and talked for another twenty minutes before returning to the barracks. By 11:30 p.m., Chris and Nichole had gone to bed.

Next door, Jon and Erin were also in bed. Erin's pregnancy had not relieved much of the tension between the couple. They continued to bicker over minor, petty things. As the weekend approached, she told Jon she needed some "me time." Early the next morning, she told Jon, she planned to take the Corolla and drive to Joshua Tree National Park to scout out locations to visit with her mom. She told Jon she'd be home before 4:00 p.m. for dinner.

Erin also told Jessie about her plans.

"She just wanted to be able to get away for a little bit," Jessie explained. "Especially since she and Jon were fighting a lot. She needed some time away."

Chapter 15

On the last day of her life, Erin awoke around dawn.

Jon was still asleep. Quietly, Erin styled her hair and applied makeup, painting her lips with tinted gloss. She dressed in a pair of pink panties and a matching pink-and-black bra underneath blue denim jean shorts and a pink tank top.

It was June 28, 2014, a Saturday.

At 7:19 a.m., Erin called her friend Jessie and said she was getting ready for her day. They spoke for a few minutes before Erin hung up.

Grabbing her cell phone, Erin walked over to the bed, knelt down, and gave her husband a kiss good-bye.

"I'm heading out for the day, Jon," she whispered. "I love you."

"Love you, too," Jon said.

Jon heard the front door of the apartment open and shut. Still in bed, he glanced out the bedroom window and saw Erin get behind the wheel of the blue Corolla, back up, and drive east toward the back Condor Gate of the combat center. Jon closed his eyes and drifted back to sleep.

In the apartment next door, Chris Lee lowered the black baseball cap on his head and descended the apartment staircase carrying his .22 Winchester rifle.

Strolling toward the carport, he opened the back of his Jeep Cherokee and shoved the weapon under a tarp. He was dressed in a pair of denim blue jeans, a white T-shirt with a blue American Eagle Outfitters brand logo, and a pair of tan, steel-toed combat boots with rough tread.

Earlier that morning, Chris had spoken with Conor outside his apartment near the carport, where the Jeep was parked. Conor said he couldn't go coyote hunting because he still had friends over, sleeping off their night of drinking.

"Dude, they can take care of themselves," Chris told Conor. "Come with me. It will be our last hurrah."

But Conor said Aisling wouldn't approve and that he couldn't come. Conor looked over at Chris's Jeep and saw a white propane tank peeking out from under the tarp.

"What are you going to do with that?" Conor asked.

"I'm going to use it to blow up a mine shaft," Chris replied with a grin. While out in the desert, Chris explained, he planned to pour gasoline on it, shoot it, and cause an explosion.

By 7.00 a.m., Chris had set off on his desert excursion alone. Before leaving base, he stopped for gas. Because he still had a quarter of a tank, he just put in thirty dollars' worth of gas.

Chris exited through the Condor Gate and navigated onto Highway 62, the main route to Joshua Tree National Park. As he turned down Gold Crown Road, he switched into four-wheel drive to traverse the rocky dirt paths over the mountain through the old mining districts. His destination was the same abandoned mining area he had been so fascinated with when he had visited the desert with his friend Joseph just six days prior.

At 8:16 a.m., Chris's phone alerted that he had received a new text. Glancing at the screen, he saw Conor had sent him a message.

"Hey, I can meet up now," Conor wrote. "My friends left."

Chris typed out a quick message telling Conor where to meet. "Tell Nichole I put my phone in airplane mode," Chris texted.

Then, Chris switched his phone off.

Inside unit D, Nichole slept late. When she got up, she texted Isabel at the ranch. The day before, Nichole had told Isabel they would be returning Saturday morning. But now Nichole texted that she was sick and staying home with Liberty, while Chris went hunting.

Next door, Jon was in the apartment living room playing video games. Hours passed, and he didn't hear from Erin. He wasn't too alarmed, figuring there was limited cellular service in Joshua Tree.

That afternoon, Lore texted Erin to follow up on their discussion about Jon's auto mechanic school.

"I think we should go out there with Jon and check out the school," Lore wrote.

Erin never replied.

About 3:30 p.m., Chris emerged from the park alone. Switching on his phone, Chris noticed he had missed calls from both Conor and his wife. First, he called Conor.

By then, Conor was irritated. After receiving his friend's text, Conor drove toward the entrance of the park but couldn't find Chris or his Jeep. Conor tried calling, but Chris's cell phone went straight to voice mail. He sent a text, but Chris didn't respond. After nearly three hours of searching, Conor gave up and returned home.

When Chris finally called hours later, Conor confronted him. "What happened? Where have you been?"

Chris said that Conor must have gotten confused about where they planned to meet.

"I was looking for a good place to find coyotes," Chris told him. "And then I got kind of lost and had no reception."

Chris also told a bizarre story about encountering a stranger in the park who shot a gun in his direction.

"You should have come with me, dude!" Chris exclaimed. "Someone shot at me!" After hanging up with Conor, Chris called his wife.

"Where are you?" Nichole was frantic and gasping for air. When she couldn't reach Chris, she had panicked, triggering an asthma attack.

"She was really upset," Chris recalled. "Because I had no service and she couldn't get ahold of me."

By 4:00 p.m., when Chris returned to the apartment, Nichole was sobbing. Embracing his wife, he tried to calm her down.

"Breathe. Breathe," he told his wife soothingly. "It's OK. Everything is going to be OK."

Once she had caught her breath, Nichole and Chris lay down and took a nap.

Later, Conor noticed the propane tank was no longer in the back of Chris's Jeep. He asked his friend if he had blown the tank like he'd discussed.

"It didn't go off," Chris replied dryly.

As the sun was setting, Jon realized it was getting late and Erin still hadn't returned. Starting at 4:00 p.m., when Erin had said she'd be home, he dialed his wife's number dozens of times, but each call went straight to voice mail. Jon told himself that Erin must have decided to stop by a friend's house.

But it was just so unlike Erin not to at least call.

In the early evening, Chris awoke from his nap beside his wife.

They passed the next few hours watching Pokémon cartoons with Liberty. Around 9:30 p.m., Chris left to pick up takeout for dinner at the nearby Santana's Mexican restaurant. The family ate in front of the television while watching one of Liberty's favorite movies, *The Pirate Fairy*.

Around 11:30 p.m., Chris and Nichole retired to bed.

By midnight, Jon Corwin was silently imploding. He had barely slept, lying in bed and clutching his cell phone, hoping Erin's number would appear on the screen.

"I called her at least fifty times," Jon remembered. "I was just so stressed and worried."

As the sun rose that Sunday morning, Jon knew something was very wrong. He called the San Bernardino County Sheriff's Department.

"My wife is missing," Jon said, his voice trembling. "I need to file a missing persons report."

Chapter 16

Rookie sheriff's deputy Danny Millan was just weeks on the job and in training at Twentynine Palms when he and his supervisor were sent to the Marine base to take a missing persons report. Arriving at the apartment complex on Jasmine Drive, Millan and sheriff's corporal Cathy Tabor climbed the stairs to the second floor and knocked on the Corwins' front door. Jon invited them inside.

"When did you last see your wife?" Tabor asked.

Jon replied that he'd seen her the morning before as she was leaving to go to Joshua Tree National Park.

"She's pregnant," Jon said, grimacing. "We just found out."

He provided Erin's phone number and the number of her mom and some of her friends in Tennessee. As they took his statement, Jon seemed relatively composed, considering his wife was missing.

A pregnant woman lost in the desert during the summer was considered high priority. The San Bernardino County Sheriff's Department was all too aware how deadly the summer heat can be in the Mojave. Each year, dozens of hikers are rescued from the desert in distress. Another dozen people perish each year from dehydration, exposure to the elements, accidents, and even murder.

After speaking with Jon, Millan and Tabor canvassed the apartment complex to talk to some of the Corwins' neighbors. Their first stop was apartment D, right next door to the Corwins. Chris Lee answered the door.

When Millan and Tabor explained they were searching for Erin Corwin, Chris didn't seem surprised or concerned. But he said he couldn't be of any help because he didn't know Erin very well. The last time they spoke, he said, was about two months earlier. He claimed the extent of any contact he had with Erin was waving hi in the hallway.

"When was the last time you saw her Corolla in the carport?" Tabor asked.

Chris glanced up at the ceiling. "Probably yesterday. I don't know. I wasn't paying attention."

Chris added that the last conversation he could remember having with Erin concerned a babysitting gig.

Next, the investigators went downstairs and knocked on the Malakies' apartment. When the deputy told Aisling that Erin was missing around Joshua Tree National Park, her stomach sank. That same day, Conor had spent hours driving around the park in search of Chris. It couldn't be a coincidence.

Aisling told the deputies about Chris's affair with Erin. As she spoke, Tabor and Millan exchanged a curious glance. The deputies returned to apartment D upstairs, but by then, Chris Lee was gone.

A panicked sense of dread washed over Jon. After deputies took his report, Jon also went downstairs and spoke with Conor and Aisling, desperate to see if they had any idea where Erin could be. Neither Conor nor Aisling had seen Erin in days.

Jon then returned to his apartment and called Lore Heavilin in Tennessee.

"Erin's missing," Jon blurted out.

"What do you mean Erin's missing?" Lore asked.

"She went to Joshua Tree to look for places to go during your trip," Jon said. "She left yesterday morning. I haven't seen her since. I'm so worried."

Lore's first thought was that Erin must have gotten stuck in the desert.

"Knowing that she had absolutely no sense of direction, I assumed she was lost," Lore explained.

With summer temperatures approaching one hundred degrees in California, Lore's immediate concern was that Erin would be dehydrated.

"How much water did she take with her to drink?" Lore asked.

A short time later, Lore's phone rang again. This time it was a San Bernardino County sheriff's deputy following up on the missing persons report.

"Do you think she might be driving home to Tennessee?" the deputy asked.

Lore laughed. She knew her daughter would never drive across the country on a whim.

"I know how much she hates to drive, has no sense of direction," Lore told the deputy. "And there's absolutely no way she would give up a trip to SeaWorld and the zoo."

Fretting about her friend, Aisling called Nichole Lee.

"Where's your husband?" Aisling asked. "Erin's missing. There's people here looking for her."

Nichole's callous response left Aisling astonished.

"I don't care what happens to that little bitch," Nichole said coldly. "Mind your own business."

Sickened, Aisling hung up the phone. Scalding

tears flooded her eyes and poured down her cheeks. Somehow, she knew something terrible happened to Erin.

Jon spent most of Sunday morning calling friends in search of his wife.

One of his first calls was to her best friend, Jessie Trentham, in Tennessee.

"Have you heard from Erin?" Jon asked.

At first, Jessie was taken aback. While she knew Jon as Erin's husband and had met him a few times at Tractor Supply, he had never called her before. Jessie explained she had talked to Erin just yesterday as she got ready to go to the park. But for some reason Jon didn't understand, Jessie was vague about the details of their conversation.

That afternoon, while detectives searched for Erin around the base, Jon rounded up more than thirty Marines to hunt for Erin.

"We literally drove around Joshua Tree National Park all day," Jon recalled, "trying to find any signs, any clues about where she might have been."

He also posted on his Facebook page: "If you hear from Erin, please contact me."

That Facebook message got the attention of several of Erin's friends in Tennessee, including Abby Gouge, who immediately called Lore.

"What in the world is going on?" Abby asked.

Lore told her what she knew, which wasn't much. Lore also messaged Jessie on Facebook, asking her to call.

By the afternoon, with no word from Erin, Lore's worry had morphed into agonizing anxiety. More than two thousand miles from Twentynine Palms, she felt helpless.

Jon also kept in close communication with his own parents. Worried, Shelia Braden wanted to be there for her son. That evening, Lore spoke with Jon and Sheila and decided to coordinate a flight for the following morning. Bill would stay behind a day to make arrangements for Alex.

As Lore hastily packed a suitcase, her cell phone rang again. This time it was Jessie Trentham. What she had to say about Erin would change everything.

Chapter 17

Chris Lee had been caught in a lie.

But while it seemed suspicious, the lie wasn't necessarily incriminating. If Chris was having an affair, he had every reason to try to keep it a secret. Although the rule is rarely enforced, in the military, cheating carried penalties of up to a year in jail, plus a dishonorable discharge resulting in forfeiture of all retirement pay.

"It's not uncommon to see a military person deny such a relationship because they know it can lead to repercussions," explained San Bernardino County sheriff's sergeant Trevis Newport.

After speaking with the Malakies, sheriff's investigators now knew Chris Lee had been concealing some sort of past affair with a missing woman. When they couldn't find him around the complex, sherriff's corporal Cathy Tabor repeatedly called Chris's cell phone. But the phone kept ringing, never connecting to voice mail, and they were unable to leave a message.

Patrolling the complex, Millan and Tabor watched and waited. Around noon, Chris pulled into the carport in his Jeep. Dressed in Marine fatigues, he stepped out of the car. The officers approached Chris and asked to speak to him again.

"We got reports of you possibly being with her last night," Deputy Danny Millan told Chris. It wasn't true, but investigators wanted to see how Chris would respond. Chris took the bait and said he now wanted to clarify his previous statement but didn't want to talk inside his apartment. Instead, he agreed to meet Millan and Tabor in the parking lot of a Vons supermarket for a recorded audio interview.

"When's the last time you saw her?" Millan asked Chris for the second time.

"I saw her a couple of times when she was outside, but I haven't spoken to her in more than a month," Chris replied quickly. "Ever since everything went down."

Chris now admitted to the affair and explained everything that "went down" when his wife uncovered the infidelity.

"A little while after she moved in, we started having a thing," Chris admitted. "The bond grew stronger, and then my wife found out and Jon found out, and the whole thing blew up."

The affair started partially because of his mental state, Chris told investigators, blaming his depression and suicidal thoughts on why he first started talking to Erin. But he added another layer to the drama, telling police that Erin wasn't so innocent.

"She's a pathological liar," Chris said. "She was lying to me about her husband—she kept telling me that he's beating her and choking her."

According to Chris's story, soon after his first kiss with Erin, she had admitted to him that she was being abused. Because Erin was afraid for her life, Chris told deputies he was trying to protect her.

After Nichole confronted Erin about the affair, however, Chris said he learned everything his lover had told him was a lie. According to Chris, Erin had admitted in front of Jon that she had never been abused.

Chris said that Nichole believed Erin had deceived him to gain sympathy.

"What she had told me was her husband was abusing her and she was afraid he was going to kill her," Chris told deputies. "But I found out that she had lied to me."

But Millan reminded Chris that he was the one who had lied earlier that morning when he'd said he barely knew Erin.

"Why at first did you tell me that you don't know her?" Millan asked.

"I just didn't think our relationship was pertinent," Chris replied.

"OK. Are you scared of getting in trouble?"

"No. I just didn't think it was relevant because it was so long ago."

The investigator asked why Chris didn't answer their calls throughout the day. He claimed his phone battery died and it was being charged inside his apartment.

"Typically, if a phone is dead, it goes to voice mail. But yours was still ringing," Tabor told Chris.

"OK, then I don't know." Chris shrugged.

Wrinkling her brow, Tabor scowled suspiciously at Chris. Probing deeper into the details of the affair, Chris said it ended a month and a half or two months earlier.

"So you understand that she's about two months pregnant right now?" Tabor interjected. It wasn't true—Erin was just a few weeks into her pregnancy. But Tabor wanted to see how Chris would respond.

"No, I didn't." Chris shook his head.

Tabor assured Chris they weren't part of the military and were not concerned about a consensual affair.

"I'm going to reiterate we're not the marriage police. We're not here to get caught up if you guys are still sneaking off," Tabor told Chris. "Obviously in the investigation, being that she's pregnant, the father's going to come out. And if it turns out the father is you, it's important that we know that now for the missing persons investigation."

But Chris said his affair with Erin was emotional and had never progressed beyond kissing.

"It won't be me," he said. "We never had sex."

The deputies asked about Erin's friends, her routine, plans, and where she could be.

"She said she kept wanting to run away or get out of there, but she was afraid something would happen," Chris said. "But like I said, I don't know if anything she says is true or not. Because she was constantly lying to me, lying to Jon, lying to everyone."

When Tabor asked about Chris's whereabouts on Saturday, he readily admitted he had been at Joshua Tree National Park in the morning and early afternoon. But he said he had gone alone to go coyote hunting after his buddies bailed on the trip.

"So you guys never met up? You never saw her? You didn't invite her? She didn't invite you?" Tabor asked. "'Cause she went missing yesterday morning."

"No. I made these plans maybe a week ago," Chris replied.

Describing his desert trip, Chris said he hadn't shot any coyotes but did take out his .22-caliber rifle and fired it at some rocks.

"So if we go up there, we're going to find .22 cartridges?" Tabor asked.

"I picked them all up," Chris said.

Chris said the casings were in his Jeep and allowed

officers to search the vehicle. Inside, they found ten spent .40-caliber bullet casings, which they confiscated as evidence. But there was no rifle.

"So you understand the seriousness of the investigation right now—she has not surfaced, we have not found her," Tabor told Chris. "So potentially, it's a homicide investigation."

Chris nodded in agreement. But Tabor and Millan sensed something amiss about Chris.

"He didn't seem like he wanted to talk," Tabor recalled. "He answered quickly."

As they were finishing up, Tabor let Chris know he wasn't under arrest but that the circumstances were suspicious.

"You initially said you were just associates. And then we find out later that you guys have this intimate relationship and that you were actually quite involved. And then we get reports that you are the last person that she had been seen with," Tabor said. "It just doesn't look good."

Before Chris drove to the grocery store parking lot to speak with deputies, he'd spoken to his wife, whispering a secret message in her ear.

That afternoon, Nichole gathered her daughter, grabbed a long black case from the apartment closet, and headed to the horse rescue. When she arrived about an hour later, Isabel was surprised to see them. Just the previous morning, Nichole had said she was sick. But that afternoon, she and Liberty looked healthy.

As Isabel tended to an injured foal, Nichole grabbed the black case and stepped into the main house on the property. A few minutes later when she stepped outside, the case was gone. At the time, Isabel didn't give it much thought.

By then, word of Erin's disappearance had made its way to the rescue. When Isabel asked about Erin, Nichole's face flushed. For the first time, Nichole revealed to Isabel that Erin had had an affair with Chris. But Nichole also claimed she didn't really believe Erin was missing. To Isabel, Nichole painted a picture of Erin as a liar who had created a ruse to somehow punish Chris.

"She's probably hiding out somewhere, trying to make Chris's life miserable," Nichole rolled her eyes. "She's setting us up. She's trying to hurt our family to get sympathy."

Nichole's nasty words left Isabel stunned.

"She said Erin was missing, and that she felt she was playing a game, and that she wished she was dead, and she wouldn't care if she was dead," Isabel recalled. "She wasn't at all nervous . . . She seemed more angry and defiant. All of this was Erin's fault anyway, Nichole believed."

After a tense interview with the deputies, Chris returned to the apartment complex. When Conor saw Chris's black Jeep pulling into the carport, he dashed outside. Despite being close with Chris for years, Conor suddenly felt uneasy about his friend and worried for Erin's safety.

"Did you do what I think you did?" Conor asked bluntly.

Chris looked directly into Conor's eyes. "What are you even talking about?" he responded, shaking his head defiantly. "You know me better than that."

"I swear to God, Chris," Conor told him. "You'd better have not done anything to that girl."

Despite his insistent denials, Conor believed Chris was lying. Even standing next to his friend now made Conor's skin crawl.

Chapter 18

What happened to Erin Corwin? Had the missing nineteen-year-old gotten lost in the vast Mojave Desert? Did she run away from home to flee her troubled marriage? Or was she the victim of foul play?

Following the interview with Chris Lee, Tabor and Millan decided the circumstances surrounding Erin's disappearance were suspicious. The San Bernardino County Sheriff's Department homicide detectives took over the investigation, supervised by Sergeant Trevis Newport.

Husky with a wide face framed by slicked black hair, Newport was a graduate from Southern Illinois University and William Howard Taft University. He first joined the San Bernardino County Sheriff's Department in 1999. After seven years, he was promoted to detective in the homicide detail, and in 2013, he rose to the rank of sergeant of the homicide detail, where he led a team of four detectives. He'd managed several high-profile investigations, including solving the recent murder of a San Bernardino County sheriff's deputy who was killed in the line of duty. Newport was a divorced father of a daughter.

Detective Jonathan Woods was assigned as the case agent, collecting paperwork and reporting to the district attorney's office. In his forties with receding hair,

Woods was married with a young son. Law enforcement was in Woods's blood. His father, Gary Woods, was a navy veteran who spent twenty-nine years working in the San Bernardino County Sheriff's Department. One of Woods's happiest memories was when his dad swore him in as a deputy sheriff. Just six months later, Woods's father died of cancer. Soon after, Woods was promoted to detective in the homicide unit and assigned his father's old badge number, 423.

His partner, Daniel Hanke, was brawny with narrow eyes and buzzed hair. Hanke had joined the San Bernardino County Sheriff's Department as a correctional deputy in 2005, working his way up to patrol. In January, he had been promoted to the homicide unit and had only handled a few cases. Growing up in the city of San Bernardino, Hanke played football in high school and college and was married with two children.

Rounding out the team were Detective Bryan Zierdt and Detective Mauricio Hurtado. Tall and lanky with light brown hair, Zierdt had worked in law enforcement in San Bernardino County since 2002. With short black hair that framed his plump face, Hurtado started his career as a corrections officer before working patrol in San Bernardino County. In 2011, he was promoted to detective in the homicide unit.

Though they were homicide detectives, the investigators still hoped to find Erin alive. But the search wouldn't be easy. The largest county in the country, San Bernardino County is massive, spanning more than twenty thousand square miles of vast deserts and mountain ranges. Each summer, the sheriff's department gets rescue calls for hikers, mountain climbers, and tourists who have suffered from heat stroke or have gotten lost. More than a dozen volunteer rescue groups work alongside the sheriff's department, including the

San Bernardino County Cave and Technical Rescue team, which specializes in desert rescues.

That Sunday, a search crew was dispatched to the park to look for signs of Erin. On June 28, the day she disappeared, temperatures had soared to ninety-four degrees in Joshua Tree National Park.

With pregnant women, heat stroke can happen twice as fast because their bodies burn more calories. If Erin was lost, she was in danger of dying from the elements.

"Obviously, we were concerned. Can we find her before she meets a horrible end?" Newport explained. "We don't know if she's being held somewhere. We don't know if she's stranded in the desert still."

In Tennessee, Jessie Trentham called and texted Erin numerous times. Each time, the phone rang once before going straight to voice mail.

"Are you OK? Your phone has been off. Holler at me and tell me how your day went," Jessie texted on June 29 at 1:57 p.m.

After speaking to Jon, Jessie had been consumed with worry. At her boyfriend's house in Sweetwater, Tennessee, Jessie spent much of the day pacing back and forth to her car and checking her cell phone.

Erin had better hurry up and get home, she thought.

Sitting on the back porch at her boyfriend's house, her phone rang again. It was a deputy from the San Bernardino County Sheriff's Department.

Throughout their friendship, Erin had trusted Jessie with her deepest secrets. Now, Jessie was about to betray that trust.

Chapter 19

When she'd first arrived in Twentynine Palms in September 2013, Erin Corwin had truly been in love with Jon. But the illusory haze of a young romance had dissolved after a miscarriage and one too many fights about money.

Both Jon and Nichole believed their spouses' momentary flirtation had been stamped out before splintering their respective marriages. But unbeknownst to everybody but Jessie, the affair had never ended.

For a few weeks after Nichole exposed the infidelity, Chris largely avoided Erin. His wife had confiscated his phone, and he didn't dare attempt to see her. Likewise, Erin was too afraid to call or text him for fear Nichole would see it.

Crestfallen, Erin felt even more isolated and alone, she told Jessie. At the time, she wanted nothing more than to return to Tennessee. The affair had only widened the divide between Erin and Jon.

"It just pushed Jon further away," Jessie explained. "It got to a point where they were just mad at each other all the time."

Next door in apartment D, Chris was busy placating Nichole. He was going to counseling and claimed to want to work on his marriage, but privately, he was conflicted. He didn't want to get a divorce and risk losing even partial custody of Liberty, but he was also unwilling to let go of Erin. As he sorted out his feelings, Chris wrote several letters and poems.

"After everything stopped, I was still pretty emotionally unstable," Chris recalled. "So I was writing, trying to figure out how I felt about her, how I felt about everything else."

He burned most of his poems to avoid leaving evidence Nichole might find. But there was one he kept, handwritten in careful cursive.

> *Like it or not you still hold a part of my heart.*
> *Ready or not we were gonna get caught.*
> *Don't give up and I won't too.*
> *Hopefully like me, you still think I love you.*

In April, weeks after they'd stopped speaking, Chris secretly slipped Erin the poem. Touched by the gesture, Erin kept it in a compartment in her jewelry box. She and Chris resumed seeing each other, only this time they were more discreet.

They both used a phone app that altered the number they called from and were more careful about when they exchanged messages. Soon after, they were seeing each other in the mornings and whenever Jon was in the field. In early May, they had sex.

"He started talking to her again, trying to be friends again," Jessie remembered. "And it progressed from there."

Juggling both his wife and girlfriend, Chris slept with both women. However, Erin and Jon had barely touched in months. The more time she spent with Chris, the deeper Erin fell in love. On calls with Jessie, Erin made it clear she was in love with Chris and started talking about moving to Alaska to be with him.

By June, she was even searching for apartments in Anchorage.

While she was excited about her new romance, Erin wasn't stupid. She knew how messy it would be for them to end their marriages and fretted about revealing the truth to her mom.

Then, Erin found out she was pregnant again. She first learned she was having a baby in early June—weeks before her emergency room visit confirmed the news to Jon. At first, Erin kept it a secret—only telling Jessie. On June 3, Erin texted Jessie about the pregnancy, referring to her best friend as "Aunt Jessie." Erin also confessed she knew the father was Chris.

"She was pretty sure it was Chris's baby," Jessie remembered. "She was like 99 percent sure it was his. Because it had been a while since she and Jon were intimate."

Sometime in early to mid-June, Erin told Chris she was having his baby. Erin had worried about how her married lover would react, afraid he might want her to have an abortion, which she adamantly opposed. But when Erin revealed the news, Chris was remarkably positive, she later told Jessie.

Ignoring the repercussions, Chris only talked excitedly about being a father again. At one point, he even brought up what to name the baby.

"She waited a little bit before she told Chris, but she did tell him it was his and they were talking about baby names," Jessie explained. "There was never any talk of not keeping the baby . . . But nothing definite about what to do about it."

Chris told Erin he feared Nichole's reaction. To give him time to sort out the mess, Chris asked Erin to wait a week before they told anyone. Erin agreed, although she had already told Jessie.

Erin also agonized about how Nichole would react to the pregnancy.

"I'm more worried about Nichole going psycho," Erin wrote. "Keep her away from the alcohol."

When Erin referenced her mom's upcoming visit, Jessie asked if she was going to tell Lore.

"Well, Chris wanted to tell everyone next week," Erin responded on June 25.

On June 22, when Jon took Erin to the hospital, he learned she was pregnant. He never once questioned if it was his baby, even calling his dad to inform him he would be a grandfather. Sadly, if he would have considered the timing of the pregnancy, he might have had suspicions.

But when he found out his wife was expecting, Jon's suggestion for how they would parent the baby left Erin further disillusioned, she told Jessie. He'd decided it would be best for Erin to return to Oak Ridge while he went to mechanic school in California.

"He wanted me to move home while he went to school in California for almost three years," Erin wrote to Jessie. "I don't think he cares too much."

Unaware of Jon's actual feelings, Jessie assumed he didn't care either.

"He probably assumes it's not his anyway," Jessie replied.

"I'm hoping he assumes," Erin wrote. "Otherwise he's straight up stupid."

"Well he's a complete asshole anyway," Jessie responded.

"Exactly. He proves to me how big of an ass he is every day," Erin wrote before launching into a tirade about one of their latest fights.

The same day Jon took Erin to the emergency room, Chris was exploring the mines outside of Joshua Tree.

Sometime early the following week, Chris told Erin he wanted to take her somewhere special to celebrate the pregnancy because he had a "special surprise" for her. Since learning she was expecting, Erin hadn't had much time alone to talk to Chris. He promised they could spend the whole day together and talk. Despite her prodding, Chris would only reveal it was "a one-of-a-kind place." They planned the getaway for a full week before setting the date for Saturday, June 28.

As the week passed, Erin fantasized about the added significance of the secret trip. *Was Chris planning to tell her he was leaving Nichole? Did Chris want to ask her to divorce Jon and marry him?* Late on the night of June 25, just three days before the excursion, Erin contacted Jessie.

"So apparently this surprise trip is super important and I finally got him to tell me it's by the national park," Erin texted Jessie at 10:43 p.m. "It apparently takes two hours just to get there. A long slow drive. Good talking time though!"

They agreed to meet that morning in a desert swath, a few miles from the back Condor Gate. From there, Erin would ride with Chris in his Jeep to their mysterious destination.

"Getting the whole day together," Erin told Jessie. "It's a first for us, the location is only half the surprise . . . And he said he's honestly not sure how I am going to react."

As for the "special surprise," Chris would not give her any hints.

"I am clueless. Lol. I'm ready to know what it is! I mean I have a couple ideas in mind but I'm not saying shit until I actually know," she wrote.

"I don't blame you," Jessie responded.

"I seriously don't know why he would drag me out

to a very special place for a dumb surprise," Erin wrote. "I feel like it's big but . . ."

Jessie replied with a string of emojis, including a diamond ring, hearts, and question marks, suggesting a possible engagement.

"Maybe!! . . . He was mysteriously playing with my ring the other night," Erin texted back. "We shall see! This day cannot come quick enough."

Later, Erin explained she actually wasn't expecting much and didn't really think he was going to propose marriage. Erin just knew how much they needed to talk about the baby.

"They were going to the desert to talk about their relationship," Jessie explained. "She thought her trip out there would bring them together, and she was hoping he'd make some kind of commitment."

Knowing Chris, Erin actually had set her expectations quite low.

"I got him to spit out it's not a tire fire," Erin wrote. "Anyway, he says he's stoked for this weekend."

In a peculiar twist, Chris had also told Erin about the cover story he planned to use to fool Nichole: a decoy hunting trip with his friend Skyler Dent. Chris's plan was to drive out to the desert with Skyler, then convince him they should separate to cover more ground and go meet Erin alone.

"Only one of them will be truly hunting," Erin wrote. "Chris said he might pull out his gun for a few minutes but his focus is on us."

It was a convoluted and bewildering plot, Erin confessed.

"I told him it's kind of a ridiculous plan," Erin told Jessie. "But if it gets him a whole day with me, oh well."

Erin added that Skyler was trustworthy, so they wouldn't get caught. As for her own cover story, Erin used her mom's upcoming visit to claim she was scouting out places in the park.

"They planned it for like a week," Jessie remembered. "She was just so excited."

Three days later—June 28—Jessie spoke to Erin for the last time. At 7:19 a.m. California time, Erin called Jessie to tell her about her day.

"She said she was getting ready and about to leave their apartment to go meet Chris to have their special day," Jessie recalled.

Jessie asked Erin to call her later to let her know how the day went. That call never came. The next morning, when Jessie got the call from Jon, she was filled with dread. It had been more than a day since Jessie had last heard from Erin, but she knew she had been surreptitiously spending time with Chris. Jessie told Jon she hadn't heard from Erin, but she was careful not to reveal too much.

"At that point, I wasn't telling everything," Jessie explained. "I'm sitting there and I'm trying really hard not to spill the beans about the affair."

It hadn't occurred to her that Erin was in trouble; she figured Erin was with Chris. Then, she got a call from sheriff's deputy Danny Millan. When Jessie spoke to investigators, at first she parsed her words.

"I was giving them the hint of where she was supposed to be," Jessie described, "but just didn't say Chris was there."

Jessie suggested that sheriff's deputies reach out to Erin's next-door neighbor Chris.

"You know, Chris might know something more than I do," Jessie told Millan.

"We just got done talking to Chris," Millan replied.

Jessie's heart skipped a beat. She went stark white and nearly dropped the phone.

"I just lost it. I was freaking out," Jessie remembered. "I knew if he was there and she was not, that something wasn't right."

All of her friend's secrets suddenly tumbled from Jessie's lips. She told the deputy everything she knew about the affair, the pregnancy, and the trip to Joshua Tree National Park. Normally a slow talker from Tennessee, Jessie now spoke with urgency.

"She was with him! I know she was with him!" Jessie shouted. "Something is wrong. You need to find her now!"

Jessie's thoughts jumbled as she considered possible scenarios. Did Chris leave Erin in the desert? Did he give her money for a bus ticket home to Oak Ridge? Was she traveling back to Tennessee?

"The last thing that popped in my mind was that he killed her," Jessie admitted. "I was just thinking, *Why is he here? Why is she not?*"

By the time Millan finished taking her statement, Jessie was trembling. Soon after hanging up with the deputy, her phone rang again. This time it was Jon. The first time Jessie spoke to her best friend's husband, she had lied. Now, Jessie revealed the truth.

"I let him know that Chris was supposed to be there with her," Jessie remembered.

Jon was devastated. Not only was Erin sleeping with Chris, she was planning on leaving him. Even more explosive: Jon was almost certainly not the father of his wife's baby. While he was crushed, Jon was also infuriated—but not with Erin. Despite the lies and infidelity, Erin was his wife. And if Chris hurt her, Jon wanted him to suffer.

"I felt like someone literally stuck a knife in my back. It was earth-shattering," Jon recalled. "I was honestly ready to go out and strangle Chris."

The next call was even more difficult for Jessie. Earlier, Lore had sent Jessie a Facebook message, asking about Erin. Now, Jessie had to tell her best friend's mother about the affair.

"It didn't really hit me until I talked to her mom," Jessie remembered. "I was scared. I knew stuff that she didn't. I knew she'd be mad."

Even as Jessie spoke to deputies and Erin's mom, it didn't occur to her that her best friend might be dead. She was more concerned Erin would be mad when she surfaced. That night, around 8:30 p.m., she sent one more text to her friend.

"Erin, I don't know where the fuck you are but you better be OK," Jessie wrote.

For the first time, Lore had learned details of her daughter's unfaithfulness. It broke her heart that Erin was struggling with such a heavy secret.

"That is very out of character for Erin," Lore remarked. "I was extremely shocked. I still have a hard time wrapping my brain around it."

While Lore was stunned, she was more worried about Erin's safety than anything else. Lore and Sheila had booked their flight to California and were leaving in the morning.

The next day, as the plane taxied out to the runway, the flight attendant announced over the speaker it was time to shut off phones and electronic devices.

Lore Heavilin had waited until the last possible minute before switching her cell phone to airplane mode for the six-hour flight to California. It was Monday morning, and Erin had been missing for forty-eight hours. Seated beside Sheila Braden in coach, Lore was frantic.

"One of the hardest things was getting on the

airplane and knowing you had to shut your phone off. And there's no contact the whole time you are in the air," Lore remembered. "I couldn't get to Twentynine Palms quick enough. The plane could not fly fast enough."

Chapter 20

In the skies above the Mojave Desert, helicopters whooshed overhead as Marines, volunteers, and search-and-rescue dogs scoured Joshua Tree National Park. That Monday, June 30, temperatures reached more than 115 degrees. The park remained open to the public, and rangers assisted investigators escorting visitors to popular scenic areas of the park, away from the search.

The information Jessie relayed to sheriff's deputies spun the investigation from a missing persons case to a probable homicide with a strong suspect. Deputy Millan passed it along to Sergeant Newport and Detectives Woods and Hanke, who later spoke directly with Jessie. She forwarded Hanke screenshots of her text messages with Erin.

Now detectives knew Chris's affair with Erin had never ended. Further, they knew that Erin believed she was pregnant with his baby.

"[Jessie] said that Erin was making plans for a life with Chris," Newport explained. "It wasn't just a friendship or a slight infidelity. It was full on. They were completely involved with each other."

In light of this new information, detectives had accelerated the urgency of their search for Erin. That Monday, the sheriff's department announced that there were special circumstances in Erin's disappearance and they were working under the theory that she hadn't disappeared voluntarily.

"We don't have any evidence yet that it's criminal," said San Bernardino sheriff's captain Dale Mondary. "We're just trying to find a missing person."

Security footage taken at the Marine base's three main gates was turned over to the sheriff's department. Sentries at each of the gates were also instructed to look for a woman fitting Erin's description. As the investigators dug deeper, they pulled Erin's phone records and bank account information and checked her social media accounts. There was no activity on any account from the time Erin disappeared. And her phone had been shut off within an hour of leaving her apartment.

Whatever happened to Erin, it seemed to detectives she would not be returning home alive.

Parked about a hundred feet from the road, the blue Corolla baked under the searing summer sun. The vehicle was parked on Ranch Road near Valle Vista Drive, just a few miles outside the back Condor Gate of the combat center. It appeared out of place in the stark stretch of desert, about five miles outside Joshua Tree National Park.

Driving her SUV with her young daughter in the passenger seat, Debbie Valik had just turned onto Ranch Road when the blue car caught her attention. It was rare to see a vehicle parked in the middle of the desert, miles from civilization.

"I noticed a car parked off to the left-hand side of the road that wasn't there the night before," Valik remembered. "I thought it was odd because there was no reason for it to be there. There are no hiking trails near my property. There's nothing to do out there."

In her early forties with long brown hair, Valik lived with her husband and daughter in a rural property in the desert.

"It's pretty barren," she explained. "It's really flat. You can see for hundreds of miles in all directions."

On that Saturday morning, a craving for doughnuts had led Valik and her daughter to drive eight miles to the nearest grocery store. She had taken the main road into town when she spotted the blue car. Although she found it strange, Valik kept driving.

About half an hour later, on their return trip home, Valik was surprised to see the car still parked in the same location. She drove up behind the Corolla and snapped three photos on her cell phone camera.

"I didn't want to get out of my truck because I didn't know what was inside the car and who it belonged to," Valik remembered. "I didn't know if someone was doing drugs in there. Or if someone was just up to no good. But I knew it wasn't supposed to be there."

At the time, Valik had no idea of how important those photos would become. Valik and her daughter returned home, ate the doughnuts, and continued about their day. Although she thought about reporting the abandoned vehicle to police, it slipped her mind.

"I think I thought my imagination was just getting the better of me," she remarked. "And somebody had probably parked the car out there for good reason."

The car sat parked in the desert for two more days.

On Monday, June 30, Valik was eating breakfast with her family when she heard the sounds of helicopters zooming overhead. Police cars swarmed the desert near where Valik last saw the car parked.

Earlier that morning, the vehicle had been reported found by an employee of the Twentynine Palms Water District. It was the same make and model of the car belonging to the missing woman, the employee told a deputy. A patrol officer responded to the scene and used his dash-top computer to run the license plate: 7CJX519. It was registered to Jon and Erin Corwin.

When she found out the car belonged to a missing girl, Valik contacted detectives and turned over the cell phone photos, which proved Erin's car had been in the desert since the morning she vanished.

Crime scene tape encircled a section of desert surrounding the blue Corolla that Monday morning. Helicopters circled overhead as crime scene investigators walked side by side in a grid pattern.

Sergeant Trevis Newport was at the scene as investigators examined and processed the vehicle for evidence. The Corolla was covered in a thin layer of dust. A single set of footprints led from the blue Corolla to the site of another set of tire tracks that snaked across the desert. Then the footprints vanished.

"Those tire impressions made what appeared to be a loop back toward the vehicle, Erin's vehicle," Newport explained. "And there were shoe impressions that appeared to walk from the driver's side of Erin's vehicle to those tire impressions that came through this area."

One of the crime scene investigators placed numbered yellow placards around the tracks while another snapped pictures. Erin's car was photographed from all angles before being impounded and towed to the sheriff's station.

The discovery of the car was a significant development. It appeared Erin had driven to this spot before getting into another vehicle and driving off with someone. Sergeant Newport now had his first solid lead of the case.

"I realized at that point we were dealing with a situation where we're being led in one direction—which is Joshua Tree National Park," Newport remembered. "Whereas, in fact, now her car is several miles north of that location. I'm obviously very concerned that we hadn't been searching the right area."

Soon after the Corolla was found, a Twentynine Palms local came forward with a bizarre story. On the morning Erin vanished, at about 10:00 a.m., Michael Beasley was driving his sister's car along Ranch Road, when he said he saw two vehicles parked just off the roadway. As he passed by, a woman Beasley said looked like Erin stepped out of the blue car and locked it. Then she walked over to a red, compact sedan driven by a man. The two appeared to chat briefly before driving away together in the red sedan.

"To me it looked like someone was broke down and somebody picked somebody up," Beasley told reporters. "There was no struggle. That girl was waiting to get picked up. She willingly got into the vehicle."

About half an hour later, Beasley was driving home when he said he saw the blue car alone.

"Next thing I hear, the weekend goes by and it's Monday morning [and] the sheriffs are looking for this girl because she ain't home yet," Beasley remembered.

His sister Jessica, who lived nearby, also recalled seeing the car. But when the Corolla was located, they both insisted to the sheriff's department that when they saw the car, it had been parked much closer to the road. Both Michael and Jessica swore someone had reparked the car to try to hide it.

"Somebody moved that vehicle," Beasley told reporters. "I know that vehicle was moved."

Beasley described the man in the red car as having

short hair and said he appeared to be less than five feet nine inches tall. However, Beasley later admitted on television he never saw the mystery driver get out of his vehicle.

Twice, investigators interviewed Beasley. For the next few days, he and his sister caused a stir in Twentynine Palms, conducting interviews with local and national media.

"Everybody is out here looking for her," Beasley said on the news. "Somebody knows something."

In interviews, Beasley also expressed the sentiment among the locals of Twentynine Palms.

"This is a Marine town," he told a reporter. "I would really hate to think someone in the corps has something to do with it."

As investigators analyzed the evidence, Beasley's story didn't quite add up. Jon had told investigators that Erin left at 7:00 a.m. But Beasley said he saw her getting out of her car around 10:00 a.m. Plus, it made no sense that someone would return to move the car just a few feet. Regardless, Beasley's statement was added to the file.

When the plane touched down at Phoenix's Sky Harbor International Airport for a layover, both Sheila and Lore fiddled with their cell phones, anxious for the pilot to announce it was safe to turn on electronic devices. For Lore, cut off from communication with anyone in Twentynine Palms, being in the air was agonizing.

Sheila's phone sprang back to life quicker, and she was first to hear the voice message from her son.

"It's Jon," Sheila whispered breathlessly, her phone pressed against her face. "They found Erin's car."

A jolt of panic shot through Lore's body.

"When they found her car without her, that's when I knew something else had happened," Lore remembered. "I think at that point in time, I knew she was not with us anymore."

Lore was forced to step back onto a plane for the next leg of the journey with the disturbing realization she might never see her daughter again.

Upon arriving in Twentynine Palms, Lore and Sheila rented a car and drove to Jon's apartment. Jon immediately wanted to go to the place where Erin's car was found. Just beyond the back gates, they found the Corolla surrounded by crime scene tape. Gawking from afar, they could only guess what police had discovered.

"We couldn't get anywhere near it," Lore remarked.

That night, Lore and Sheila stayed at Jon and Erin's apartment, right next door to Chris Lee and his family. They were up late dissecting potential scenarios for what could have happened to Erin.

For Lore, it was heartbreaking being in her daughter's home, surrounded by Erin's things. In the kitchen, she opened the pantry. A few days before, Lore had told her daughter all the ingredients she would need to cook her favorite dishes.

"All the ingredients were in her kitchen when I got there," she remembered.

Chapter 21

The disappearance of a pretty, pregnant Marine wife sparked a massive search across four different California counties, spanning multiple agencies, hundreds of volunteers, and hundreds of thousands of dollars. While the San Bernardino County Sheriff's Department headed the investigation, the FBI, Border Patrol, and neighboring Los Angeles and Kern Counties sheriff's departments participated in the search.

The Naval Criminal Investigative Service, or NCIS, also assisted on the military aspects of the investigation. But because the crime occurred off base and involved a civilian, it would not be handled by military police.

"We're assisting them as far as some of the more military aspects of the investigation," an NCIS spokesman told reporters. "The military world is sometimes very confusing to nonmilitary investigators. We help them connect the dots and find a way through the red tape."

Volunteers in shorts and tank tops, carrying water bottles, combed the streets of Twentynine Palms and Joshua Tree National Park—1,200 square miles of wilderness, an area slightly larger than the state of Rhode Island. That first Saturday, more than eighty volunteers showed up. During the week, the search was scaled back as volunteers returned to work.

In the withering desert heat, the chances of finding Erin alive dwindled, and with such an enormous area to cover, the search dragged on.

"The investigation and search for Erin will continue until she is found," a sheriff's department spokesperson told the media. "They are following up on any and all leads, speaking to numerous people, in an effort to find Erin."

Detectives follow a certain protocol with missing persons cases. To find Erin, they needed to understand her life. They started by interviewing those closest to her and then widened the circle. Detectives Woods and Hanke were tasked with interviewing her family.

On Tuesday morning, Bill Heavilin and Tommy Corwin landed in California and made their way to Twentynine Palms. Tommy and Sheila stayed at the Corwins' apartment. The Heavilins rented rooms at a nearby hotel, where they would live for the next sixteen days. At home, friends and family cared for Alex.

On Tuesday night, Jon, his parents, and his in-laws reported to the sheriff's department in Joshua Tree. They were separated into different interrogation rooms and questioned.

While the initial evidence pointed to Chris, detectives weren't ready to rule out Jon. The fact that Erin had been unfaithful only raised their suspicions about her husband. He was interrogated for hours about his marriage, the affair, and her pregnancy.

"Anytime you have a spouse who is missing and you hear that there might be some infidelity involved," Sergeant Newport explained, "it's just human, not just as an investigator but as a human being, to question whether or not that person might possibly be involved with the significant other going missing."

The stunning development about Erin's pregnancy gave the detectives pause. If Jon had learned it wasn't his baby, it was possible he had killed his wife in a jealous rage.

"Jon realized that it was very likely not his kid. Which again brings motive to a spouse," Newport remarked. "That's why we wanted to question him so much."

In the tiny interrogation room, Jon sat up straight and looked Detective Woods directly in the eye. Worry marred his youthful face. A hollow sadness pulsed behind his eyes as he talked about his missing wife.

"I had no idea she was still seeing Chris," Jon told Woods. "Until I talked to Jessie."

Detective Woods grilled Jon about his whereabouts on Saturday, and Jon admitted he did not have anyone to verify his alibi—he had been in their apartment alone for most of the morning and afternoon.

"I never left the base," Jon said.

But Woods thought it was odd that Jon didn't immediately call police when Erin didn't return home.

"It's a little suspicious that you waited until the next day to report her missing," Woods told him.

Jon lowered his head. "You see these kind of things on television you can't report a person until twenty-four hours after they had gone missing," he said calmly. "I truly believed that."

Detectives also questioned why Jon had gone searching the park on his own on Sunday, as criminals often return to the scene of the crime.

"Obviously, as an investigator, you have to wonder, is this person trying to put themselves there?" Newport explained. "Is this person trying to give us a reason why they would be there where the last person was seen or possibly contacted?"

In the interrogation room, Woods leaned forward and looked Jon in the eyes.

"You didn't know exactly where she was going?"

"She just said she'd be in Joshua Tree." Jon shrugged.

"Would you be willing to take a polygraph test?" Woods asked.

"Absolutely," Jon replied quickly.

Still, Jon's reserved demeanor didn't do him any favors. Throughout much of the interview, he was unemotional and distant.

"Jon was kind of withdrawn. He was concerned, but he was withdrawn," Newport recalled. "At times, we wondered if it was his military background. When you have a spouse who is not extremely frantic, why aren't they super excited? Why aren't they super upset?"

Through interviews with Erin's family, neighbors, and friends, the detectives were able to gain a glimpse of Erin's life in Twentynine Palms. It appeared to them that Erin's marriage to Jon was crumbling.

"Their relationship wasn't intertwined," Newport remarked. "We knew that it was a relationship that was probably starting to dwindle."

The timing of Erin's pregnancy seemed significant. Newport knew the sickening statistics. Homicide is the leading cause of death among pregnant women. While desperate infertile women sometimes kill expectant mothers to steal their babies from their wombs, it is most often husbands and boyfriends who slaughter their pregnant lovers.

Is that the reason Erin is missing? Newport wondered. *Did Jon kill his wife because he discovered Erin was carrying her neighbor's baby? Or did Chris lure Erin to the desert to prevent his wife from discovering the affair?*

In Newport's mind, the pregnancy gave both Jon and Chris an equal motive for murder. Having spoken to Jon, Newport decided it was time to pay Chris a visit.

Chapter 22

Police cruisers lined the block outside the apartment complex on Jasmine Drive, rotating lights casting red-and-blue splotches on the sidewalk. Yellow crime scene tape cordoned off the wrought iron railing leading to the second floor of the complex. More than a dozen sheriff's deputies and detectives swarmed the balcony between units D and F, occupied by the Lees and Corwins.

Just after midnight on July 1, a Joshua Tree court judge signed off on four search warrants for two apartments as well as Erin's Corolla and Chris's Jeep, which four teams of investigators simultaneously executed. They were looking for computers, phones, electronic records, personal journals, and letters—anything that might hold clues about Erin's life. Crime scene investigators were also on the hunt for biological evidence: fingerprints, blood, and hair.

The Corwins' apartment was clean with modest furnishings. In the bedroom, sheriff's detective Daniel Helmick picked up Erin's laptop computer. Stuck to the inside screen was a Post-it note with small, feminine handwriting reading *Providence, Trailside Heights Apartments*. Later, Helmick searched the words on Google, revealing that the Trailside Heights Apartments were located in Anchorage, Alaska—Chris Lee's hometown. It was a curious discovery. It showed that

Erin might have been contemplating following Chris to Alaska.

In Erin's jewelry box, detectives found another note—a love poem written in cursive in a different handwriting. When they later asked Jon about the letter, he made it clear it was not in his handwriting, and he denied ever seeing the note.

Meanwhile, next door, Nichole scowled at the detectives as they invaded her apartment. Incensed, she folded her arms and told them, "You're not going to find anything!"

Not only was Nichole livid, she seemed entirely uninterested in finding her former friend. Speaking briefly to detectives, Nichole didn't want to talk about Erin, contemplate her whereabouts, or even discuss if she was still alive. She was just inconvenienced that her husband's mistress's disappearance was now upending her life.

"Extremely uncooperative, angry," Newport described Nichole. "Just not what you would expect of somebody who is trying to assist in an investigation."

When asked where she was on June 28, Nichole said she was at her apartment all day with Liberty. As for Chris, she verified his account of going coyote hunting Saturday morning until 4:00 p.m. After that, she said he only left the house once to pick up takeout for dinner.

At that point in the investigation, detectives were speculating that Erin might be found somewhere around Joshua Tree. The leading theory was that Erin had been shot and killed in the desert. If her body was found with bullet wounds, crime scene analysts might be able to match any bullets or bullet fragments to a particular gun. The search warrant allowed the detectives to confiscate any weapons located in either apartment.

"It is highly likely that Erin could have been harmed by an unknown firearm," investigators wrote in the affidavit. "Detectives believe if Erin was injured and left at an undisclosed location, she would not be able to call for help."

A quick search showed Christopher Lee was the registered legal owner of two firearms: a Winchester bolt-action .22-caliber rifle and a .40-caliber weapon. As crime scene analysts pored over her belongings, sheriff's detective Bryan Zierdt approached Nichole. "Where does your husband keep his firearms?"

Nichole's answer was short. "In the closet."

Detectives searched all the closets inside the home but found no hunting rifle. Meanwhile, Detective Dan Hanke pulled Chris aside.

"Hey, man," Hanke told Chris. "We're just trying to find your neighbor. Would you mind coming down to the station for an interview? It could really help."

Chris's eyes widened. He flinched and ran one hand over his buzzed brown hair. "Yeah, sure. Anything I can do to help."

As Hanke led Chris downstairs, they passed by the carport on the way to the detective's cruiser. Swarming around the Jeep was a small assembly of crime scene technicians. Out of the corner of his eye, Chris watched as his Jeep was loaded onto the back of a tow truck. Hanke held open the rear driver's–side door, and Chris crouched down into the cruiser.

As Hanke drove away from the apartment, Chris stared out the window, watching the desert. He appeared remarkably collected and chatted casually with Hanke about his background in the Marines, his marriage to Nichole, and the investigation into Erin's disappearance.

"I really want to do everything I can," Chris told Hanke. "I really want to help you guys find her. As much as she lied to me, I still cared about her."

Chris's black Jeep was transported to an evidence bay at the station where Erin's Corolla was also being examined. Impressions of the Jeep's tires would be taken for later analysis and compared to the tracks in the desert near where the Corolla was found. If those were a match, it would be highly incriminating against Chris Lee.

Because the investigation was ongoing, the judge sealed all four probable cause affidavits associated with the warrants, and no details about the case had been publicly released, meaning Chris's affair with Erin was still unknown to anybody but the detectives, Erin's and Jon's families, and residents of the apartment complex. The Marines and locals around the base were left to speculate why Chris's apartment and Jeep were also being searched.

"It was a search warrant in connection with an ongoing investigation; however, we have not named a specific person of interest or a specific suspect," a sheriff's department spokesperson told the media. "It's an ongoing investigation, and with that investigation, there are a number of people who have been interviewed."

Chapter 23

Detective Dan Hanke ushered Chris Lee into the narrow interrogation room inside the Joshua Tree station of the San Bernardino County Sheriff's Department just after 1:00 p.m. A table sat in the corner of the space, flanked by three cheap black seats and one leather high-backed chair on rollers. Chris passed by the stationary chairs and plopped down in the leather one with his back to the wall. He wore tan shorts, flip-flops, and a tight shirt that clung to his bulky frame. Detective Hanke, dressed in a button-down olive-green shirt and tie, took one of the cheap seats, directly across from Chris.

Chris placed his cell phone on the table in front of him, nervously scratched his leg, and then crossed his arms defensively in front of him.

Earlier that morning, before serving the search warrants, Hanke had met with Sergeant Newport to discuss a strategy for the interview. They agreed Hanke would feign ignorance about the investigation and let Chris explain his case. One of his first questions to Chris was to identify the missing woman's last name.

"Ummm," Chris said, knocking on the table like the name was escaping him. "It's Jon's last name, too," he mumbled under his breath. "Corwin!"

As Hanke probed into the illicit details about his

affair with Erin, Chris related a similar story to the one he'd told sheriff's deputies—that the affair ended a few weeks after their spouses found out. Again, Chris blamed the affair on his depression and confessed to multiple suicide attempts, claiming that after returning from Afghanistan, he played Russian roulette each morning for days at a time. Most notably, Chris credited Erin for helping save his life by counseling him through his depression.

"She was a secret, so I could tell her my secrets," Chris told Hanke. "She was my happy place."

Chris had gotten along so well with Erin that he thought they were meant to be together. Many times through texts and in person, Chris professed his love for Erin, he admitted to Hanke.

"When you told her that you loved her, did she tell you that she loved you?" Hanke asked.

Chris nodded. "She did. And honestly, I kind of think she meant it."

After attending marriage counseling with Nichole, Chris had convinced himself his infatuation with Erin was superficial. He described their relationship as a "fantasy" or like "watching a movie." Looking back, Chris told Hanke, he now knew he was not thinking clearly, had never intended to leave Nichole.

"It was my make-believe life. I thought I was in love with her." Chris paused. "But like it was just make-believe."

Without much prompting, Chris had a lot to say about Erin's marriage to Jon, repeating what he'd told sheriff's deputies about Erin's claims of abuse.

"She said her husband was beating her and choking her, and, like, she was scared for her life," Chris said. "She'd say that he would choke her whenever, like, he would get mad."

In his irrational mental state, Chris thought he could rescue Erin.

"I was like, 'I can fix this,'" Chris said. "Broken pieces fix each other, so we just started developing a bond that grew stronger."

Hanke brought up Erin's pregnancy, but Chris maintained that they never had sex. Given what investigators discovered from her best friend, Jessie, however, they knew Erin believed she was having Chris's baby. For a moment, Hanke humored him.

"And how many times did you guys kiss?" Hanke asked.

"Four tops." Chris sighed. "Maybe some hands up and down while we were kissing. But nothing real heavy."

"OK. So clothes never came off?" Hanke asked.

"No." Chris shook his head. "The furthest we got was making out with hands moving across each other's bodies."

Hanke pressed, telling Chris he must be concerned about admitting the infidelity and getting in trouble with his wife or court-martialed from the Marines.

"I'm not the military, I'm not your wife," Hanke said. "I don't care about affairs. That's not what I'm worried about. That's not my job . . . I don't care if you guys had sex."

But Chris again denied he ever had sex with Erin and maintained he could not be the father of her baby. Still, he admitted he talked to Erin about building a future together.

"So you guys talked about actually leaving Nichole?" Hanke asked.

"When me and Erin were at our strongest, I probably would have," Chris replied. "Because, like, everything seemed like it was perfect."

Ultimately, though, he said he chose Nichole for Liberty's sake.

"In my mind, I knew what I was doing was wrong," Chris said. "I told her I would not leave Nichole for her."

After they broke up, Chris learned a big part of his bond with Erin was based on lies and that she hadn't really been physically abused, he told Hanke.

"She lied to me about this and this," Chris said. "I don't even know who she was really."

That's when he and Erin stopped speaking, Chris claimed. Their last conversation was more than a month and a half earlier: around this time he started attending counseling when he recognized he had a problem, he told Hanke.

"After we stopped talking, I realized, hey, I'm not myself. I don't know what's going on. I was falling apart so fast that it was crazy that I didn't realize I needed help," Chris said. "It was like an avalanche going downhill."

Through time and counseling, Chris told Hanke he arrived at the realization that he had never actually loved Erin. He had just been caught up in the thrill of a new romance.

"She was just a distraction from everything that was going wrong in my mind. Something I could focus on and fix," Chris said. "It was an escape. That's really what it was, something to focus on. I could pretend my problems weren't real."

As Hanke tried to nail down specific details, many of Chris's answers were unclear. Chris said he could not give clear dates and times for when his relationship with Erin began and ended. He blamed the fuzziness on a bad memory, which he told Hanke resulted from concussions on the football field and training for the battlefield.

"It seems like forever ago, it really does," Chris said. "Just because I was in such a bad state. The last six months of my life almost seem hazy. It's weird."

Suddenly, Hanke noticed a cut on Chris's finger. "Did you do something to your finger?"

Chris glanced down at his right middle finger and flung his wrist dismissively. During his coyote hunting trip, he said, he'd accidentally cut himself.

"I had a knife in my back pocket," Chris said. "And I went to grab it and I sliced my finger."

Steering the conversation toward the hunting trip and the weekend Erin vanished, Hanke asked Chris to explain his whereabouts in specific detail. Chris mentioned how he'd originally planned to hunt with his Marine buddies Skyler and Conor. When his friends couldn't join him, Chris said he set off alone, stopping briefly for gas.

Flipping over a piece of paper, Hanke handed Chris a pen and asked him to draw a map of the route he took that morning. Scribbling lines across the paper, Chris explained how he took Highway 62 to Gold Crown Road and off toward the mining districts.

Shortly after 8:00 a.m., Chris said he received the text from Conor about meeting up outside the park. For some reason, after Chris replied, he shut off his phone.

"I put it in airplane mode right after I tried to send a message to Conor," Chris told Hanke. "And I guess he was looking for me in the national park somewhere . . . He misunderstood where I was going. So he couldn't find me."

"Why did you put your phone on airplane mode?" Hanke asked.

"Because it conserves the battery," Chris said matter-of-factly.

The journey to the desert took more than an hour.

"By that point, I was pretty sure the coyotes would be gone," Chris said. "Since Conor said he couldn't go, I wanted to go off-roading, too."

He ended up outside Joshua Tree National Park in a barren stretch of desert peppered by hundreds of mine shafts. It was an area Chris admitted he had been to before—just one week before Erin's disappearance.

For this hunting trip, Chris said, he brought his Winchester bolt-action .22-caliber rifle. After parking his Jeep near some abandoned mining equipment, he wandered around the desert.

Asked about the rifle, Chris admitted that after being confronted by officers Sunday, he'd asked Nichole to stash the gun at Isabel Megli's ranch.

Exploring the desert that Saturday, Chris told Hanke he was alternatively hunting coyotes and snakes.

"I was really looking for snakes," he said. "I got out and hiked for a while. And I was looking for a good place to find coyotes. And then I got kind of lost."

Although he didn't shoot any coyotes or snakes, Chris said he fired his rifle four or five times at some rocks.

As he crested a hill, he noticed a man wearing a brown shirt and khaki-colored pants that almost looked like beige camouflage Marine fatigues. Suddenly, the man aimed a pistol in Chris's direction.

"I came over the ridgeline and I saw him. I heard four shots. And it was fired in my general direction," Chris said animatedly. "I said, 'Fuck this.' And I got out of there as fast as I could."

Racing back to his Jeep, Chris said he took off,

When she was just a baby, Erin Corwin was adopted by Bill and Lore Heavilin. She was raised in a tight-knit household with five brothers and sisters and dozens of pets, including dogs, cats, guinea pigs, rabbits, and fish. *(Heavilin Family)*

A shy, small-town girl from Tennessee, Erin Corwin was a sweet soul who trained her cat to do tricks, taught a rabbit to walk on a leash, and tamed a thousand-pound quarter horse. "She was like the animal whisperer," said one of her best friends. "She could train any animal to do whatever she wanted." *(Heavilin Family)*

As Erin entered her teens, she transformed into a pretty young woman with an alabaster complexion, striking blue eyes, and a demure smile. *(Heavilin Family)*

While she adored all animals, through the 4-H club Erin discovered a true passion for horses. When she got her beloved horse, Rye Leigh, she spent hours at the barn learning to barrel race. *(Heavilin Family)*

As an adult, Erin was very close with her mother, Lore Heavilin. "I often said that she was a breath of fresh air amongst our normal chaotic life," Lore remembered. "We were blessed to be chosen to be her family." *(Heavilin Family)*

Erin first met Jon at the barn. When Erin turned sixteen, Jon asked her on a date and they quickly became a couple. Here, she poses proudly with Jon at his high school graduation. *(Heavilin Family)*

In 2011, Jon took Erin to his senior prom. When Erin descended the staircase in her purple gown, Jon knew he'd fallen deeply in love. *(Heavilin Family)*

Erin was proud to be dating a Marine and became increasingly patriotic as Jon absorbed himself in the military. "She was tickled to death that he was in the Marines," said a family friend. *(Heavilin Family)*

Erin was just eighteen when she married Jon in Las Vegas. Her parents were concerned by how fast the relationship was moving, even asking Jon to wait two years before proposing. "That didn't happen," Lore said. "They wanted to be together." *(Heavilin Family)*

(top left) Jon excelled in the Marines, rising from the rank of private to corporal. He was a skilled shooter and was well respected by his fellow Marines and commanding officers. *(Heavilin Family)*

(middle left) When Erin and Jon moved to Twentynine Palms, their relationship grew rocky. Their young marriage was quickly challenged by financial stress, Erin's homesickness, and a devastating miscarriage. *(Heavilin Family)*

(bottom left) After his second tour of duty in Afghanistan, Chris Lee returned to Twentynine Palms depressed. He started drinking more and gained weight. His mental state took a toll on his marriage. "I got to the point where I was shutting everybody out. I wasn't talking to my parents anymore. It was bad," Chris said. *(White Rock Horse Rescue)*

(above) To help Chris battle his depression, his wife, Nichole, brought him to the White Rock Horse Rescue and introduced him to the owner, Isabel Megli. Chris found solace at the rescue and he and Nichole adopted two rescue horses. *(White Rock Horse Rescue)*

(middle right) When they first met, Nichole and Erin bonded over their mutual love of horses. But once Nichole learned of her husband's attraction to Erin, she abruptly ended their friendship. *(White Rock Horse Rescue)*

(bottom right) Chris collected knives and guns and talked often about setting fires and blowing things up in the desert. In the summer of 2014, he was arrested and charged with possession of a destructive device. *(San Bernardino County Sheriff's Department)*

(above) Hundreds of volunteer cavers, including Doug Billings (pictured here), assisted police in the search for Erin. By the time Erin's body was found, nearly five thousand volunteer hours had been spent searching countless mines and horizontal passages—known as adits—in the old mining districts just outside of Joshua Tree National Park. *(Doug Billings)*

(middle left) Doug Billings, known as "Cave Doug," played a crucial role in recovering Erin's body, due to his near-encyclopedic knowledge of the caves in and around Joshua Tree. "Just by the grace of God, this girl disappeared in a spot where I happened to probably be the world-leading expert in exploring that area," Billings said. *(Doug Billings)*

(bottom left) Caver Luca Chiarabini was the first to volunteer to descend into the mine containing Erin's body. Years later, tragedy would strike again when he lost his life during an expedition. *(Luca Chiarabini)*

(above) The search for Erin originally covered two thousand square miles, including three hundred square miles of desert dotted with thousands of abandoned mine shafts. The San Bernardino County Sheriff's Department flew cavers to and from the search sites by helicopter. (Doug Billings)

(middle right) After seven weeks of searching in the grueling desert heat, Erin's remains were discovered at the bottom of a 140-foot-deep mine shaft. Her body was in the late stages of decomposition, her skin withered and blackened. *(San Bernardino County Cave and Technical Rescue)*

(bottom right) The ten-by-ten-foot mine shaft where Erin's body was found was little more than an anonymous, unmapped hole in the desert. The caving crew positioned a tripod device and a maze of rope in order to descend into the mine to retrieve Erin's body. *(Doug Billings)*

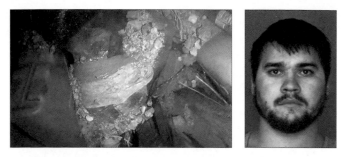

(above left) Erin's decayed remains were partially concealed at the bottom of the mine by rocks, debris, and a discarded tire. A propane tank and an empty, translucent green Sprite bottle sat on the side of the mine. *(San Bernardino County District Attorney's Office)*

(above right) When Chris was arrested in Alaska, he appeared disheveled, his hair mussed and scruff covering his full cheeks. When he appeared in court, former friends were struck by the dramatic change from the clean-shaven Marine they knew: "He looked miserable . . . I almost didn't recognize him," one friend said. *(Anchorage Police Department)*

About five miles adjacent to the mine where Erin's body was recovered, a desert garden now grows in her memory. Hikers often stop by the garden to leave gifts, including sculptures of horses. *(San Bernardino County Cave and Technical Rescue)*

heading back to the base. By then, it was late in the afternoon, and Chris was thirsty. He suddenly realized he had forgotten to bring water, so he drove toward the ranger station hoping to find water. Eventually, he stopped a hiker to ask for water. The man pulled an extra bottle of water from his backpack and tossed it to Chris.

Around 3:30 p.m., Chris switched back on his phone and saw he had missed calls from Conor and Nichole. He spoke to both of them briefly. Conor was annoyed after having driven around for hours searching for his friend. Nichole was having an asthma attack and was frantic with worry.

"When I got back, she was crying," Chris told Hanke.

By 4:00 p.m., Chris was back at the apartment and left just once, around 9:30 p.m., to get Santana's Mexican food for dinner.

It was a detailed and bizarre account, especially the inclusion of the mysterious desert shooter. But for Hanke, it sounded like fiction.

"He was very descriptive about this guy and his clothing and where he was at on the ridgeline. And that he was reloading and fired four rounds at him," Hanke remembered. "It was just a very unusual, wild story that I thought he was telling me."

Detective Hanke didn't betray his skepticism. Instead, he stared into Chris's eyes.

"Did you make any other phone calls when you were out?" Hanke asked.

"No, I couldn't," Chris said. "I literally lacked the ability to because of the area we were in."

The statement struck Hanke like a slap to the face. Chris had slipped, using the pronoun *we*, not *I*.

"That was a big tell for me," Hanke recalled. "He had told me this entire time that he was by himself."

More than an hour into the interrogation, Detective Hanke revealed to Chris that investigators had recovered Erin's Corolla.

"Are you familiar with the area of Valle Vista Drive and Ranch Road?" Hanke asked.

"Hmmm." Chris paused. "I think so."

After some prompting, Chris identified it as a dirt road where he often raced his Jeep and shot pellet guns with Conor. The last time Chris was out there was about a week earlier, he said.

"Have you and Erin ever met in this dirt area?" Hanke asked.

"No," Chris said.

Hanke leaned forward, resting his elbows on his knees. "Because we found her car."

"Oh, did you?" Chris's eyebrows raised.

"It was parked in that area," Hanke said, pointing to the hand-drawn map.

"OK." At that revelation, Hanke noticed a shift in Chris's reaction.

"He seemed surprised that we had found the car," Hanke recalled. "I could see him definitely get more tense in his body."

Locking eyes with Chris, Hanke let a few moments of silence pass. Chris squirmed in his chair. "Any reason why she would have been parked in that dirt?"

"No. Not that I can think of." Chris shook his head. "Maybe she was meeting with somebody."

Placing his hands in his lap, Hanke laced his fingers. "Would there be any reason why we have some evidence linking you to that scene in the dirt by her car?"

"Not really." Chris shrugged. "I mean besides the fact that I'm over there multiple times a week."

Another quiet moment passed.

"If you guys met here, and there's some evidence that leads me to believe that you did meet up here, I need you to be honest with me," Hanke pressed.

The detective suggested perhaps the stranger in the park had actually shot and killed Erin. Or maybe Chris was hunting and his rifle accidently misfired.

"If she got hurt, if she got shot out in the mountains, I need to know about that. Her family needs to know about that," Hanke said. "I don't know if that's what happened. You have to tell me."

Despite the detective's digging, Chris remained quiet. "I didn't meet her on Saturday," he said repeatedly.

Next, Hanke tried bluffing. Investigators were still analyzing the tire tracks and footprints found in the dirt next to the Corolla. But Chris didn't know that. So Hanke lied, telling him that the tracks were a conclusive match to his Jeep.

"Your tire tracks are there, as well as her tire tracks," Hanke told Chris. "And your tire tracks drove over hers, showing that you met her there."

Hanke scooted his chair closer to Chris so that the two men's knees were practically touching. Chris inched back farther toward the wall.

"It could have been a different vehicle," Chris said, looking straight at Hanke. "Because I wasn't there Saturday."

Sighing, Hanke dropped his chin in his palm.

"It's your vehicle, Chris," Hanke said. "You got to be honest with me."

"I'm sure I'm not the only one with those kind of tires," Chris argued. "They are a pretty common brand."

Hanke explained that every tire wears differently over road, dirt, concrete, and gravel surfaces. Investigators would be able to tell the distinction. Slumping into his chair, Chris didn't respond.

Switching tactics, Hanke brought up Liberty.

"I know you're afraid that your wife's going to find out and you're going to lose your daughter. I understand that," Hanke said. "I know how important your daughter is."

Because of Chris's love for Liberty and his service to the country, the detective said he could tell Chris wasn't a "bad guy."

"That's the difference between you and a cold-blooded killer," Hanke said. "They care about nobody but themselves."

But Chris didn't say anything. After a long pause, Hanke reached out and touched Chris's knee.

"You care about your daughter," Hanke continued. "You're afraid of what people are going to think. You think people are going to think you're a bad guy."

The detective's gaze bore down on Chris. "I don't think you're a bad person. And I know you want to tell me the truth." Pointing at Chris, Hanke said, "I can see it in your eyes. You need to tell the truth."

A poisonous silence filled the room. Hanke glowered at Chris, daring him to look away. Several more moments crept by before Chris finally blinked.

"I didn't see her on Saturday. I just saw her vehicle," Chris suddenly blurted out.

Chris now abruptly changed his story. While he maintained he never saw Erin on Saturday, he now admitted he'd seen her car parked near the dirt road.

"And I drove past there to see if she was in there," Chris said. "But she wasn't."

Chris claimed he had driven to the area to look for

tires and blown-out treads by the side of the road to start a "tire fire" in one of the mines. He said he was "curious" to see how long it would burn. But when asked what he did with the tires, Chris said he left them in the desert because he "didn't want them."

As for why he lied about seeing Erin's car, Chris said he was scared.

"I was worried that if I told you guys I saw her car, because of my previous relationship with her, you would've automatically assumed I did something," Chris said.

Hanke took a deep, audible breath, exhaling through his nose.

"We're getting there." Hanke smiled sadly. "We're halfway there."

Detective Hanke briefly stepped out of the room to speak with Sergeant Newport. For a few moments inside the interrogation room, Chris was alone. At first, he stayed still as a statue, not moving, barely breathing. He reached for his coffee but didn't take a sip. He picked up his cell phone from the table and immediately set it back down. Then he sank farther into his chair and remained nearly motionless for the next ten minutes.

Around 2:00 p.m., Hanke returned to the interrogation room and sat back down directly in front of Chris. He now had a new strategy: confront Chris with what the investigators had learned from Erin's best friend. Asked about Erin's friends in Tennessee, Chris said the only person she ever mentioned was Jessie.

"Do you know if she talked to Jessie about you?" Hanke asked.

"I don't," Chris replied.

"Here's the deal, man," Hanke said. "We know that

you met with her on Saturday morning, the day that she went missing. We know that."

Hanke then revealed to Chris that Jessie Trentham had told police that Erin intended to meet Chris on Saturday.

"We've talked to Jessie," Hanke said. "We know you were going to meet her on Saturday. We know you were going to take her on a long drive and that there was going to be a surprise."

But Chris had a ready response, once again claiming Erin was a liar. "She could have told Jessie anything."

Hanke tried to get Chris to admit he was with Erin on Saturday, but Chris was defiant. His new mantra: "I never saw her on Saturday. I just saw her vehicle."

After all the lies, Hanke was done humoring Chris.

"OK, we're past that," Hanke said. "Something bad happened after you met her. And I need to know exactly what happened."

Before Chris could answer, Newport stepped into the interrogation room and took a seat in one of the plastic chairs.

With his gaze darting between the detective and sergeant, Chris again disparaged Erin, portraying her as an attention-hungry liar and manipulator.

"What did she lie to you about?" Newport asked.

"She told me that her husband was beating her and that she was afraid for her life," Chris replied, almost robotically. "And the only reason she couldn't go home was because he wouldn't let her."

Repeatedly, Chris called Erin a "pathological liar."

"She openly lied to people in her life," Chris said. "A pathological liar is a liar. They don't care who they lie to."

But Chris was the one who had been deceiving the sheriff's department, Newport told him. He asked Chris why he had initially lied about seeing Erin's car.

"I was afraid that since I saw her vehicle that you were going to automatically assume that I did something, that it's my fault she's missing," Chris said.

"So you've been thinking about that?" Newport said. "It worries you, huh?"

"That she's missing?" Chris asked.

"No," the sergeant said. "That you think we think you had something to do with it."

"It does."

Newport then informed Chris they had obtained text messages Erin sent to Jessie in which she discussed meeting with Chris on the day she vanished. The two investigators sat silently for a moment, letting that information sink in.

"So no reason at all why she would message people saying she was planning to meet you on Saturday?" Newport asked.

Chris now suggested that Erin, the animal lover, was upset she wasn't invited to hunt coyotes and must have lied to Jessie. Erin had to have been eavesdropping from her bedroom window when he was talking to his friends, Chris claimed.

"Like, she very well could have overheard when me and Conor were talking or me and Skyler were talking," Chris said. "She easily could have overheard what my plans were."

At the ludicrous suggestion, the investigators exchanged a glance.

"So you think she set you up and disappeared?" Newport asked.

"No." Chris shook his head. "I just don't think she

got over the fact that we had stopped seeing each other, and I think she was trying to maintain that appearance with her friends."

Hanke grimaced. "Was she stalking you or something?"

"I honestly don't know," Chris replied. "Because sometimes when I would come home, I'd see the blinds move."

Both Newport and Hanke pointed out the discrepancies in this new version, but Chris just kept calling Erin a liar. Sergeant Newport returned to the subject of Erin's pregnancy.

He informed Chris that Erin had gone to the hospital a week before she disappeared and a blood test had determined she was pregnant. When the detectives found Erin's body, DNA experts would be able to determine the father, Newport told Chris.

"I don't know what must have been going through your head when you found out she was pregnant," Newport said. "Any man facing that sort of situation has a lot to worry about. Any man."

But Chris was adamant. "She wasn't pregnant with my child."

"Maybe you really don't know, I don't know." Newport shrugged. "That's what she was telling everybody."

The sergeant added that Erin had even spoken to Jessie on Saturday morning while she was getting ready for the surprise trip.

"I mean, come on, Chris." Newport snorted.

Once again, Chris repeated, "I never saw her on Saturday."

"You're pretty sure you got this all figured out, right?" Newport smirked. "The only problem is there's so many different versions of your story that no one can believe you, honestly."

Chris didn't move, didn't speak.

"It's not going to go away, dude," Newport continued. "We're not going to stop. We're going to find Erin."

In the days since Erin had vanished, the investigation had mushroomed and now included the FBI, NCIS, and law enforcement agencies in several different California counties, Newport told Chris. He added that the San Bernardino County Sheriff's Department were experts at finding people in the desert.

"We're damn good. And I feel very confident about this one," Newport said. "But this one isn't going to be luck. This is going to be tenacity."

At that very moment, Newport said, volunteer caving groups were specifically searching the mines around Joshua Tree. At the mention of the mine, Chris flinched, a look of concern briefly passing across his face.

"Do you think Erin's still alive?" Newport pressed.

"I hope so," Chris whispered.

Newport asked if Chris would be willing to take a lie detector test, but he refused because he said he was "emotionally unstable" and feared giving off a false reading. Newport asked if his team would discover suspicious searches on Chris's computer, like how to beat a polygraph or hide a corpse.

Releasing a shallow breath, Chris confessed that about a month earlier he had looked up ways to dispose of a body while having a conversation with a fellow Marine.

"It came up randomly," Chris said. "You know, random Marine talk."

Chris told Newport that he had used his phone to look up the information on Google. But when pressed, he couldn't remember the name of the Marine he spoke to.

"What were the results you found out?" Newport asked curiously.

"Pigs," Chris blurted out.

"Pigs?" Newport asked dumbstruck. "What did it say pigs do?"

"They eat them." Chris smirked.

"Are you serious?" Newport glanced at Hanke.

Chris said the internet forum also mentioned burning a corpse, but the idea was disputed because it takes too long to effectively cremate human remains. "The best answer the forum gave was to eat them."

"Eat the person?" Newport recoiled. "Like cannibalism?"

Chris nodded, adding that the killer would later have to grind the bones into dust to avoid being caught. Newport appeared repulsed, but Chris didn't seem to read his expression. Without prompting, he delved deeper into the subject.

"Someone said one way is to dig a vertical hole and then put the body in the vertical hole and then put a dead animal on top of that and then bury the animal," Chris continued.

"What did it say about mine shafts?" Newport asked. Across the room, Hanke gave Newport a sideways glance.

"It didn't say anything about that." Chris grew quiet again.

"We've had a lot of cases like that, mine shaft ones, here in San Bernardino County," Newport prattled on. "It's a pretty good idea. Problem is it's been done so much."

When Newport asked how the conversation of disposing a body came up, the interview took an even more bizarre turn.

"I think it was a dead baby joke," Chris explained.

In an inexplicable moment of the interrogation, without prompting, Chris began sharing some examples.

"What's the difference between a Corvette and a pile of dead babies?" Chris didn't wait for a response. "I don't have a Corvette in my garage. What's the difference between a pile of dead babies and a pile of bowling balls? You can't move a pile of bowling balls with a pitchfork."

Perhaps Chris didn't assess the seriousness of the situation, but his sick sense of humor wasn't endearing him to the investigators.

"Oh my God . . . Geez, man," Newport gasped. "Is this a Marine thing? Is this what Marines do?"

For nearly five hours, detectives interviewed Chris without an attorney. He voluntarily submitted his fingerprint impressions, and his cheek was swabbed for a DNA sample. His Samsung Galaxy S cell phone was also confiscated.

Throughout the investigation, Hanke and Newport had caught Chris in several lies. But they still didn't have proof he had committed a crime, much less homicide. When the sergeant told Chris he was not under arrest, he seemed surprised. Detective Hanke said he would drive Chris back to the Marine base. Newport would follow behind them in his own cruiser. Before they left the interrogation room, Newport asked about Chris's plans to return to Alaska in less than a week.

"Well, who knows? Maybe we'll go up to Alaska and visit you, buddy," Newport's cheery tone belied the connotation of his words. "It will give us an excuse to get out of the office for a couple days, right?"

Climbing back into Hanke's police cruiser, Chris's mood darkened. He was no longer chatty with the detective, stewing silently and staring out the window. After a few moments, he spoke up.

"Have you ever not found anybody?" he asked quietly, his voice trailing off.

"I personally have never not found anybody," Hanke said, adding he was sure Newport had also closed all of his missing persons cases.

Chris asked why he wasn't being taken directly to jail. Under his breath, he muttered, "So what are you guys waiting for?"

Hanke didn't answer. About half an hour later, both Hanke and Newport arrived in separate cars at the apartment complex. Newport parked, got out of his cruiser, and approached Chris.

"We're just trying to make sure we have everything covered, buddy," Newport told Chris. "Hey, can you think of anyone who would want to hurt Erin in any way?"

Chris responded hastily, "I don't want to say Jon. Because she's the only one who told me he was violent toward her, but that's it."

"Chris, you're supposed to help us out here, man," Newport said. "We were hoping to have it all situated."

Hanke mentioned Chris's question about how many bodies they had not found. Newport chuckled.

"We're good," he said confidently. "We're used to the deserts out here. You can count on that."

Before he walked away, Newport let Chris know they weren't going to give up.

"We're going to find her." Newport paused. "I know I'll find her."

Chapter 24

He's so dumb he can't keep his lies straight," Nichole hissed, shaking her head in disgust.

Isabel Megli's eyes widened as she glanced at Chris, who was standing just feet away and in earshot of their conversation. A look of shame eclipsed his face. Hunching his shoulders, he returned his attention to his horse.

It was early evening on July 2. Standing with Isabel on the porch of the main house at the White Rock Horse Rescue, Nichole complained bitterly about her husband. Mostly, however, she worried that he had said something incriminating.

"She was very concerned that he would get his story confused," Isabel recalled. "Because he wasn't in control of the facts as much as she was."

Just hours earlier, police had stormed the Lees' apartment armed with a search warrant and Chris had been escorted off base in a police cruiser. While Chris was interviewed at the station, Nichole had briefly remained at the apartment. She scowled at sheriff's detective Bryan Zierdt when he asked again about Chris's hunting rifle. At first, she had stated it was in the closet. But after scouring both closets in the apartment, investigators found no gun. When confronted a second time, Nichole huffed, "It's at the ranch."

Nichole told the detective that Chris was the one

who had taken the gun from his Jeep and stashed it at Isabel Megli's horse rescue. It was a contradiction to what Chris had said in his interrogation, when he'd told Hanke that Nichole brought the gun to the ranch Sunday at his prompting.

Detective Zierdt then escorted Nichole and Liberty to the rescue to retrieve the weapon. When Isabel saw Nichole with a sheriff's detective, she was dumbfounded.

"Hey," Isabel said, concerned. "What's going on?"

Nichole said Chris had left a gun in her closet. Isabel furrowed her brow, deepening the wrinkles in her forehead. She hadn't been told about the rifle and didn't even allow guns on her property.

"I had no idea. I was very disturbed," Isabel recalled. "I can't imagine somebody hiding something in my house and not telling me."

Isabel consented for the detective to retrieve the gun, and Zierdt followed Nichole into the house, down the hallway, and into the guest bedroom. A few minutes later, Zierdt emerged carrying a black case containing a long, wooden rifle with a scope.

"I had nothing to do with that," Isabel told the detective. "I wasn't involved. I didn't even know anything."

The detective left with the rifle, but Nichole stayed behind at the ranch. By then, Nichole was incensed that her home was being searched. Following his interrogation with Hanke, Chris had joined Nichole at the rescue. The police were still combing the couple's apartment, and the Lees wouldn't be allowed to return until the evening, so he'd gotten a ride to the rescue.

In front of Isabel, Nichole berated her husband for not having an alibi and for telling so many different stories. Nichole bragged that she was able to keep her story straight and that detectives learned nothing from her.

While Nichole was anxious that Chris didn't have an alibi, she reassured herself and Isabel that there would be no way her husband would ever face murder charges. Without a body, detectives didn't have a case, Nichole said. And there was no way they would find a body.

"She said that we watched enough of those CSI movies to know: no body, no case," Isabel remembered.

Nichole also mentioned that the detectives had missed something during the search.

"They never checked the garage," Nichole whispered to Isabel.

Over the next few days as Nichole came and went from the rescue, she talked often of Erin. Nichole even bragged about threatening to kill Erin during their confrontation over the affair, according to Isabel.

"Nichole hated Erin. There was no grudge. There was hate," Isabel remembered. "It was so bitter, what came out of Nichole's mouth about her was evil."

As she listened to Nichole grumble about her husband's lack of an alibi and attack the character of a missing girl, Isabel was revolted. But while the couple frustrated her, Isabel didn't consider that they could have possibly killed Erin. She decided not to say anything.

"I was starting to get more angry at Chris and Nichole," Isabel recalled. "Because now I'm part of it and I didn't even know I was part of it."

Now under suspicion for the murder of his girlfriend, Chris Lee was ready to put Twentynine Palms in his rearview mirror for good.

The family had to be out of their apartment by

Friday, July 4—Independence Day. But Chris would not be discharged until July 7. Isabel Megli had previously agreed to allow the Lees to stay in her guesthouse. Despite her irritation concerning the hunting rifle, she did not rescind the offer.

Chris and Nichole began storing their possessions in a pink bunkhouse at the rescue, adjacent to the main property. Because police had impounded Chris's Jeep, Isabel lent them her green Honda Civic and cream Ford F-250 to assist with the move.

On moving day, they also rented a U-Haul truck, which Nichole parked outside the apartment complex on Jasmine Drive. Next door, Lore peeked out the apartment window, watching curiously as Chris and Nichole wordlessly brought boxes down the stairs. Kleenex in her hand, Lore wondered if she would ever see Erin again.

Lore had been in constant communication with the investigators, mostly Dan Hanke, who developed a close relationship with the family. Though many of the details were kept secret to avoid compromising the ongoing investigation, Lore had gathered enough information through Jessie Trentham to know her daughter had expected to meet Chris the morning she vanished. Aisling Malakie had also told her about Nichole's cruel reaction to Erin's disappearance.

"At that point in time, I knew next to nothing," Lore remembered. "But I thought maybe he had something to do with it."

As Chris came and went from the apartment, Lore watched him suspiciously, trying to catch his gaze, curious as to how he would react. When he noticed her, Chris dipped his head and stared at the ground.

Nichole, meanwhile, was openly hostile to Lore.

One afternoon, Lore went for a walk and saw Nichole sitting outside near the playground. As she walked past her, a venomous scowl darkened Nichole's face.

"Nichole gave me a 'drop-dead' look," Lore remembered. "For some reason, it didn't surprise me."

Meanwhile, the Heavilins could only wait and worry. Even in Twentynine Palms, they felt helpless. Bill and Lore spent their days shuffling from their hotel to Jon and Erin's apartment, waiting desperately for the phone to ring.

Each evening, the Corwins and Heavilins met at Jon's apartment for dinner, taking turns cooking meals. On several occasions, Aisling and Conor joined them. The conversation was always stilted, and they talked mainly of Erin and where she could possibly be.

Aisling felt sympathetic toward Jon and brought her son, Brian, to see him almost every day. The more time Aisling spent at Jon's apartment, the more she grew to adore Erin's parents.

"Whenever Jon was home, I'd try to take his mind off of it," Aisling recalled. "It's not that we didn't care. We just didn't want him to sit in his apartment all day long doing absolutely nothing."

To stay busy, a few times Jon's dad took him to the movies or the bowling alley. One afternoon, they passed a few joyless hours at a water park in Palm Springs. But Lore remained at the hotel, never out of sight from her cell phone.

"I wasn't going to be someplace I couldn't get a phone call," Lore explained.

Wrestling with grief and racked by guilt, the first few days following Erin's disappearance were horrible for her best friend, Jessie Trentham, in Tennessee. As word spread across Oak Ridge, people who knew her from church, the barn, and work flocked to the Tractor Supply Company.

"I had customers coming into work asking about her," Jessie recalled. "I didn't want the affair to be the topic of the conversation. I wanted the topic of conversation to be Erin."

Jessie also kept in close contact with the Heavilin family and followed the investigation closely.

"I was checking in with her mom quite a bit," Jessie remembered.

Jon quietly internalized his pain. He didn't cry much, pushing through his days in a fog of tortured resilience. He always maintained that he was distraught over Erin's disappearance, even if he didn't show it outwardly.

"I'm definitely not one to speak about my emotions," Jon explained. "I've always kept them bottled up my whole life."

At the time, however, Jon was unable to convey that to the public and the media, who had turned their cameras suspiciously in his direction. He had been instructed by his commanding officer not to speak to the media. He had also been ordered not to assist with the search for fear he may contaminate it. Even with his parents and the Heavilins by his side, Jon felt alone.

It seemed like everyone on base knew his wife was missing. Because few details had been released, the affair was still just Marine gossip. But as the cuckolded husband of a missing woman, Jon knew many considered him the prime suspect. Around base, he noticed the lingering stares.

"You could tell they would look at me differently," Jon recalled. "I ended up staying at home because of it."

As part of his job, Jon handled artillery. His superior officers suddenly expressed concern that he was under too much stress to work around weapons. Jon was removed from active duty.

"At the time, they considered me to be mentally unstable," Jon explained. "They took me away from everything pretty much because we handle firearms every day."

Jon's absence from his job only fueled suspicion. A rumor spread around the base that in the days after Erin's disappearance, Jon had gotten so drunk that he had trashed his own apartment. It wasn't true, but it didn't make the menacing rumors any less painful.

On Facebook and Twitter, people were labeling Jon a murderer, Aisling recalled.

"As someone who cared about Jon, it killed me what people were saying on social media," she explained. "You could tell all the dirty looks got to him."

At first, whenever Jon ran into one of his Marine buddies, they offered their sympathies and support. But as the situation grew bleaker, most of those friends abandoned him. Even some of Erin's friends were questioning if Jon was involved in the disappearance of his wife.

"I did think maybe Jon. And I think that's normal," recalled Erin's Oak Ridge friend Abby Gouge. "That doesn't make it right. But I think it's a normal human response to think the spouse."

While strangers and acquaintances turned on him, Jon had the support of his parents, as well as the Heavilins. Lore never questioned her son-in-law's sincerity.

"That's just Jon," Lore remarked. "That's who he is."

While he knew he was a suspect, Jon said he was never worried about himself. He knew when the truth was revealed that he'd be proven innocent.

"Everybody who knew me personally knew there was no way I could do that," Jon explained.

Weary of the gossip surrounding her son and knowing he couldn't defend himself, Sheila Braden spoke to the media on Jon's behalf.

"I know there has been a lot of speculation about the husband, but Jon loves Erin, Erin loves Jon," Sheila told reporters. "I know there's no possible way that he had anything to do with it—that thought never crossed my mind."

Sheila said her son had no intention of leaving Twentynine Palms because he "wants to stay really close to where the investigators are."

"It's apparent he's torn up inside over Erin being missing and wants his wife back, and he's still hoping and praying that that's going to happen," Sheila said on camera as she fought back tears. "It's heartbreaking."

Despite the triple-digit heat, the family continued to cling to the faintest hope that Erin was alive. And Sheila prayed that somehow everything would be all right and she would soon be a new grandparent.

"We hope every day that we have us a grandbaby," Sheila said. "We are faithful people, and we are praying every moment of every day for that."

Meanwhile, back in Tennessee, Erin's family gave a few interviews to try to keep interest in her disappearance. Her sister-in-law, DeeAnna Heavilin, told local reporters she was still praying that Erin had gotten lost somewhere.

"She's just really timid, and she has a terrible sense of direction," DeeAnna said. "We were all scared for her to travel home on her own because she had to go through airports by herself, and it can be kind of overwhelming if you don't have a good sense of direction."

Chapter 25

The black Jeep that Chris Lee used to race around Twentynine Palms—the same vehicle detectives believed Erin rode in on her last road trip—was towed to an evidence bay in the sheriff's department's Scientific Investigations Division. On July 3, crime scene investigators processed the vehicle for evidence. Deputies had previously collected ten .40-caliber shell casings from the Jeep. Sorting through the vehicle's contents, they found mostly trash, including some twine.

Crime scene technicians compared the impressions taken of the tire tracks found near Erin's Corolla to Chris's Jeep. At first glance, it seemed like a match—they appeared to have a similar tire width, tread pattern, and wheelbase. To confirm those results, the Jeep was temporarily kept in evidence for further testing.

That same day, two detectives also returned to Isabel Megli's horse ranch. After Chris's hunting rifle had been found stashed at the ranch, Sergeant Trevis Newport dispatched detectives to interview Isabel Megli.

Standing outside under the patio of the main house, Isabel revealed everything she had overheard the past few days, including Nichole's comments about "no body, no crime." Since Erin vanished, Isabel said, Nichole had been anxious. And the day of his interrogation, Nichole had fumed at Chris for being "too dumb to keep his lies straight." Nichole also told Isabel she had searched the internet for some very specific information.

Chris had researched "how to dispose of a body, a dead body," Isabel told the detective.

At first, Nichole had not revealed the affair to Isabel. But when she finally opened up about the infidelity, Nichole had confessed about confronting Erin. By then, Nichole hated her husband's mistress.

Isabel also recalled one other strange story. About a week before Erin had vanished, Chris had stopped by the ranch and spoke animatedly about a recent excursion around Joshua Tree. Chris seemed particularly enamored by one mine on the northern edge of the park. It was so remote and isolated, Chris thought the mine had long been forgotten.

"He said, 'We found a lot of mines, but I found this one mine that no one will ever find,'" Isabel told investigators.

Just then, as Isabel was speaking with detectives, Chris pulled up to the rescue driving Isabel's Ford truck. Nichole trailed behind him in a white U-Haul truck, next to Isabel's thirteen-year-old volunteer ranch hand Jaelynn Watson.

While Chris parked beside the main house, Nichole stopped the U-Haul outside the gate. Glancing briefly at the detectives observing from several yards away, Chris reached into the car, grabbed a large black duffel bag, tossed it over his shoulder, and walked quickly toward the main residence. A few moments later, he emerged from the house empty-handed. Nichole parked the U-Haul and ran up to him, whispering something in his ear.

"What are they up to?" one detective wondered out loud.

Before they left, one of the detectives interviewed

Jaelynn Watson. The girl explained she was a friend of the Lees and was helping with the move. When asked if she had seen any weapons stashed in the apartment, the girl mentioned the potato launcher Chris stored in his garage. Last she saw, Jaelynn said the potato launcher was disassembled in the back of Isabel's green Honda Civic, parked near the main house.

"He asked me to grab a bag of potatoes to blow up later," Jaelynn told the detective.

Chris Lee didn't realize it at the time, but he was about to get arrested for committing a crime against a potato.

Chapter 26

A pigtailed toddler's American-flag dress fluttered in the wind as she scampered across the park, her face painted with glitter and gold stars. A horde of teenagers traveled in a pack, navigating around the lawn chairs planted in the grass while munching on funnel cake and watermelon slices. On a large blanket, an elderly couple snuggled and looked upward as a bloom of color illuminated the night sky.

In a patriotic Marine town like Twentynine Palms, Independence Day is a big celebration. Each Fourth of July, about five thousand people flock from all over California to Luckie Park for live music, games, food, entertainment, and the largest display of fireworks in the Morongo Basin. The combat center contributes to the patriotic displays, with Marines from the color guard marching with flags.

In 2014, however, the disappearance of a Marine wife had rattled the town and cast a shadow over the celebration. To show their support and help raise awareness, city leaders invited Erin's family and loved ones to the celebration.

"Her mom, father, husband, and his family were all there," remembered Cynthia Truitt, the director of the local chamber of commerce. "It was pretty emotional."

At the Fourth of July celebration, Lore and Bill

Heavilin met many of the detectives and rescuers assisting with the search.

Burying her personal sorrow, Lore warmly expressed gratitude to the searchers.

"Thank you so much for looking for our daughter," Lore told the searchers, shaking each one of their hands.

None of the volunteers searching for Erin would ever get the chance to meet the girl. But many had a chance to meet Lore and her family and were touched by what good, spiritual people the Heavilins were. The volunteers were fueled by a desire to bring answers to her family.

Meanwhile, July 4, 2014, was not a day for celebration for Chris or Nichole Lee. That morning, Isabel Megli was preparing horse feed at the rescue when she noticed a string of cop cars kicking up dust on the main road leading up to the ranch. One by one, the cruisers parked out in front of her property. One of the detectives approached Isabel, a stack of papers in hand.

"Hi, ma'am," the detective said. "We have a search warrant in connection to the disappearance of Erin Corwin."

Isabel's eyes went saucer wide. "She's not here."

"We have to follow up on every lead that might be possible," the detective told her.

It had been almost a week since Erin had vanished, and there was still no sign of her. So Sergeant Trevis Newport turned his focus to the horse rescue, which seemed to hold so many secrets.

"Erin Corwin and Jon, Chris Lee and his wife—they were all tied to that ranch," Newport explained. "We were looking for any evidence that we could find—anything linking anybody to Erin's disappearance."

Detectives asked Isabel where the Lees were staying, and she identified the pink bunkhouse adjacent to the main property. The couple was detained as their room was searched.

"We had no idea what they were looking for," Isabel recalled.

The warrant also covered all the vehicles on the property, including the U-Haul and Isabel's two cars. Deputies were hunting for weapons, electronics, and personal effects.

Crime scene technicians sorted through the packed boxes in the back of the U-Haul while another team combed the main residence. In the living room, detectives retrieved a pair of tan boots and men's beige camouflage shorts. Inside the pocket was a peculiar piece of evidence: a blue latex glove. Detectives would later theorize that Chris had worn gloves during the murder to avoid leaving fingerprints.

From the white Ford truck, they seized a pair of tan boots, a black Pelican case containing several .223 rounds, one Springfield .45-caliber magazine with rounds, a Gerber utility knife, and a Canon digital camera. They also located a black Samsung cell phone left on the front porch and confiscated an iPod Touch from Nichole's purse.

One of the detectives searched the green Honda. In the trunk of the car—exactly where Jaelynn Watson last saw it—was the disassembled potato launcher. A spud launcher uses air pressure and flammable gas, such as propane, to launch projectiles at high speeds. It is a dangerous weapon, illegal to own in the state of California. When detectives removed the launcher from the back of her Honda, Isabel was stunned.

"The detective was like, 'You didn't know that's a

weapon?'" Isabel recalled. "I said I had no idea it was even in my car."

Newport and his team decided they would use the potato launcher as leverage to arrest Chris. They didn't yet have enough to charge him with homicide. However, they could book him on charges of possession of a destructive device.

Chris was arrested and cuffed to a chair on Isabel's patio while the search continued. Hours later, he was booked into the Morongo Basin Jail. Because he had already spoken to detectives at length, he wasn't questioned again.

Chris Lee was fingerprinted, photographed, and held on $25,000 bail. Nichole spent the day desperately calling Chris's parents, who wired money to California to help with bail. When bail was posted, Chris was released. The next day, July 7, was the last day of his Marine contract, and he was officially honorably discharged from the Marines.

As part of his discharge, Chris had enrolled in the Individual Ready Reserve, a designation for former active-duty members of the armed forces. As a reservist, he would receive no pay or have any obligation to participate in drills or annual training. However, if called to serve, he would be required to return to active duty.

Because he'd put up bail, Chris was free to leave the state and return to Alaska, but would be required to return for any future court hearings. Before leaving Isabel's property, Chris told her he'd be back for any future legal hearings in reference to the potato gun.

On the morning of July 8, Chris and Nichole fled with Liberty to Anchorage. They loaded their two horses into a trailer, attached it to the U-Haul, and navigated onto Highway 62. From there they headed north, crossing through Oregon, Washington, and Canada. Chris didn't have to be back in Alaska until July 17, when he was obligated to be the best man in a friend's wedding. So the Lees decided to make the sixty-hour journey a long, slow trip with lots of detours. On the drive, they passed through the redwood forest and visited Nichole's best friend in Oregon.

If investigators had gambled that the arrest would spook Chris, they were mistaken. When Nichole, according to Isabel, had said, "No body, no crime," she was right. If they were unable to find a body or a crime scene, it would be almost impossible to obtain a conviction against Chris.

After more than two frustrating weeks in Twentynine Palms without answers, Bill and Lore Heavilin decided to return home to Oak Ridge. Lore had already purchased a return plane ticket from California to Tennessee, which she had intended to use to fly home after Erin's birthday visit.

"There wasn't anything we could do but sit around and wait. We decided to use that ticket to come back," Lore explained. "Because at least we could get busy at home, and maybe not dwell on it so much."

In Oak Ridge, the community rallied around the Heavilins. Many of their friends from church wanted to help, and several family friends brought casseroles and meals by the house.

"So many people would ask, 'What can I do?'" Lore recalled. "And there's really nothing anyone can do."

When the pain seemed unbearable, Lore found comfort in God.

"I said the most important thing they can do is

pray," Lore remembered. "And if they think of me, or think of Erin, send me a private message or text that said, 'I'm thinking of you and praying for you.'"

Over the coming weeks, Lore would receive hundreds of encouraging texts, calls, cards, letters, and emails from people who loved Erin.

"Every time I would get a text, it would just touch my heart," Lore commented. "It helped me know that we weren't in this alone. There are still people there with us."

Over the next eight weeks, the high-profile investigation into the missing Marine wife garnered extensive local and national media coverage. In a military town like Twentynine Palms—where murders and abductions are uncommon—Erin's disappearance had quickly consumed the attention of the locals.

"It was a topic of discussion probably every day at breakfast, when you're out for lunch," recalled Cynthia Truitt, the executive director of Twentynine Palms' chamber of commerce. "The question in the community here was, 'Where's Erin? Where's Erin?'"

Flyers were posted throughout the military base, displaying photos of Erin Corwin and details about where she was last seen. In coffee shops and bars, people who'd never met her discussed intimate details of her life. Many residents expressed fear and paranoia that some sort of killer was on the loose.

"I think they're more cautious than they were and more vigilant of where they're at, what they're doing, who's around them," said Marilyn Forman-Sieburs, a longtime Twentynine Palms resident.

The residents of Twentynine Palms and the Marine base would organize several fund-raisers and candlelight vigils to raise awareness about the search for Erin.

One woman, who had never met her, launched a ribbon campaign around the base. Having seen photos of Erin online, in her prom and senior photos, in which Erin is dressed in purple, and thus believing it was her favorite color, the Good Samaritan cut and folded purple ribbons and handed them out.

Though Erin's favorite color was pink, pink ribbons typically represent breast cancer awareness. So Lore later decided it was appropriate. The color purple became the official shade representing the search for Erin.

Back in Alaska, Chris and Nichole stayed with her brother in the Anchorage community of Jewel Lake. They spent much of their time visiting with their families. Because his Jeep was still in police custody, Chris regularly borrowed his mom's white Chevy Suburban to get around town.

Chris revealed to his parents all the details of his legal troubles and everything that had unraveled during the last year in Twentynine Palms. He explained how he had come back from Afghanistan depressed and sought comfort in the arms of another woman. Like he had told Nichole, Chris claimed he and Erin never had sex and had only kissed a few times before he was caught and came to his senses. When Erin went missing, he had gotten snared in a murder investigation. But he swore to his mom and dad that he was innocent.

The Lees, a private, working-class family, were stunned that their son was a homicide suspect. Dennis and Karen didn't consider it possible that Chris could commit murder. But knowing the seriousness of the charges, they scraped together money to afford a retainer for a defense attorney. In late July, the Lees hired

David Kaloyanides, a top-rated California criminal defense attorney and experienced trial lawyer based in Chino. In his fifties, Kaloyanides was lean and spry with silver hair and a ruddy complexion.

Kaloyanides earned his license to practice law in 1992, at Loyola Law School in Los Angeles. He'd joined BakerHostetler LLP, one of the largest law firms in the world, before launching his own firm, specializing in about 90 percent criminal defense. In his twenty years representing accused criminals, he had handled more than two hundred cases, including drug crimes, violent crimes, homicides, white-collar crimes, and fraud.

Kaloyanides reached out to the San Bernardino County Sheriff's Department to let the detectives know he was Chris Lee's attorney. Speaking with detectives, Kaloyanides got the early impression that the case was stalled as they sought out a body or crime scene. Kaloyanides told the Lee family it was possible the case would never see the inside of a courtroom.

During the first three weeks of the investigation, spokespersons from the San Bernardino County Sheriff's Department declined to provide details of the case to the media. While rumors circulated across base about Erin's former neighbor, the department wouldn't even confirm if there was a criminal investigation into her disappearance. In fact, in July, the department put out a news release stating, "There are no suspects or persons of interest identified."

Then, on July 21, details of the investigation were leaked to the media through a mistakenly shared affidavit outlining the sheriff's department's probable cause to search Isabel's ranch. Local and national news outlets reported for the first time that Chris and Nichole Lee had been the focus of a July 4 search warrant at the White Rock Horse Rescue.

The sheriff's department released a statement.

"Further information regarding the facts outlined in the search warrant will not be discussed," the statement read. "It is unfortunate such extensive details were released regarding this investigation because it can affect the outcome of the case."

For the first time, the department announced that detectives were looking for evidence of foul play in Erin Corwin's disappearance, and Chris was identified as a suspect. Television news programs, including ABC's *20/20* and NBC's *Dateline,* ran episodes on the search for Erin and the suspicions swirling around Chris. The media obtained photos of both Chris and Nichole posted on Isabel Megli's rescue website. Soon, Chris's picture was on the front pages of the local papers and national magazines.

On July 30, *People* magazine ran a cover story about the search for Erin. "Mystery of the Marine Wife, Pregnant and Missing. Did a military love triangle lead to tragedy?" was splashed across the magazine in bright writing beside a photo of Jon and Erin from the Marine ball and a picture of Chris in a cowboy hat.

"As the search for Erin continues, questions surround the nature of her relationship with her neighbor, former Marine Cpl. Christopher Lee," the story read.

The last thing Newport wanted was to alarm Chris and risk compromising the investigation. Following the leak, the sergeant conducted an interview in which he downplayed the significance of the report.

"Obviously, detectives decided that there are several people—not just a few in particular—who have been looked at and are being looked at in this case,"

Newport told reporters. "They're not going to miss any potential evidence or leads involving some of these people."

While he declined to officially state if Chris or Nichole were considered suspects or persons of interest, suspicion in the community had now firmly engulfed the Lees.

"We cannot rule out that foul play is involved. We cannot rule out that Erin may have taken off on her own accord and just doesn't want to be located," Newport said. "We have to look at potential people who may have had recent contact with the missing person. We have to look at potential relationships that others may have had with this missing person. So it's not uncommon for investigators to have many different aspects of an investigation going on at once."

Meanwhile, in Anchorage, Dennis Lee was at the grocery store when he noticed his son's photo staring back at him from the magazine racks. He picked up the *People* magazine and thumbed through the pages before setting it down on the conveyor belt and buying the issue.

At home, when Karen Lee noticed the magazine, she was aghast. She stashed it in her bedroom closet to keep it away from Liberty's view.

As the days turned to weeks with no sign of Erin, Jon Corwin clung to a dark kind of hope. While he never lost faith Erin would be found, he had admitted to himself that it was very likely his wife was no longer alive.

"I had some hope, but overall, I expected the worst," Jon remembered. "It's basically the only thing you can do after so much time."

In Oak Ridge, Bill and Lore Heavilin alternated

between worry and despair. Erin's disappearance had sent the family on an emotional roller coaster. As the search stretched on, Lore had come to believe her daughter was dead somewhere in Joshua Tree National Park.

"I felt like she was probably in a mine shaft somewhere," Lore explained. "I really kind of felt like we might be waiting years to find her."

Nights were the hardest. Lore would lie awake, fretting about Erin. One night, a few weeks into the search, Lore had just drifted off to sleep when Erin visited her in a dream.

"She walked up to me in the dream, and she just said, 'Mom. It wasn't supposed to be this way. I had so many plans for my life,'" Lore recalled. "And then she turned around and walked away."

Chapter 27

The blistering summer sun bore down on the volunteer cavers scouring the mines outside Joshua Tree National Park. In the face of grueling conditions in the remote Mojave Desert, hundreds of volunteers had made it their mission to find Erin Corwin.

The San Bernardino County Cave and Technical Rescue team, operating under the umbrella of the sheriff's department, was the main caving group working directly with homicide detectives. They were highly trained and had specialized equipment for rappelling into mines and caves. It was a strictly volunteer organization, and members had to provide their own equipment and go through unpaid training before joining the team.

These volunteers were joined by searchers from other groups around San Bernardino County, including the Desert Dog Troglodytes, the Desert Dog Stomp Club, the Southern California Grotto, and the San Diego Grotto.

The search for Erin originally covered two thousand square miles. By July, it had been narrowed to three hundred square miles of desert dotted with thousands of abandoned mine shafts. Before it would conclude, around five thousand volunteer hours were spent searching for Erin.

The dirt road leading to the mining districts cut

through Joshua Tree National Park and snaked through the rocky and sandy terrain with frequent deep dips carved into the unforgiving hillsides.

"The terrain was rough: sharp rocks, cactus," remembered Sonny Lawrence, a physician and volunteer caver.

Even their four-wheel-drive vehicles had difficulty traversing the terrain. Tires on two separate vehicles popped, and the transmission on another truck broke down. In some of the mines, rescuers encountered venomous desert creatures, including snakes and scorpions. At the bottom of one mine lay a dozen mannequins someone had used for target practice.

"So many weird things happened out there," one caver recalled.

On one particular sweltering day, the group's team leader left the windows down on his truck. When he and his partners returned, the car was full of bees. Someone set some brush on fire and eventually smoked the bees out, but a few people got stung.

"Some of us became pessimistic. I know I did," Lawrence said of the weeks-long search. "It's difficult to keep the enthusiasm up."

Dozens of deputies and homicide detectives worked alongside the searchers, checking off each mine on the list. The homicide team was joined by dozens of officers and law enforcement officials from different departments and bureaus across California.

"We were digging holes, we were searching. I was wearing a T-shirt and jeans, going into mine shafts," remembered Detective Hanke. "We wanted to find her, so we were doing anything we could to help."

Police chief Dale Mondary of the Joshua Tree station spent weeks working ten- and twelve-hour days in the desert. He arrived early each morning but never seemed to beat the sheriff's homicide team. One morning, Mondary raced to work, determined to be the first there. Instead, he saw the detectives clambering out of their vehicles, dressed and ready to resume searching at sunrise. Mondary realized the homicide detectives were sleeping in their cars.

"They were just incredible," he commented. "And I was just lucky enough to be associated and be a part of that."

After weeks of searching the rugged terrain of the park, the rescue teams paused to reevaluate their search plan. By then, more than two hundred square miles of desert had been explored. The search was complicated by the fact that there were so many mines—some unmarked, spread across the park. Some pits were so vast a car could fall into them.

Despite the lack of clues, investigators were determined to use every resource available to find Erin. Ceasing the search would mean Erin's remains might never be uncovered and her killer would never be brought to justice.

"Everyone was definitely very aware that if a body wasn't found, there may never be enough evidence to make an arrest," remembered searcher John Norman. "And whoever killed this girl would never be punished."

Chapter 28

Seated at the desk in his office overlooking the desert of Victorville, deputy district attorney Sean Daugherty skimmed the phone directory in front of him, searching for the name of a detective whose last name began with the letter *H*. It was a typical afternoon for the San Bernardino County prosecutor. He was reviewing a homicide case and had a question only sheriff's detective Daniel Helmick could answer. But when the person on the other end picked up, Daugherty heard an unfamiliar voice.

"This is Detective Hanke," the man said.

Glancing at the phone list, Daugherty realized he had mistakenly misdialed Dan Hanke. "Hey, man, I'm sorry. I was trying to get ahold of Helmick."

But for Hanke, the unexpected phone call seemed serendipitous. After weeks searching Joshua Tree, the crew was reevaluating the case.

"That's cool. No problem," Hanke told the prosecutor. "Check out what we're working on."

Hanke told Daugherty about the details of Erin Corwin's disappearance and the case they were building against Marine corporal Chris Lee.

The detective knew Sean Daugherty wasn't just any prosecutor. He was the deputy district attorney charged specifically with prosecuting murders and major crimes that occurred in the desert surrounding San Bernardino, including Joshua Tree National Park. The desert encircling the cities and towns of San Bernardino County was so often the setting for murder that an entire division was devoted to those crimes.

Typically, a homicide case wouldn't reach the prosecutor's office until a body was found or a suspect was in custody. But after being briefed by Hanke, Daugherty thought it sounded like a potential homicide. Bringing it to his supervisor, Daugherty was assigned as the prosecutor on the case.

"Given the high-profile nature, it probably would have ended up with me either way," Daugherty explained. "But I kind of hit the ground before they submitted it for filing and while she was still missing. It was a pure stroke of luck."

Tall with a shaved head and prominent jawline, Daugherty was a married Mormon father of twin boys and two girls. More than fifteen years earlier, his path toward becoming a prosecutor had also seemed to come about by luck, or perhaps fate.

About two hours north of Twentynine Palms, off old Route 66, lies the quaint community of Victorville. Like Twentynine Palms, Victorville is in southern San Bernardino County, surrounded by the Mojave Desert, and operates in the orbit of the military, near Edwards Air Force Base. Old Route 66—the main street of America—used to run through the heart of downtown Victorville, but when Interstate 40 was completed in 1984, it bypassed the city completely, cutting off major developments.

Growing up in Victorville, Daugherty never considered a career as a lawyer. He attended Utah's Brigham Young University and received an undergrad degree in zoology. Returning to his hometown in the high desert, he spent a couple of years teaching elementary school and contemplating his next career move. Then one day he was sitting in church when it hit him out of nowhere: Why not try to be a lawyer?

"I had never once thought about it, never looked into it," he explained. "But it hit me like a lightning bolt."

Six months later, Daugherty was in the top of his class at Western State University College of Law in Fullerton, in northern Orange County. Learning the law came naturally for Daugherty. In 2001, he graduated at the top of his class and got a job practicing civil law at a firm for which he had clerked while in school. By then, he was married with twin boys on the way. But while he enjoyed being a lawyer, he quickly discovered it was unfulfilling to litigate solely about money.

Months later, on September 11, 2001, the Twin Towers collapsed in New York City. Watching the first responders on television running into the building and saving lives, Daugherty's perspective abruptly shifted.

"When 9/11 happened, that for me was a pivotal moment," Daugherty recalled. "I realized I wanted to do something that actually helps people, that actually impacted people's lives, as opposed to their pocketbooks."

That's when he found his calling as a prosecutor. He was hired at the San Bernardino County District Attorney's Office with the goal of one day prosecuting crimes against children and murders with special circumstances so heinous the defendants were eligible for the death penalty. He started out handling misdemeanors out of a small office in Barstow, working his way up to prosecuting juvenile offenders and ultimately homicides in Victorville.

On his first felony drug case, Daugherty lost. In another homicide trial, the jury returned with a guilty verdict on a far lesser offense. But in more than fifteen years handling homicides, he never lost a murder case to a not guilty verdict.

After conferring with Hanke, Daugherty began working closely with detectives on the Erin Corwin investigation and stayed apprised on the updates in the case. By then, attention was focused solely on Chris Lee.

One aspect about Chris's initial reaction to deputies raised the prosecutor's eyebrows. At first, Chris had claimed he barely knew Erin. Later, he began disparaging his neighbor as a pathological liar. It was something Daugherty had seen before from murder suspects.

"I think the thing that initially stuck out was there was no reason for him to lie at the door," he explained. "This is not a way to react when the police are questioning you and your neighbor is missing."

But the massive amount of desert the detectives had to search seemed so daunting that Detective Hanke worried about what would happen if they never found Erin. However, Daugherty thought it might be possible to prosecute Chris even if Erin's body was never found.

In past decades, homicide cases without the victim's body had been difficult to prosecute. It was challenging to prove if the victim was actually dead and even harder to prove the victim had been murdered. But in the previous fifteen years, new technology—DNA, cell phone records, and social media—have made these cases more winnable. In the previous two hundred years, 450 no-body homicide cases have been filed in the United States—more than half of which were filed in the last decade and a half.

In 2009, Daugherty had even negotiated a second-degree murder conviction in a no-body homicide involving a married California man named Jeami Chiapulis, who was convicted of murdering a Barstow woman.

Daugherty recommended the detectives build a circumstantial homicide case by interviewing witnesses and gathering evidence to show Erin did not leave voluntarily.

"Does she have a passport? Any other bank accounts?" the attorney asked.

Without a body, it's necessary to show the corpus, or body, of the crime, meaning the sheriff's department first needed to prove a crime had actually occurred.

"Obviously, keep looking," Daugherty told Hanke. "But let's also start gathering evidence of all the reasons Erin would stay. Everything that she loved and what she wouldn't have left behind."

While simultaneously handling the prosecution in Erin's murder, Daugherty would also be prepping for the high-profile homicide of a family of four. In February 2010, Joseph McStay, his wife, Summer, and their sons, four-year-old Giovanni and three-year-old Joseph Jr., went missing from their home in Fallbrook, in northern San Diego County. Four days after the family had last had any contact with loved ones, their white Isuzu Trooper was discovered abandoned in a parking lot near the Mexican border. For years following their disappearances, there was widespread speculation about a dark and grainy surveillance video, which seemed to show a couple walking with two small children across the border into Mexico. The case was initially investigated by the San Diego County Sheriff's Department, and at one point, officials even announced that the McStay family had voluntarily disappeared.

Then in 2013, the skeletal remains of all four members of the family were found in a shallow grave near Victorville, in a stretch of desert Daugherty could view from the window in his office. The San Bernardino County Sheriff's Department took over the investigation, and one year later, on November 5, 2014, they arrested Joseph McStay's business partner, Charles Merritt, on multiple counts of murder. Prosecutors were seeking the death penalty.

For Daugherty, both the McStay murders and Erin Corwin's disappearance would become personal.

"When someone loses their life at the hands of someone else, you can't help but for it to get a little bit personal," Daugherty explained. "These cases are all sad and they're all incredibly intense and they all affect you as a human being and a prosecutor . . . The best we can do is seek justice, whatever form that takes. And that's just kind of how I approach things."

Partly on the prosecutor's advice, the detectives worked two angles in searching for Erin: hunting for Erin's body and building a case against Chris if she were never found. One team of law enforcement officials and volunteers searched for Erin in the desert, while another team interviewed Chris's and Erin's friends and collected evidence.

Both Aisling and Conor Malakie cooperated with the investigation. By then, the couple had come to believe that Chris knew what happened to Erin. During an interview with detectives, Aisling described Chris as having a dark and disturbing mind.

"No one else I knew talked about snapping necks and hiding bodies with coyotes," Aisling told detectives.

Before Erin went missing, Chris had been bragging about searching for ways to hide a body—much in the same way he'd admitted to detectives in the interrogation room. Aisling didn't remember how the conversation started but said Chris had described the "perfect" way to hide a body.

"He would just put the body down, cover it with a little bit of dirt, and put the coyote on top and bury it, so if they ever came across it they would dig it up and think it was just someone coyote hunting," she told detectives.

While Chris made her uncomfortable, Aisling never thought her neighbor was dangerous. It was only after Erin disappeared that his comments took on new meaning.

In a separate interview, Conor told detectives how he was supposed to go with Chris that day to go coyote hunting but had to cancel. He explained how, that morning, he had noticed something in the back of Chris's Jeep.

"I saw a bunch of items covered by a tarp, and I saw a white propane cylinder," he described.

When Conor asked what he intended to do with it, Chris had said he was "going to blow up a mine shaft" by pouring gasoline on it and shooting it.

In mid-July, after learning that a fellow Marine in his unit had been linked to a missing girl, Corporal Andrew Johnson contacted detectives. Tall and strapping with buzzed dark hair, Andrew had first enlisted in the Marines in 2010 and was in the same company as Chris.

In mid-June, shortly before Chris took his last leave, he worked a twenty-four-hour post position on base. To keep Chris company, Andrew visited him, who at the time seemed preoccupied, searching something on his cell phone. In a creepy encounter that stuck with Andrew, he told detectives how Chris asked about ways to hide or get rid of a body. Specifically, he wanted to know about the salt evaporation canals and ponds in the unincorporated town of Amboy and whether a body could be submerged in the chloride pits.

"Who do you want to kill?" Andrew asked his friend.

With a sinister smile, Chris responded, "Don't worry about it."

Grabbing a notepad, Chris began scribbling furiously. Andrew pointed out there were probably surveillance cameras around the Amboy salt pits. Nixing that location, Chris then switched his focus to burying bodies in the desert.

"He did mention the benefits of hiding a body in a vertical position so ground-penetrating radar wouldn't be able to see the outline of a body," Andrew told detectives.

As Chris talked, Andrew caught a glimpse of what he was writing in the notepad. Chris had drawn two columns. One section was a list of tools, including a shovel and chemicals, possibly lye. The other column was the price of the items.

The next day, Chris returned, looking for the notepad.

Detective Mauricio Hurtado also tracked down Chris's hunting buddy Joseph Hollifield. While Joseph readily admitted to exploring the desert with Chris on June 22, the auto mechanic didn't volunteer much more information. When the detective tried to nail down the exact location they had traveled to, Joseph was vague.

"We were just out past the airport," Joseph said, referring to the small Twentynine Palms Airport.

Beyond admitting he hung out with Chris, Joseph denied knowing anything about Erin's murder. Hurtado asked another question: "Do you currently have your phone with you?"

At that, Joseph balked, an inscrutable expression on his face. "Do you have a warrant?"

As detectives interviewed witnesses, crime lab technicians examined evidence collected during the investigation. Erin's cell phone had not been found in her apartment or in her Corolla. Still, the FBI's Cellular Analysis Survey Team was able to obtain phone records from the cell phone providers for Erin, Jon, Chris, and Nichole.

Special Agent Kevin Boles was tasked with analyzing those cell phone records. When a call is made from a cell phone, it typically routes to the nearest cell tower, which is recorded by the service provider. Boles was able to use those cell tower records to place the phones at an approximate location at a particular time.

By comparing Erin's and Chris's records, Boles surmised both were traveling in an easterly direction from the Twentynine Palms Marine Base around 7:30 the morning of June 28. About six minutes later, Chris was within 1,600 meters of Ranch and Valle Vista Roads, where Erin's Corolla was abandoned. At 8:04 a.m., Erin's phone registered its final activity, after which it was turned off or out of service. The phone was never used again.

Less than twenty minutes later, at 8:22 a.m., Chris's phone was also shut off. It didn't register activity again until 3:13 p.m., shortly before Chris called Conor Malakie. At the time of that call, Chris was just outside the entrance of Joshua Tree National Park.

The evidence seemed to be stacking up against Chris. But the question for detectives was what Nichole knew.

Nichole's angry outburst and nasty comments about Erin were alarming. She not only hated Erin, she had threatened to kill her after learning of the affair, according to the interview with Isabel Megli. Perhaps Nichole followed through on that threat, Newport wondered.

"Hearing a statement like that obviously just raises all kinds of red flags," Newport explained.

Although detectives didn't announce it publicly, they considered Nichole a person of interest. Theories included that she knew of the murder plot or perhaps coaxed her husband to kill his mistress.

When detectives spoke to Nichole, however, she was adamant she had been in her apartment on base the day Erin vanished. To prove or disprove her story, the detectives turned to electronic records.

Sheriff's detective Daniel Helmick—the detective prosecutor Sean Daugherty originally tried to contact when he'd reached Dan Hanke—also assisted on Erin Corwin's investigation. In July, Helmick examined the laptop computers belonging to the Lees and Corwins, which had been confiscated during the search warrant.

Scanning through the computer records, Helmick was able to show a possible alibi for Nichole. The investigators believed Erin had been murdered on the morning or afternoon of June 28. That morning, Nichole's computer was used between 11:00 a.m. and noon. Cell phone records also put her on base that morning and early afternoon.

Although the records indicated that Nichole likely did not physically kill her neighbor, Newport wasn't ready to rule out her involvement.

"It really makes you wonder, did this person pay somebody to harm Erin?" Newport wondered.

Nothing incriminating was discovered on Chris's laptop, which was broken and hadn't been used for nearly a year. But Helmick combed through Erin's laptop and discovered something interesting. Erin had been researching pregnancy as early as June 14—eight days before Jon learned his wife was expecting during the emergency room visit. It seemed to corroborate that Erin was pregnant at the time she vanished—a potential motive for her murder.

Finally, Helmick reviewed Jon's laptop. Speaking with detectives, Jon said he had been in his apartment playing games and watching television on the morning Erin left for the park. Reviewing the log on his laptop seemed to confirm his story. The computer had been used on June 28 from shortly after 7:00 a.m. until 10:00 a.m.

Through these records, detectives officially cleared Jon Corwin of anything related to his wife's disappearance. Throughout the search, Jon had been helpful and cooperative. He was interviewed on several occasions, for more than twenty hours, and volunteered to take a polygraph test, which he passed.

Detectives also found no evidence that Jon had ever been abusive toward Erin. While at first it seemed he might have had a motive, the evidence kept leading away from Jon and toward the Lees.

"Jon didn't do it. He was on his computer all day as best as we could tell," Daugherty explained. "His cell phone never left that area of the apartments on base housing."

For Jon, it was a relief. For the past year, he had been cuckolded and publicly suspected of killing his wife. The entire time he had been unwavering in his belief he would be vindicated.

"I knew what was true, and I gave them my honest answers," Jon recalled. "I never lied to them, and a light shined through."

Chapter 29

Fortune hunters once journeyed to the California desert in covered wagons loaded with pickaxes, chisels, hammers, axes, and shovels, looking for a chance to strike it rich.

The prospectors panned gold, silver, and copper from the streams and riverbeds. Using the pickaxes and shovels, they dug holes in the ground, filled them with dynamite, and scooped out the loose rock, birthing thousands of deep mine shafts just outside Joshua Tree.

More than a century later, most of the vertical mine shafts are dilapidated and dangerous. The wood frames rotted from time and termite damage, the floors covered in trash and debris. Hundreds of the mines are unmapped.

By 2014, there were more than twelve thousand abandoned mines in the Bureau of Land Management's California Desert District—which encompasses more than ten million acres of land, from Bishop to the Mexican border and the Arizona border to the Pacific Ocean. The high-desert mining districts overlap in areas that are public, private, and county lands.

"It's like finding a needle in a thousand haystacks," Detective Jonathan Woods explained.

Yet everything seemed to be leading detectives to the mines. In his police interrogation, Chris had talked about exploring the mines on his coyote hunting trip.

Just one week before Erin disappeared, on the same day her pregnancy was confirmed, he'd also explored abandoned mines with a friend. Later, Chris even excitedly boasted to Isabel Megli that he had found a mine so remote that it would never be found.

Then, the detectives caught a break. When Detective Mauricio Hurtado first interviewed Chris's friend Joseph Hollifield, the auto mechanic didn't want to turn over his phone. So detectives obtained a search warrant. Joseph wasn't necessarily uncooperative; he was just a proponent of personal rights and informed detectives if they thought his phone had evidence, they needed to obtain a search warrant. After securing the warrant, detectives borrowed his smartphone and made a digital copy.

Subsequently, a crime scene technician examined the contents of the cell phone. What he uncovered would be a virtual gold mine for investigators.

Sorting through the phone, a crime scene technician recovered dozens of photos of the desert and mines outside Joshua Tree National Park. The pictures were embedded with metadata indicating they had been taken on the morning and early afternoon of June 22.

At first glance, there wasn't anything unusual about the photos. The crime lab technician turned the pictures over to homicide detectives, who distributed some of them to members of the caving team.

Examining the phone, the technician found something else interesting. On June 28—the day Erin went missing—Joseph had sent Chris a text: "How are the mines?"

Chapter 30

In more than four decades as a caver, Doug Billings had camped underground for up to five days at a time. He had squeezed his lean body through crevasses so tight he could barely fit and had been so deep beneath the surface of the earth the oxygen levels dipped dangerously low. With a team of veteran explorers, he had discovered caves that had never been seen by humans.

"Quite often, my team has been the first to place their footsteps on the ground," Billings explained. "It's very exciting. I relate it to being an astronaut on earth. You're going where no man has gone before."

In his fifties with shaggy hair and narrow eyes, Billings, known as "Cave Doug," is one of the leading cavers and explorers in the high desert. Growing up with a second home in Joshua Tree, Billings found his passion exploring the abandoned mines across the Mojave. As a teenager, he co-founded an exploration club, read books on caves, reviewed geological studies of the area, and personally explored nearly every mine in the area, developing a near-encyclopedic knowledge of the caves in and around Joshua Tree.

"I've been down nearly every one of these mines," Billings recalled. "I know how deep they are, I know what's inside of them."

When he's not running his family's hardware business, Billings travels the world as a cave surveyor and mapper, leading teams of cavers in places like Belize and across North America. It's tough work—requiring physical fitness, survival skills, and courage in the face of darkness, heights, and confined spaces.

Through his caving experience, Billings had befriended several of the volunteers from the San Bernardino County Cave and Technical Rescue team, including team coordinator John Norman.

On July 1, days into the search for Erin, Norman first contacted Billings.

After receiving copies of some of the mine photos from Joseph Hollifield's cell phone, the cave team had spent the day in the desert trying to identify the location where they were taken. But even officials from the park service department didn't recognize the areas in the pictures.

Billings had volunteered to let the cave team stay at his cabin in Joshua Tree, about an hour's drive from where they were searching. Because of Billings's expertise, Norman called and asked Billings to meet him at the cabin.

"Hey, we have these photos, and no one could recognize where they were taken," Norman told him. "Maybe you can pop out here and help us out a little bit."

Without hesitation, Billings grabbed his gear and headed out to Joshua Tree. At the cabin, the first picture they showed him was of a mine in the foreground and an abandoned water tower in the back.

"I immediately recognized the tower," Billings recalled.

One picture looked directly into a vertical mine shaft.

"They showed me another picture, and instantly, I realized exactly where it was," Billings remembered. "Every picture they showed me, I knew where it was."

The next morning, Billings joined the crew in Joshua Tree and met with Sergeant Trevis Newport and Detectives Dan Hanke and Mauricio Hurtado.

When Newport first saw the long-haired, wiry man, he looked him up and down. "Who are you?" he asked.

Billings didn't have a formal title. Thinking fast, he made one up. "I'm the mine expert," he said. "I was asked to come offer my assistance."

It was true—Billings knew these mines better than anyone else on earth.

"Just by the grace of God, this girl disappeared in a spot where I happened to probably be the world-leading expert in exploring that area," Billings explained.

On his laptop, Newport pulled up the more than twenty photos to see if Billings could help identify the locations where they were snapped.

"Without skipping a beat, Mr. Billings almost immediately identified each photograph, and we began plotting them on a topographical map," Newport recalled.

Based on the time stamps in the photos and the location of the sun, Billings was able to reconstruct the route Chris and Joseph took on their trip, using landmarks that could be identified in the photos.

"Doug kind of pieced together everything," prosecutor Daugherty remembered. "You could almost follow the trail they went that Saturday, following that direction and the time stamps. He was so good and knew the area so well."

That Saturday, Billings took the crew to where the photos were taken, a canyon on the northern edge, just outside of Joshua Tree National Park.

That morning, they searched only the mines in the pictures. They explored each tunnel by foot and walked cadaver dogs around the vertical mine shafts. Later, the crew returned and rappelled into each mine, but Erin wasn't found.

Once outside the park, the homicide detectives realized what an extensive undertaking it would be.

"How many mines are there?" Newport asked.

"There are at least one hundred mines in that valley alone," Billings explained.

As the sun was setting and they were packing up their gear to leave for the day, Billings spotted a mine down the canyon that wasn't on his map. A few things made the mine stand out to him—it was accessible by car and directly next to the area where most of the pictures were taken.

"There's one more mine I'd like to search," Billings called out over the radio.

"Is it in the pictures?" a detective asked.

"No."

"We'll have to wait another day," the detective told him.

As he drove away, Billings snapped a photo through the window of his truck. Later, he emailed the picture to the search director. Billings thought the mine had been searched and cleared, but at that point, the investigation was splintered and chaotic.

The mine in the photograph was unnamed and unmapped. It was suspected it had been dug out in the 1980s, during a second wave of fortune hunting when the price of gold had tripled in value.

Later, he'd learn that this was the mine that served as Erin's tomb.

"I was literally standing a hundred yards from her the first day, looking at it, saying we need to go down there," Billings remembered. "But every time I said that's where she is, something prevented me from going out there."

The search area had been narrowed to three mining regions in the Mojave: the Dale Mining District, the Brooklyn Mining District, and the Eagle Mountain Mining District. The area was a rocky, two-hour drive from downtown Twentynine Palms, depending on the driver's speed and experience with off-road terrain. Aerial searches had identified hundreds of mine shafts that could possibly conceal a dead body.

"The detectives didn't know where to go until they saw the pictures of the mines," Billings recalled. "And once I identified the mines, it changed the whole direction, all the way to the outside of the park."

Many of the mines were horizontal adits that could be easily searched by foot. But vertical holes or shafts required one of the cavers to rappel down the shaft, which could take hours for a team to rig the rope and safely search the mine.

Working on his own, Billings drafted a map of the region, cataloging more than six hundred potential sites where Erin could have been discarded. He color-coded the map, identifying mines most likely to conceal a corpse.

"There was so much evidence pointing in so many directions," Billings explained. "I decided I needed to catalog every mine feature within a reasonable area."

The map was so useful that detectives kept in close contact with Billings. Billings volunteered with the crew, going to Joshua Tree more than a dozen times and even searching for Erin alone. He personally searched a hundred mines and became obsessed with the case.

"I'm the type of person that when I get assigned a

mission, I don't give up," Billings remarked. "I was staying up at night just going crazy studying everything. I would not have given up. I believe in closure, too."

For the next seven weeks, searchers checked every single mine on this list. Often, they were unaware of the condition of the mine until arriving at the site. Many were little more than crumbling holes in the ground. Breaking into teams of three, each day the volunteers were assigned a list of ten to twenty mines to check. Billings led a team of two cavers. It was a race against the sun—trying to check off as many mines in the shortest possible time before darkness fell.

"I didn't have to look at a map," Billings remembered. "I knew where I was at any time in any of the mines so I was able to direct the rescue team."

In a strange coincidence, a relative of Billings' was a Marine who had served with Chris Lee and knew of his reputation. What he had to say about Chris was chilling.

"He did it," Billings' relative told him. "And he didn't shoot her. He would have killed her with his hands."

"Why do you think that?" Billings asked.

"That's just the way he was. There was something wrong with him."

The case became personal for Billings. When he was younger, he had lost a cousin to murder and witnessed firsthand how it tore his aunt and uncle apart. The tragedy became even more heartbreaking when he met Lore and Bill Heavilin.

"I was up late at night talking to detectives, studying maps, obsessing on it, thinking about the family and how upset they must be," Billings explained. "I was determined to find her."

Still, the enormity of the operation was overwhelming.

"At first, I didn't really quite grasp it," Billings recalled. "But once we'd been out here, pounding this area for several weeks, it started going through my head, *Oh my God. When is this going to end?*"

During the third week in August, temperatures hovered around 115 degrees in the Mojave. John Norman of the Cave and Technical Rescue team coordinated with sheriff's deputies and detectives. He maintained the map, prioritized the search area, divvied up the rescuers into teams, and assigned them lists of mines.

"This was one of the most prolonged, protracted, technically difficult searches," Norman recalled. "It was definitely the longest and most difficult search I've ever been on."

After eight weeks, the detectives had grown weary and pessimistic. It was decided that Saturday, August 16, would be the last day of the search. While volunteers from the search-and-rescue teams pledged to continue conducting training exercises in the areas, the search would be scaled back considerably, and they would no longer be actively searching for Erin.

That Saturday, the crews planned to check and clear the remaining highlighted mines on Billings's list. The cavers were separated into teams of three and each given a list of twenty-five mines to clear. The crews started with the ones farthest away, working their way closer to the mines featured in the photographs.

Veteran caver Luca Chiarabini spent several weekends driving more than two hours from his home in San Diego to help with the search. On the morning of August 16, he arrived before sunrise and teamed with volunteers Sonny Lawrence and Pedro Ligorria.

The detectives hadn't told the searchers much about the case other than that they were looking for a dead body. Chiarabini knew Erin was the wife of a Marine and that she was pregnant. The volunteers had also been told that detectives had a strong suspect but needed to find the victim's body before an arrest could be made.

"We think we know who did this," a sheriff's deputy told Chiarabini. "I know you will find her."

The sun was beginning to set when Chiarabini and his teammates approached one of the last mines on their list. There was something about this hole that distinguished it from the others.

"There was a strong smell of gasoline coming up this vertical shaft," Chiarabini remembered. "We couldn't just go down and take a look like we had with the other mines."

Lawrence was the first to notice the smell of gasoline emanating from the mine. Near the collar of the mine, Ligorria spotted the brass bullet casing. With a gloved hand, he placed the casing in a plastic evidence bag. Meanwhile, Chiarabini called for backup. "We found something."

Sheriff's corporal Robert Whiteside, the program coordinator of the San Bernardino Sheriff's Department's Search and Rescue Unit, arrived at the site soon after, called the homicide detective, and secured the area. Meanwhile, the caving team used the bucket camera to confirm Erin was at the bottom of the mine.

It would take three more drops into the hole before detectives were positive they had found Erin. The mine was estimated to be at least 250 feet deep. Her body had fallen the equivalent of fourteen stories and landed on a plank of wood wedged to create a false floor, blocking passage to the bottom of the mine.

Facedown in debris, 140 feet underground, Erin's body had been left to rot for eight long weeks.

Chapter 31

Just after midnight in Oak Ridge, Bill and Lore Heavilin were awakened by a phone call from Detective Jonathan Woods. Sitting up in bed, Lore grabbed the phone.

"We think we found Erin," Woods told her. "We came across a body in a mine, and we're almost positive it is her. We're bringing in crews to recover her tomorrow morning."

As soon as her body was positively identified, Woods said, they'd be arresting Chris for murder in Alaska. In the meantime, it was important that Chris didn't learn they had found the body.

"We're keeping a close watch on him in Anchorage," Woods told Lore. "But we just need to keep it quiet for now, so don't tell anyone. We don't want him to disappear."

Hanging up the phone, Lore and Bill hugged each other. Lore worried about telling their other children about Erin's death. Because of Woods's warning, they decided they would pretend nothing was wrong.

"Bill and I decided we needed to act as if everything was normal," Lore explained. "We couldn't tell anybody."

Lying back down, they somehow slept a few more hours. The next morning—Sunday—Lore was up getting ready for church when a text came through from Detective Daniel Hanke: "Are you awake?"

Hanke had sent the message late the night before, just a few moments after his colleague Woods called to inform her Erin's body was found. But she didn't notice it until the morning. Lore called him back, but he didn't answer. So she and Bill headed to church.

"I went to church and was feeling extremely numb," Lore recalled.

Typically, Lore switched her phone to vibrate for church. But that morning, she left the ringer on. A few minutes into the service, that same obnoxious cell phone ringtone sounded in church. Gingerly, Lore stepped outside and took the call.

By then, Hanke had grown close to the Heavilin family and was concerned about their reaction. "I'm sorry I wasn't the one to call and tell you personally," Hanke said.

Hanke told Lore that once Chris was arrested, law enforcement would hold a press conference. However, Lore expressed concern that her other children would hear about Erin on the news.

"Dan, my kids cannot find out at a press conference that their sister's body was found," Lore said.

"OK, go ahead and tell them, but you have to tell them not to say anything to anybody else," Hanke said. "You all have to go on and live like everything is normal."

Bill and Lore decided to wait to tell their children until a positive ID was confirmed. In a daze of despair, Lore somehow managed to get through the rest of the day.

Meanwhile, in the Mojave Desert, detectives and rescue crews surrounded mine number 108, about twenty miles southeast of Twentynine Palms. The area was so difficult to access that even many of the four-wheel-drive vehicles had difficulty reaching it.

"It is very rough terrain out there," Newport commented. "It is a very dangerous area. There are lots of mine pits out there. And it's very remote."

It was 106 degrees when the recovery effort began. Firefighter Brenton Baum was the first in the mine that afternoon, collecting the propane tank, water jugs, climbing rope, and the Sprite bottle. As he was preparing to exit the mine, a rock came loose and hit him. When he reached the surface, he was treated for a minor injury and dehydration and held overnight at Arrowhead Regional Medical Center.

It was nearly 6:30 p.m. by the time the second firefighter fished Erin's remains from the mine. Her body was clothed in the same outfit she'd worn when she left the apartment on June 28—a pink top and jean shorts—but she was barefoot. Her shoes, purse, cell phone, engagement ring, and car keys were not located in the mine shaft and would never be recovered.

That evening, Detective Hanke called Lore again. This time, he had a question.

"Did Erin have her wisdom teeth removed?" he asked.

"Yeah, she did," Lore confirmed.

After they hung up, Lore realized that the X-rays the sheriff's department had were likely the ones the dentist had taken to see if Erin needed her wisdom teeth removed. The teeth had since been extracted. Lore sent Hanke a text with that information.

Hanke called back five minutes later. "It's a positive ID," he said somberly.

Chapter 32

The decayed, emaciated remains of what used to be Erin Corwin were deposited on an autopsy table in the San Bernardino County coroner's office late Sunday night.

After two months in the summer heat, the body was markedly decomposed and extensively skeletonized. Blackened, desiccated flesh sheathed the skeleton like a grotesque suit of skin. The upper and lower teeth were exposed, dirt clumped in the otherwise empty orbital cavities.

Such severe decomposition created unique complications for the county medical examiner, Dr. Frank Sheridan, who performed the autopsy. After firefighters brought Erin's body to the surface of the earth, an awaiting helicopter had transported her to the coroner's office.

A beam of light shone down on the autopsy table as Sheridan examined the body. Thin and balding with salt-and-pepper hair and a beard, Sheridan was originally from Ireland and spoke with a lilting Irish brogue. For more than two decades, he'd worked for the California medical examiner's office and performed thousands of autopsies.

From the observation bay, separated by glass, Detective Jonathan Woods watched as a forensic technician photographed the body, swabbed the withered flesh, and plucked strands of hair. Samples were collected and bagged for DNA testing.

Wearing blue latex gloves and a long white coat, Dr. Sheridan noted the condition of the cadaver.

"What appeared to be a female, very decomposed," Sheridan explained. "She had a pair of blue denim shorts on, a pink shirt, a pink-and-black-colored brassiere, pink underwear."

Sheridan immediately noticed the handheld garrote looped around her neck and partially entangled in her hair. After the weapon was photographed, Sheridan unwrapped the garrote and sealed it in an evidence bag.

Inspecting the neck, it was difficult to determine much about the wound. As the body mummified, a hardened layer of flesh had blackened and attached to the bone. The discoloration of the skin made it difficult to spot any trauma.

Examining the body externally, it was unclear if Erin might have been shot or stabbed. To document the internal injuries, Erin's body was x-rayed. Sheridan reviewed those images and found fractures to Erin's left clavicle and left first rib. The back of her skull was also cracked and broken in multiple places.

Because of the location of her body, Sheridan knew some of the broken bones were the result of a 140-foot fall down the mine. When Erin's body hit the floor, it appeared she had landed on her left side, causing the fractures. Studying the pattern of the breaks, he determined they likely occurred postmortem.

But one of the breaks to the skull seemed different to Sheridan. On the left side of Erin's head, just above the ear, was a large concave break in the bone. Given the severity of the fracture compared to the chips and fractures to the back of the head, Sheridan believed Erin had been hit with some sort of heavy object, either while she was alive or very shortly after brain death.

Next, Sheridan began the internal examination. Six days before Erin vanished, a doctor at the emergency room had determined she was pregnant. Detectives believed it was Chris's baby and potentially the motive for the killing. Woods was hopeful the autopsy would solve the mystery of who fathered Erin's baby.

Starting at the top of each shoulder and meeting at the breastbone, Sheridan made a Y-shaped incision across Erin's chest with his scalpel and cut away at the dried skin, opening the chest cavity. But after two months in a mine shaft in the summer, the internal organs had digested themselves, liquefied, and decomposed. Insects, including blowflies, fed on the soft tissue.

Because of the extent of decomposition, Sheridan had trouble collecting what remained of the organs. When he did find the uterus, he examined it for signs of pregnancy—but it was too decomposed to even determine if she had ever been pregnant, much less obtain DNA from a fetus. Erin's fetus had rotted away until it essentially disappeared.

When there is nothing left to visually identify a body, coroners often use dental records because the teeth are the most resilient substance in the body. To show the body belonged to Erin, Sheridan relied on the dental records previously provided by the family. Examining the dirt-smeared mandible, Sheridan opened up her jaw and took impressions of Erin's teeth. After establishing with Lore that Erin had since had her wisdom teeth removed, Sheridan compared the images to the dental records and confirmed: This was Erin Corwin.

Because of the trauma to the skull and the garrote,

Sheridan ruled the cause of death as homicidal violence, with evidence of strangulation and possible blunt-force trauma to the head. While it was impossible to place the time and date of death, the condition of the body fit with the time frame of when she went missing.

As for the manner of death, because of the garrote, Sheridan believed Erin was strangled to death, not choked. It was an important distinction. When choked to death, a victim's airway is cut off and he or she cannot breathe, leaving the victim struggling for up to five minutes before the heart stops and the brain dies. But if Erin was strangled to death, the cord would have cut off blood flow to the jugular vein in her neck. Within about twenty seconds, she would have lost consciousness. Within four minutes, her brain would have died.

Because the coroner couldn't determine with certainty whether Erin was pregnant, her remains were classified as evidence and stored in the custody of the sheriff's department. Erin's remains would not be laid to rest for four more months.

Chapter 33

It was about 9:00 p.m. on Sunday night in Anchorage, and Chris was driving his mom's Chevy Suburban with Nichole in the passenger seat. They were headed back to Chris's parents' home when he looked up and noticed flashing red-and-blue lights in the rearview mirror.

Chris pulled the Suburban to the side of the road, and a uniformed Anchorage police officer approached the driver's side under the guise of a traffic stop.

"I need you to step out of the vehicle," the officer instructed.

Seemingly dazed, Chris rose, turned around, and put his hands behind his back.

"Christopher Lee," the officer said, "you are under arrest for first-degree murder."

Chris was placed in the back of a police cruiser. Unbeknownst to him, for the previous twenty-four hours, he had been secretly monitored by the Anchorage Police Department's Special Assignment Unit and the Anchorage Safe Streets Task Force, who were assisting in his apprehension. The San Bernardino County Sheriff's Department had teamed with the FBI and Alaska State Troopers to monitor Chris. Just thirty minutes after Erin's body was identified in California, homicide detectives sent word to their Alaskan counterparts. Meanwhile, Detective Jonathan Woods had boarded a plane for Anchorage to bring back the murder suspect.

Chris was taken to a holding cell at the Anchorage Correctional Complex, where he was fingerprinted, photographed, and placed in protective custody in a private cell. In his mug shot, he appears disheveled, his hair tousled and a scruff covering his full cheeks. With an inscrutable expression, Chris stares directly into the camera with a stony gaze.

The Suburban was impounded until a search warrant could be obtained. Nichole, who was not under arrest, returned home to her family.

When he arrived in Anchorage, Detective Woods and the crime scene investigators examined the Suburban. In the back of the car, they found several items that looked familiar: two spools of paracord and blue climbing rope, similar to the blue rope tied around the propane tank they'd found inside the mine. They also confiscated knives Chris apparently stored in the vehicle.

But their next discovery stunned detectives. Hidden underneath the passenger seat was a homemade garrote constructed from braided paracord, two pieces of PVC piping, and black electrical tape.

"I had only seen one of those in my life," Woods recalled. "And that was the one that was wrapped around Ms. Corwin's neck. And for the second time in the same week, I saw a second one."

After Detective Hanke called once again to confirm the arrest, neither Bill nor Lore slept much for the rest of the night. At 7:00 that next morning, Lore began the agonizing task of calling all of her children to tell them the devastating news: Their sister had been found. Lore knew their oldest adopted daughter, who was sensitive, would be a wreck, so she decided to wait to call Taylor last. Just as the story was breaking online, Lore called her at work.

"If I tell you something, can you go on like life is normal and continue with the rest of your day?" Lore asked Taylor.

"Yeah," Taylor replied. "What is it? What happened?"

But after Lore told her, Taylor came to the house and stayed with her mom all day.

For weeks, many of Erin's closest friends had been in regular contact with the Heavilin family. Lore also spoke to Jessie Trentham. Gripping the phone, Jessie dissolved into tears.

At the Marine base, Jon learned of the arrest directly from detectives.

"The day we got the phone call, neither one of his parents were around," Lore remarked. "He was by himself."

After learning his wife's body had been found, Jon went downstairs and knocked on the Malakies' door. When Aisling opened it, Jon was holding a case of beer.

"Where's Conor?" Jon asked.

Conor came to the door and invited Jon inside. For a moment, Aisling sat to join them, but Jon looked over at her with a despondent expression. "Hey, I need a minute," he told Aisling.

As Aisling walked down the hallway, she glanced back at Conor.

"He just stood there and looked at me and shook his head," Aisling remembered. "And I knew that they had found her."

A throng of reporters gathered at the San Bernardino County courthouse on Monday at noon for a press conference. Photos of Erin, the mine shaft, and Chris's mug shot were displayed on a long folding table. About a dozen San Bernardino detectives, the sergeant, district attorney, and fire chief lined up in the front of the room alongside San Bernardino sheriff John McMahon, who stood behind a podium and addressed the media. McMahon told reporters that Erin Corwin had been found and that her neighbor, former corporal Chris Lee, had been arrested for her murder.

"The murder of Erin Corwin was solved by solid investigative work and devoted volunteers committing thousands of hours during the eight-week search," said McMahon. "We can't erase the pain felt by Erin's loved ones, but we will do everything in our power to imprison the criminal responsible for her murder . . . Although the results are not what anybody was looking for, at least there is some closure."

Sergeant Trevis Newport explained how the location of Erin's body was determined using cell phones, photographic evidence, police interviews, and detective work.

"There was a compilation of many electronic devices we used in this investigation that led us to Erin's location," Newport told the press. "It was very, very hard investigative work that led us to the potential location of Erin Corwin, as well as the technology."

Newport also credited the tireless work of the volunteers, who were critical in the massive search.

"It is a very, very difficult process and very time-consuming, very draining on personnel," Newport said. "Our volunteers for San Bernardino County Sheriff's Department played such a large role in that. There is no way Erin would have been found without their assistance."

San Bernardino County district attorney Michael

Ramos told reporters Chris would be charged with first-degree murder with a special circumstance allegation of "lying in wait," meaning prosecutors intended to argue that he'd planned Erin's death and lured her into a trap. If convicted, he could face the death penalty.

"He concealed his purpose. The facts indicate they were going on a little trip in the desert," Ramos said. "He waited and watched for an opportunity to do this. And he created that opportunity. It was a surprise attack on the person. He had a position of advantage on this person. We feel the facts will indicate that, of course, she was surprised at the time of the killing."

Through his attorney, Chris denied the charges and special allegations.

After the press conference, the Heavilins sent a message of thanks to law enforcement and the civilians who'd volunteered their time and offered prayers and words of support.

"While we were praying for a different outcome, we cannot begin to express the gratitude we have for every person that has been involved in the search for Erin," the family's statement said. "The countless hours that have been spent by volunteer search crews and multiple branches of law enforcement are more than we could have asked for and are ultimately what led to finding her."

The family concluded, "Please continue to pray for our family and for justice for Erin and her unborn baby."

The arrest had come as a surprise to Chris and his attorney. After Chris was led away in handcuffs, Nichole called her in-laws, who contacted attorney David Kaloyanides. The lawyer later spoke to the media.

"Based on the recent silence from the sheriff's department, we weren't sure where this was going," Kaloyanides told reporters. "I mean, we knew he was a suspect. The DA's office and sheriff's department made that very clear. But we did not anticipate the arrest."

At that point, Kaloyanides had yet to receive evidence against Chris and was waiting to evaluate it, but expressed skepticism about what it would prove. It seemed to Kaloyanides that the police had been targeting Chris. And he had thoughts about Lee's original arrest in July for possession of a potato gun.

"I don't know of anyone who's ever been actually arrested and held on a charge of possessing a potato gun," Kaloyanides said.

Chris would be held without bail in the Anchorage jail until his next preliminary hearing. Meanwhile, his family was sticking by him. Outside their Anchorage home, Dennis Lee spoke briefly to an Associated Press reporter.

"Let's just wait until the facts come out before jumping to conclusions," he said.

On the Monday evening after Chris's arrest, about a hundred friends and strangers trickled through a candlelit vigil, offering condolences to Erin's family. Many of the mourners wore purple, the color that had come to represent the search for Erin. Others tied small purple ribbons to a fence on the southeast corner of Luckie Park in Twentynine Palms.

Throughout the search, Jon had not spoken to the media. Now, for the first time, he answered questions from reporters. For such a quiet, private man, it was difficult to be in the spotlight. He told reporters he was struggling to find forgiveness for the man he'd once called a friend.

"Obviously, I hate the actions that he did. But I feel like, if I let him bring hatred to my mind every time I see him, he is just going to pull me down," Jon said. "When I first figured out about the affair and everything, he was still my next-door neighbor. There was a part of me that wanted to go take care of him. But if I did that, I would be in the same boat as him—I would be a bad guy."

Jon said he was grateful for the volunteer searchers who had spent countless hours looking for Erin. Because Jon had come to believe Erin was dead, he felt more relief than loss.

"I have closure now. I know she is in heaven," Jon said. "She is in a better place, in no more pain."

For Shelia Braden, Chris's arrest provided respite from suspicion directed at her son. Never once did Sheila question if Jon killed his wife. But Sheila had feared that Erin might never be found and that Chris would escape justice.

"That was one of the worst feelings," Sheila told reporters. "The feeling of, 'Is he going to get away with this?' It was heartbreaking, and we were scared. We knew what he had done, but there was a possibility that he would live his life free."

After the details of the investigation were released, the family also learned about the overwhelming evidence against Chris. Sheila said she was baffled to hear about some of Chris's statements to police during his interrogation. It seemed he had led detectives to the mines.

"It kind of blew my mind," Sheila said. "Did Chris think he was that smart? Or was he that stupid? I didn't know which one it was. I think he must have thought they were never going to find her, and he was just that cocky."

Shackled and handcuffed, Chris Lee hobbled into the Anchorage Correctional Complex courtroom wearing a faded red jailhouse jumpsuit. A messy thatch of hair hung down his forehead, a thin beard covering his cheeks and neck. The bailiff grasped Chris by the elbow and ushered him into the courtroom. As he passed by the gallery, Chris exchanged a quick glance with Nichole, who was seated next to his parents, Dennis and Karen Lee.

It was August 22, just days after his arrest, and Chris was appearing for the first time in court on charges of being a fugitive from justice. Because the crime occurred in California, Chris didn't face murder charges in Alaska. Instead, he was arrested on a federal extraditable warrant, filed with the intent of bringing Chris back to California.

During the brief hearing, Chris barely spoke. When the judge asked if he planned to fight extradition, he said he would first speak with his attorney before making a decision. At that, Anchorage assistant district attorney Heather Nobrega interjected.

"Your Honor, it's not clear he has an attorney," she said.

From the back of the courtroom, Chris's parents spoke up. "He has an attorney."

However, because defense attorney David Kaloyanides practiced in California, the judge had assigned a local public defender to represent Chris in hearings in Alaska. At that, Nichole tried to make a comment but was hushed by Chris's parents. Nobrega requested bail be set at $2 million cash only, which the court granted.

From his offices in Victorville, San Bernardino

prosecutor Sean Daugherty worked with Nobrega and filed paperwork to accelerate the process.

After privately consulting with Kaloyanides and the public defender, Chris learned the extradition was inevitable—fighting it would only delay proceedings by four to six weeks. Days later, Chris was brought back to the Anchorage courtroom, where he told the judge he would not fight the order.

Detective Jonathan Woods, who had flown to Alaska, escorted Chris back to California. Once Chris left Anchorage, the charges of being a fugitive from justice were dismissed in Alaska.

A brick building off Highway 62 houses the Joshua Tree courthouse. In 2014, there were just two judges in Joshua Tree who heard criminal cases. Judge Bert Swift was assigned the odd-numbered cases; Judge Rodney Cortez got the even-numbered cases. Because the murder of Erin Corwin drew an even number, the case fell to Judge Cortez.

In early September, Chris made his first appearance in the Joshua Tree courthouse. Wearing a dingy bluish-gray jail jumpsuit, with an ID badge clipped to the outside shirt pocket, Chris's hands were cuffed in front of him. His long dark hair was parted to the side and his beard neatly trimmed. At his side, in a gray suit and tie, was his attorney, David Kaloyanides.

On the other side of the courtroom, Sean Daugherty got a glimpse of the defendant for the first time. Keenly interested in the dishonored Marine, the prosecutor curiously observed Chris. Chris sat with his fingers laced, staring straight ahead but not focusing on anything.

Seated quietly in the back of the courtroom, Jon Corwin sat beside his father, Tommy.

The hearing lasted just a few minutes. Judge Cortez addressed Kaloyanides.

"How does your client plead?" he asked.

"Not guilty," the attorney said.

After the hearing, Kaloyanides spoke briefly to a small assembly of reporters gathered outside the courthouse. He said he expected the case to creep slowly through the justice system.

"It's going to take a while, in a case of this magnitude, to get any information from the DA's office so we can evaluate what the evidence is," Kaloyanides told reporters. "There are a lot of different angles to investigate, and we need to see what they have."

On September 16, Chris made his second appearance in a California court. By then, Nichole and Chris's parents had traveled from Alaska to be there. The charge of possession of a destructive device—the potato gun—was dropped, and bail for that charge was exonerated.

Because the defense had just received a huge discovery of 1,500 pages of documents, Kaloyanides asked the court for a continuance of the case. A dozen more motions and legal maneuvers by the defense would postpone the trial for two more years.

Chapter 34

Hundreds of flickering candles illuminated the night summer sky at the East Tennessee Riding Club in Oak Ridge. An arrangement of flowers hung near the barn. Purple balloons and ribbons adorned the bleachers overlooking the riding arena, where Erin had once spent hours barrel racing with her horse Rye Leigh.

For nearly ten years, the riding club had been like Erin's second home. It was where she'd tended to her horses, bonded with her brother Alex, and first met Jon. On Friday, September 19, about 250 people gathered at Erin's favorite spot in Tennessee to mourn her death. Many of those close to her wore T-shirts bearing the words *SUPPORT ERIN,* with a biblical verse on the back. Photos of Erin were displayed alongside guest books, which were soon filled with loving messages.

A local artist had welded horseshoes into the shape of ribbons and painted them purple, which were sold at the memorial. The money was donated to the Heavilin family for future funeral expenses and to defray the costs to attend any upcoming hearings in California. Those gathered told stories about Erin, prayed, and sang "Amazing Grace."

Following the memorial, a separate Celebration of Life ceremony was held for family and close friends at Calvary Baptist Church. After the services, Bill and

Lore Heavilin briefly spoke to the media. Standing in front of cameras and reporters, Lore said the family found some comfort knowing Erin had been found and they did not have to live with the fear that she was suffering somewhere or part of some sex-trafficking scheme.

"I have no doubt that she's in heaven," Lore said. "I miss her terribly. But at least we aren't sitting here for years and years and years wondering what happened."

Lore also thanked the detectives and volunteer rescue crew who worked to find Erin. Though it was horrifying to know exactly how Erin died, Lore said she was glad to know her killer would be brought to justice.

"In a way, it helped me know deep down in my mom's heart what I knew, that he had manipulated her and lured her," Lore told reporters.

While Lore didn't believe there would ever be closure, the vigil provided some solace, knowing how much her daughter was truly loved. Many of those at the memorial had never even met Erin but had been touched by the loss. Lore said she wanted people who'd never met Erin to know she was a good-natured, gentle animal lover.

"She was sweet, kind, very naïve. Anyone that knew her loved her," Lore said. "Tonight, here at this candlelight vigil, I'm almost overwhelmed with how many people came. It was just incredible to see how many people came to support Erin."

Erin's obituary ran in the *Knoxville News Sentinel* and *Oak Ridger,* describing her as a wife, daughter, granddaughter, sister, aunt, niece, and friend. The date of her death was listed as the day she went missing: June 28, 2014.

"Erin's love for animals, especially horses, will live on in the memories of those closest to her," the obituary read. "Erin's nurturing soul led her to become the mother of dozens of animals in her short life. Her 'children' ranged from fish and guinea pigs to cats and dogs."

In lieu of flowers, the family asked for donations to be made to the search-and-rescue teams that assisted in the recovery of Erin's body.

More than a decade before Erin's murder, Lore had faced the unimaginable pain of losing her daughter Trisha to a tragic illness. Now, her beloved Erin was gone.

"Losing one is hard enough," she explained. "Having to lose the second one is even harder, and with the way she was taken from us, it makes it much harder because it just doesn't make sense."

As she grieved, Lore wanted a reminder of Erin. That November, Lore decided to get tattoos representing both of the daughters she'd lost. On her right wrist, she had an image of a horse with a purple mane, surrounded by ribbons, to represent Erin. On the left wrist, she had a pink heart with angel wings for Trisha.

Whenever she looked down at either wrist, she thought of the daughters she treasured but would never see again.

For four months after Erin was retrieved from the mine shaft, authorities had been unable to answer the one question that may have solved the motive for the murder—whether Erin was pregnant with Chris's baby.

Because of the coroner's uncertainty during the initial autopsy, the court had ruled that her body would remain in evidence for an independent forensic examination.

"There was no evidence of conception—the best we could have determined was she could have been," Daugherty explained. "She was just too decomposed."

If Erin's pregnancy could have been proven, the charges against Chris might have doubled. In California, prosecutors can file murder charges in the slaying of unborn fetuses. But further testing was also inconclusive, and the matter was dropped. So, during a December 2 court hearing, Judge Cortez ruled Erin's body be released to her family, rescinding previous court orders. Erin was cremated in California, and her ashes were returned home to Oak Ridge.

Meanwhile, it seemed to defense attorney Kaloyanides that most of the residents in Joshua Tree had already made up their minds about his client's guilt. During that same December 2 hearing, Kaloyanides began laying the groundwork to have the case moved out of Joshua Tree, arguing that widespread media coverage had irreversibly tainted potential jurors. But he was contemplating filing a change-of-venue motion.

"We are considering that because of the pretrial publicity that is already out there," Kaloyanides told Judge Cortez. "But I haven't made that decision yet."

As the murder case crept through the justice system, homicide detectives continued to collect and examine evidence. Items recovered from the mine—the propane tank, water jugs, empty Sprite bottle, torch, and rope—were sent to the San Bernardino County crime lab for examination. The items were filthy and stank of death. Dennis B. Key, a criminalist and DNA specialist with twelve years of experience, was tasked with processing the items for DNA.

After two months in the mine, any biological evidence linking Chris to the crime scene had potentially deteriorated past the point of being usable. With gloved hands, Key carefully examined the long wooden stick with green cloth tied around it—a crude, homemade torch. Detectives believed the torch was part of Chris's plan to blow up the mine and incinerate Erin's body. Perhaps the killer had been sloppy and left his DNA on the handle.

First, Key used a chemical test to check for foreign substances, like petroleum-based liquid or gasoline. Peculiarly, the results showed there were only a few drops of gasoline on the torch. Not only had the torch never been lit, it had never even been doused in flammable liquid. Unraveling the twine, Key unfolded the green cloth, revealing a man's cotton T-shirt. If worn and unwashed, it was possible that the shirt contained DNA. A chemical test showed biological evidence near the collar of the shirt. Key marked it for further testing.

Next, Key surveyed the two large water jugs. From the stamps on the containers reading *Property of the U.S. Government,* it seemed clear they belonged to the Marine base, another clue for detectives that a military member committed the crime. Examining the contents of the containers, Key found trace amounts of gasoline. Dried blood crusted on the outside of one of the jugs was swabbed for testing.

The propane tank was scratched, covered in grime, and badly dented. The label on the side, reading *Blue Rhino,* had faded and was sun bleached. Key swabbed each section of the tank. It appeared biological material was present on the knob. A sample was marked for further testing. The Sprite bottle also contained biological material on the mouth of the container.

Finally, Key studied the garrote looped around Erin's neck. Body fluid and scraps of skin had saturated the cord but had since dried and hardened. The rope contained DNA that would almost certainly belong to Erin. But Key also found biological evidence on the handles. If they contained DNA belonging to the killer, it would be like a smoking gun. That DNA was collected and marked for further testing—although the results of those tests could take weeks or even months.

During the investigation, both Jon and Chris had voluntarily submitted fingerprints and given a buccal swab, providing their DNA samples. In the autopsy, DNA was also collected from Erin's corpse.

If the DNA evidence on the items returned a partial or complete DNA profile, or a mixture of profiles, the samples could be compared to the known reference samples to determine a match.

The defense's strategy in the murder case seemed focused on legal technicalities and damage control. Throughout 2015, the defense filed several motions aimed at mitigating the damning evidence against Chris and improving his reputation with potential jurors.

The majority of the motions were attempts to exclude evidence. Kaloyanides asked Judge Cortez to only allow the coroner to testify about Erin's autopsy, which would prevent Detective Woods from telling the jurors what he personally witnessed from the observation deck. The defense objected to Erin's text messages to Jessie being allowed in court because they were hearsay. Through Kaloyanides, Chris also requested to wear his Marine uniform in court. Judge Cortez ruled against all the motions.

The defense also unsuccessfully attempted to have the search warrant quashed, a legal maneuver that is rarely successful. When that, too, failed, Kaloyanides repeated his assertion that he planned to seek a change of venue due to extensive media coverage of the case.

"The public has already seen things they probably shouldn't have seen and learned things they probably shouldn't have learned," Kaloyanides said.

Meanwhile, prosecutor Sean Daugherty told Judge Cortez the district attorney still had not decided if the state would pursue the death penalty against Chris.

Before Chris Lee could stand trial for murder, there would be a preliminary hearing to determine whether there was enough evidence against the defendant. During the hearing, prosecutors and defense attorneys presented a dry run of their evidence and testimony. It would be up to Judge Cortez to decide if there was probable cause to proceed.

On April 3, 2015, inside the Joshua Tree courtroom, Sean Daugherty questioned eleven witnesses, including Jon Corwin, Jessie Trentham, Aisling and Conor Malakie, and several of the detectives and law enforcement officials who worked the investigation. Shackled at the defense table, Chris occasionally whispered to his attorney but otherwise said nothing.

On the stand, staring at the man who had destroyed his marriage and killed his wife, Jon Corwin was remarkably composed. But he winced as he testified about the last time he saw her on the morning of June 28.

"I told her I loved her," Jon said sadly. "She gave me a kiss, and then she left."

Jessie revealed details about her friend's affair with Chris and her plans to leave her husband. In a soft, shaky voice, she also was asked by the prosecutor to read out loud her texts to Erin. While on the stand, she couldn't stop herself from staring at Chris, curious to see the man she had never met but who had caused her so much pain.

Aisling was pregnant with her second child and

battling morning sickness when called to testify. As she walked past the defense table and saw Chris, she started to tremble.

"I was just shocked about how different he looked. He looked miserable. His hair was grown out. He looked greasy, and he had a beard," Aisling recalled. "He just didn't look like the Chris I knew . . . I almost didn't recognize him."

On the stand, Aisling testified about how often Chris spoke of disposing of a dead body. Conor talked about the day of the supposed hunting trip when he'd seen a propane tank in his neighbor's Jeep, which Chris said he planned to use to blow up a mine shaft.

Detective Jonathan Woods identified the homemade garrote found wrapped around Erin's neck during the autopsy. He told the court how a similar garrote was found in the Chevy Suburban Chris was driving in Anchorage when he was arrested.

Detective Mauricio Hurtado testified about the tire tracks found near Erin's abandoned Corolla, which preliminary tests seemed to match to Chris's Jeep. Hurtado also told the judge about the photos recovered from Joseph Hollifield's cell phone. The detective explained how caver Doug Billings used those pictures to identify the exact area where Erin's body was found ten days later.

Sheriff's corporal Robert Whiteside described the massive search for Erin and explained the recovery efforts involved in retrieving her body. Finally, Detective Dan Hanke spoke about his lengthy interrogation with Chris at the sheriff's station, during which Chris admitted to having an affair but denied seeing Erin on the day she disappeared. On the drive back to base, Chris had seemed surprised he wasn't under arrest, Hanke told the court.

"He seemed nervous, because he also asked why I wasn't taking him to jail," Hanke testified. "It was a little odd."

Even the discarded tire in the mine shaft took on a new resonance. In his police interrogation, Chris said he drove to the area near Erin's car because he had been collecting tires for a "tire fire." It was another circumstantial piece of evidence that seemed to put Chris at the mine and the location where Erin's car was found.

After almost five hours of testimony, Judge Cortez decided there was enough evidence to continue Chris's case. On April 22, 2015, Chris was formally arraigned in court where he once again pleaded not guilty through his attorney.

Sitting through the preliminary hearing was exhausting for Lore. Just as she had begun to return to her new sense of normalcy, the pain came rushing back. It was a reminder what a long road ahead the family had.

"Not only did the emotional scab get ripped off, but somebody was rubbing salt in that wound," Lore told a reporter. "But then I start thinking that the salt is healing, so I can heal from this."

Everyone grieves differently. Bill Heavilin didn't want to speak to the media or sit through a trial to hear the horrid details of his daughter's death. Instead, he mourned with quiet dignity. Lore, however, was the type of person who needed answers. Even if Chris had pleaded guilty, Lore would have wanted to sift through the evidence with a detective. Now, Lore braced herself for the trial, which she planned to attend every day.

"I wanted to be there for my daughter," Lore explained.

Following the preliminary hearing, prosecutor Daugherty filed notice with the court that he would no longer be pursuing the death penalty against Chris. Before making the decision, he spoke with the Heavilin family, who didn't want that sort of punishment in this case. It wouldn't bring Erin back. Besides, if convicted in a death penalty case, a defendant is guaranteed multiple appeals that can stretch on for decades.

"I didn't want to go through any more than we already had to," Lore commented.

In 2015, the DNA test results of the items in the mine were provided to homicide detectives and prosecutors.

The biological evidence found on the collar of the green T-shirt had produced a full profile for a male contributor, which crime scene analyst Dennis B. Key was able to compare to both Jon and Chris. The results were conclusive—they belonged to Chris Lee. While there was also a small mix of another partial DNA profile, it wasn't sufficient to determine a match, and excluded both Erin and Jon Corwin as possible contributors.

The bloodstain on the outside of the water jugs was a definitive match for Erin. Her DNA was also found on the knob of the propane tank. The profile excluded both Jon and Chris.

Swabs taken from the mouth of the Sprite bottle were found to be a mix of two DNA profiles, which can be challenging to analyze and interpret. One was a male, the other a female. Comparing the two profiles, it was determined the female was Erin and the male contributor was Chris. It seemed like Erin and Chris had split a Sprite out by the mine. Sadly, this was the same drink Jon had once used to propose to Erin.

Key also found DNA consistent with Erin on both the paracord and rebar handles on the garrote around her neck. While Key had searched for a secondary profile on the handles of the weapon, the DNA mix proved inconclusive.

Some of the evidence from the mine was also tested for fingerprints, but there were no decisive matches. After more than two months in a mine shaft, any fingerprint evidence would have been lost.

But there was one piece of evidence that they could test for fingerprints—the handwritten poem found in Erin's jewelry box. It was written in cursive, and Jon denied he was the author.

The letter was dusted for fingerprints. On a corner of the paper, Key was able to lift a print that matched Chris's. The letter was also tested for touch DNA, which conclusively linked Chris to the paper. It was one last piece of proof that Chris had lied repeatedly about his relationship with Erin.

Crime scene specialist Susan Jaquez also processed evidence through the lab. Comparing samples of the twine found wrapped around the torch with the twine found in Chris's Jeep, she determined they were of the same color, construction, and composition, and likely from the same source. Jaquez also determined that the blue climbing rope found in Chris's Jeep matched the rope tied around the propane tank recovered from the mine.

Finally, a ballistic expert compared shell casings fired from Chris's hunting rifle to the casings found near the mine. Under a microscope, criminalist Christi Bonar examined the firing pin marks on the casing and compared it to the known sample from the rifle. She determined that the same gun had fired both bullets.

But there was also one big blow to the case. A visual comparison of the tire tracks near Erin's Corolla found them to be an early match to the tires on Chris's Jeep. But criminologist Jason McCauley looked closer at the divots and nicks in the tire treads and determined they did not match.

"Everybody out there—the crime scene techs, the detectives—said those tires were consistent with the tires on the Jeep," Daugherty recalled. "They visually appeared to be the same when you just looked at them in the dirt, but when you looked closer, they were just not the same tires."

Chapter 35

More than three years after leaving Oak Ridge for the Marines, Jon Corwin returned to Tennessee in the fall of 2014 a very changed man.

At twenty-one, he was a widower. His stepfather, Michael Braden, had also passed away in 2013 after a long battle with ALS.

Back in Oak Ridge, Jon moved in with his brother and enrolled in a trade school to train to be a welder. Slowly, he began to heal and learned to trust again. Living so close by, he often saw Lore and the Heavilins.

"When Jon and I see each other, we pick up where we left off," Lore explained.

The Heavilins were too paralyzed with grief to move forward. Bleak emptiness haunted each member of the family in different ways. For Lore, the grief was suffocating, sucking the joy from things she once loved. She no longer enjoyed cooking like she once had. While she had always been an avid reader, she now struggled to keep focus on a book, often starting over and over again to grasp the words.

At home, she was in such a fog that she couldn't concentrate and became easily distracted. For a while, she laughed it off, joking she'd turned into a "dumb blonde" from one of those tired gags. But over time, the grief had taken an extreme toll—she was just so unlike her normal happy self.

Then the panic started. The smallest thing would shatter her with anxiety. Her doctor diagnosed her with depression, anxiety, PTSD, and panic attacks. She was put on an antidepressant, which kept her comfortably numb for a while. But she never wanted to be medicated and soon weaned herself off the drugs.

Erin's young nieces and nephews grappled to understand what had happened to their beloved aunt. When Lore's oldest grandson came by the Heavilin home, he would stare at a framed picture of Erin for long periods of time.

During one visit, Erin's eight-year-old niece suddenly announced, "I miss Aunt Erin. She made the best chocolate chip cookies, and she would always sit and play." The girl frowned. "I won't have Aunt Erin's cookies anymore."

The youngest of the Heavilin grandchildren no longer remembered Aunt Erin. And since her death, Erin's brother Keith and sister-in-law DeeAnna had a child who would never meet her.

The Heavilins also had to prepare for the financial burden of the trial. Lore knew it would be costly to fly to California and stay in a hotel for long stretches of time. To save money, they didn't take vacations or make any major purchases for nearly two years.

"Erin's murder has cost us in so many different ways," Lore explained. "How do you make plans to go to your niece's or cousin's wedding when you don't know if you are going to be in California for the trial? We basically have been not doing much of anything that costs money because we didn't know how much all the flights, car rentals, hotels, meals, et cetera for the trial would cost. We have spent thousands of dollars to support Erin."

For a while, the Heavilins found comfort at the East

Tennessee Riding Club. Lore would take Alex to the barn to care for the horses.

"It brought back a lot of good memories," Lore explained. "We spent so much time there. Back when they had horses and they were riding."

But after an allergy test determined he was allergic to grass and hay, Alex was forced to give it up, and he stopped going.

Defense attorney David Kaloyanides never did file a change-of-venue motion based on a potentially tainted jury pool. He didn't have to.

Instead, he managed to get the trial moved out of Joshua Tree using a different legal strategy. In May, shortly after the preliminary hearing, Kaloyanides petitioned to have Rodney Cortez removed from the case, claiming the judge had a bias against Chris. The peremptory challenge motion allowed for either party in a criminal hearing to disqualify a judge without providing any clear reason.

But because Kaloyanides had waited so long to file the motion, Judge Cortez quashed it as being untimely. Undeterred, Kaloyanides took the case to the appeals court. More than a month later, on July 9, the Fourth District Court of Appeals granted the motion, and the case was transferred to the courtroom of the other criminal judge in Joshua Tree, Judge Bert Swift.

Shortly after, Kaloyanides used a similar motion to disqualify Judge Bert Swift. Since there were only two criminal court judges in Joshua Tree, it effectively meant Chris's trial would be transferred out of the precinct. In September 2015, the case was moved eighty miles away to the superior courthouse in the city of San Bernardino. Over the next year, the case would go through two more judges—Glenn Yabuno and Dwight

Moore—before being assigned to Judge J. David Mazurek.

A former prosecutor with the San Bernardino County District Attorney's Office for nearly a decade, Mazurek had been appointed as judge by former governor Arnold Schwarzenegger in 2006. Born in Pittsburgh, Pennsylvania, the judge was the son of Fred Mazurek, a lawyer and former wide receiver for the Washington Redskins and Detroit Lions. Following in his father's footsteps, Mazurek played football as a student at Cornell University until he was sidelined by an injury. After earning a J.D. from the University of La Verne College of Law, Mazurek started in civil practice in 1993 before joining the prosecutor's office in 1996. Plump with a round face framed by dark hair graying around the temples, Mazurek was a well-respected judge with a jovial demeanor on the bench.

Before the trial could proceed, Mazurek fielded a few more motions to suppress evidence in the case. After a procedural error was discovered, Kaloyanides requested the judge dismiss the case completely. The motion was also denied.

Finally, on September 21, 2016, jury selection began, and twelve men and women were seated. The trial date was set for mid-October.

Meanwhile, the two lead attorneys had been preparing to do battle in court. So far, Kaloyanides had been remarkably muted about the possible direction of the defense. Given the fact that Chris had already given multiple contradictory statements, the defense thought it best not to hint at their upcoming strategy. On Kaloyanides's advice, Nichole and the Lee family also declined media interviews.

Unaware of the defense, prosecutor Daugherty had to prepare for any possibility.

"I wasn't sure exactly what the defense had been planning simply because the defense has attorney-client privilege and were playing close to the vest," Daugherty explained.

In homicide cases, there are really only four possible defenses: that the defendant didn't commit the crime; that he or she did the killing but there was some sort of justification; that there isn't enough evidence for a conviction; and finally that "the devil made me do it"—or mental defect defenses, according to Daugherty. Because of Chris's talk of suicide in his police interrogation, the prosecutor wondered whether Chris would claim PTSD. So Daugherty contacted the Marines. The military makes mental health services available to Marines and residents of Twentynine Palms. But the prosecutor learned Chris had never sought help for any issues.

"There was no psychological evidence that I was aware of that he had PTSD," Daugherty explained.

While the case was considered circumstantial, Daugherty was optimistic. The evidence linking Chris to the crime was damning.

"There was so much connecting him, out there at that mine shaft, even the very location of that particular mine tied him to the crime," Daugherty recalled. "That for him not to have done it, he would probably be the unluckiest man ever."

In murder trials, it is rare for a defendant to testify in his or her own defense. But something about Chris's arrogant demeanor gave Daugherty pause.

As the case headed to trial, the prosecutor tried to prepare for a cross-examination against Chris Lee that he wasn't sure would ever come.

But there was no way that anyone could be prepared for the twisted tale Chris Lee was about to tell.

Chapter 36

More than two years after the murder of Erin Corwin, the trial of the *State of California v. Christopher Brandon Lee* began on Tuesday, October 11, 2016.

Looming over the palm tree–lined streets in downtown San Bernardino, the superior courthouse is a sleek, eleven-story glass-and-brick building featuring thirty-six modern courtrooms. A wood-paneled courtroom on the fifth floor of the courthouse would be the setting for the scandalous ten-day trial.

Perched above the court on the bench and flanked by the American and California flags, Judge J. David Mazurek scrutinized the proceedings through rectangle wire-framed glasses.

At the defense table, Chris Lee wore a white-collared button-down shirt and striped tie. His hair had been clipped short, and his face was clean-shaven. Chris had slimmed down significantly in jail and no longer appeared like the slovenly bearded man from his mug shot. Throughout the testimony, Chris appeared calm and attentive, occasionally whispering to his attorney, David Kaloyanides, who sat to his left dressed in a designer gray suit.

On the first day, Karen Lee sat silently in the gallery with Chris's youngest brother, Steven. Nichole Lee was not present.

On the other side of the courtroom, deputy district attorney Sean Daugherty fiddled with the open laptop in front of him. He was dressed in a black suit and purple tie, mirroring the purple ribbons supporters wore in tribute to Erin.

Sitting in the gallery directly behind the prosecution, Lore Heavilin was surrounded by a few close friends from Tennessee, who had traveled with her for the trial. She would attend every moment of the proceedings. At times, when the testimony became too horrific, she dropped her head and prayed.

After some technical difficulties with his PowerPoint presentation, Daugherty rose from the prosecution's table to deliver his opening statements around 11:00 a.m.

"Ladies and gentlemen, at its core, this is really a very simple case." Daugherty paused, standing in front of the jury box, locking eyes with several of the jurors. "All the evidence in this case points to one person. And that one person is the defendant."

Daugherty then presented a series of photos and videos. First, an image of Erin and Jon appeared on the projector, visible to the courtroom. It was a *People* magazine cover, featuring the photo of the couple at the Marine Corps ball they'd attended just hours before eloping.

Daugherty described for the jury the events of June 28, 2014—the last day of Erin's life. That morning, she left to meet Chris outside Joshua Tree, a few miles from base. Stepping into his car, the lovers drove away in Chris's Jeep, leaving behind Erin's Corolla.

"8:04 a.m. was the last cell tower communication with her phone," the prosecutor said.

Erin had lied to Jon about why she was going to the park, but investigators later learned she had really planned to meet Chris, Daugherty explained. Copies of Erin's text conversation with Jessie, during which she had discussed her desert trip with Chris, appeared on the screen.

"This day cannot come quick enough," Erin had written. "It apparently takes two hours just to get there."

Next, Daugherty showed segments from Chris's police interrogation with Detective Dan Hanke. In one clip, Chris admitted to having an emotional affair with Erin. In another, he spoke about the best way to dispose of a corpse.

Astonishingly, Chris had put himself at the scene where Erin's Corolla was recovered on the day she vanished. In the interrogation, Chris discussed his strange, solo coyote hunting expedition, which the prosecutor called "ridiculous." A midmorning hunt for a nocturnal animal in the summer heat made little sense and was simply an attempt to concoct an alibi, Daugherty said.

"He told deputies he was coyote hunting that day," Daugherty said of Chris's original statement. "In July, in the middle of the desert, coyote hunting."

Next, Daugherty showed the jury a map of Joshua Tree National Park, identifying the Marine base and the route leading to the mine where Erin was found.

"It's a long way out there," he said. "I can't stress that enough."

It was also a location Chris had been to before six days prior to Erin's disappearance, Daugherty told the jurors. The prosecutor explained how photos taken by Chris's friend during that trip were used to identify the mine in which Erin was found.

The next video clip Daugherty played for the jury was captured by a homemade bucket camera as it was lowered down the mine. On the screen, Erin's crumpled body appeared. A tire, propane tank, water jugs,

Sprite bottle, and a homemade torch surrounded her body.

The prosecutor also told jurors about the crude garrote found around Erin's neck and the matching one located in Chris's mother's Suburban in Anchorage.

"He used this garrote to strangle Miss Corwin," Daugherty said as he held up the weapon to show the jury.

Days after Erin vanished, Chris fled California and returned to Alaska.

"He was going to leave, move past all that," Daugherty said in a deep, resonating voice.

The prosecutor also described evidence he planned to introduce throughout the trial, including Chris's and Erin's DNA on the Sprite bottle and Chris's DNA on the green shirt used to fashion the torch.

The motive for the murder was simple, Daugherty explained. When Chris learned Erin was pregnant, he realized it would likely destroy his marriage and future. It was easier for him to kill Erin than clean up the mess he had made.

"He did it because she was an obstacle for him," Daugherty said.

The prosecutor concluded his opening statement, stating he was confident the jury would return a guilty verdict for the first-degree murder of Erin, with enhancement for killing by means of lying in wait.

"All the evidence points to one person who planned, prepared, and executed the murder of Erin Corwin," Daugherty said. "I will ask you to find the defendant guilty and hold him accountable."

In a trial, it's typical for an attorney on each side to make an opening statement to provide an overview of their case for the jury. Although it isn't mandatory, seldom does an attorney skip it, because it is such an effective legal tool. In an unusual move, David Kaloyanides chose not to present an opening statement, reserving the option to speak directly to the jury after hearing the prosecution's case.

The prosecution's first witness was Lore Heavilin.

Her testimony was heartbreaking. The prosecutor asked about the last conversation Lore had with her daughter two days before she vanished. Lore explained how she had planned to cook all of Erin's favorite foods while visiting for her birthday. When Lore arrived at the Corwins' apartment to search for her missing daughter, all the ingredients were still in the kitchen.

When Kaloyanides stood for cross, Lore felt a twinge of apprehension, unsure what the defense attorney could possibly ask.

Strangely, his questions focused on Lore's other dead daughter, Trisha. Kaloyanides asked about Erin's relationship with her sister, her reaction to her passing, and if she exhibited any bizarre behavior following Trisha's death.

"She cried. She always wanted to be a big sister," Lore said. "That was her biggest thing. I assured her she was still a big sister."

At the time, Lore wasn't sure what the defense was hinting at. Later, it would all make disturbing sense.

Jon Corwin was next called to the witness stand, wearing a gray collared shirt and tie. In an even tone, he explained how Erin's affair with Chris was exposed.

"I learned that the defendant and Erin were having an intimate relationship behind my and his wife's back," Jon said. "I was appalled, disgusted, and shocked."

Over the next couple of months, Jon believed he and Erin were repairing their marriage. When she learned she was once again pregnant after the devastating miscarriage, he was exhilarated.

"Were you and Erin trying to work it out?" the prosecutor asked.

"Yes," Jon said woefully.

Then, on June 28, Erin said she was spending the Saturday alone at Joshua Tree National Park to scout scenic locales. He told the jury about his final conversation with his wife.

"She told me, 'I'm heading out, Jon. I love you,' and I said, 'I love you, too,' gave her a kiss, and she left," Jon testified.

Through the subsequent missing persons investigation, Jon lived under a cloud of suspicion. It wasn't until Erin disappeared that Jon learned how deeply he had been betrayed.

On cross-examination, the defense didn't ask much about Erin. Instead, Kaloyanides continued to focus on Trisha. Jon explained that by the time he met his wife, Trisha had been dead for years and Erin didn't dwell much on the loss.

The last witness of the first day was Erin's best friend, Jessie Trentham.

On the stand, Jessie felt numb. She had spent much of the day in the hallways outside the courtroom waiting to testify, thinking about her dead best friend. In the two years since Erin was murdered, life had changed for Jessie. She had recently gotten engaged and returned to school, intending to pursue a chemical engineering degree.

As she testified about her conversations with Erin, the loss hit her once again—she wouldn't have her best friend at her wedding. Speaking in a soft, quivering voice, Jessie described how Erin had confided in her about the affair with Chris.

"Did she tell you how she felt about Christopher Lee?" Daugherty asked.

"She made it known to me that she loved him more than she loved her husband," Jessie replied quietly.

By May, Erin told Jessie that she was sleeping with Chris.

"It was a relationship that became intimate," Jessie testified. "She said that they on occasion had sex when Jon was away."

"Did she discuss with you her plans?" Daugherty asked.

"She stated that she believed that she would be divorcing her husband or that a divorce would come and that she was hoping to be able to stay with him," Jessie said.

Then, in early June, Erin confided in Jessie that she was pregnant with Chris's baby. Soon after, Erin mentioned that her mom was visiting. Jessie texted: "Are you going to tell her?"

"What did you mean when you sent that text, 'Are you going to tell her?'" the prosecutor asked.

"That she was pregnant," Jessie said.

Erin had texted back. "Well, Chris wanted to tell everyone next week . . ."

On the morning of June 28, Jessie was also the only one who knew the real reason Erin was going to Joshua Tree National Park.

"She said that he was going to surprise her with a trip out to the desert," Jessie said.

"How did she sound?" Daugherty asked. "What were her feelings about that?"

"She was excited about being able to spend time with him," Jessie replied.

Daugherty asked Jessie to read her text messages out loud in court in which Erin explained her trip to the desert. Jessie had suggested the surprise would include a marriage proposal.

"Basically, I asked if it possibly could be an engagement ring," Jessie said. "She said, 'Maybe.' With a lot of exclamation points."

Jessie had even been on the phone with Erin that morning as Erin got ready, at about 7:19 a.m. California time.

"She said she was about to leave their apartment to go meet Chris to have their special day," Jessie testified.

"What was your response to that?" Daugherty asked.

"I was excited for her," Jessie said.

"Why?"

"I wanted her to be happy."

"Did you guys make plans or talk about her calling you later?"

"She was supposed to call and let me know how it went." Jessie glanced down.

"Did you ever get that phone call?" the prosecutor asked.

"No," she said quietly.

The next morning, Daugherty called caver Doug Billings to the stand.

When Billings received the subpoena that he would be called to testify, he wanted to concretely place Chris at the crime scene. So he journeyed back to Joshua Tree with a friend.

"We went out and re-created every single picture that his friend took on his phone—the same angle, everything," Billings recalled. "I wanted to say, 'I know where he was, and I can prove it because here's my pictures that match his pictures.'"

On the stand, Billings presented the evidence to the jury, along with a map with GPS coordinates for every photo taken. It was persuasive evidence that proved Chris had visited the area where Erin was killed.

On cross-examination, Kaloyanides tried to question Billings's knowledge of the Mojave.

"What if there was an earthquake out there?" Kaloyanides asked. "You wouldn't know how that affected the terrain."

In fact, Billings had extensively studied the 1999 Hector Mine earthquake, a 7.1 magnitude quake in a remote section of the Mojave Desert.

"Actually, I know exactly the impact earthquakes have on mines," Billings replied confidently. "I did a report on it. What would you like to know?"

"I overwhelmed the defense attorney with every question he had with technical responses that were 100 percent accurate," Billings recalled. "He had no way to respond. He was grasping at straws because I had his client nailed. It was hilarious."

Aisling Malakie walked swiftly to the witness stand. She wore a purple shirt, her freshly dyed long black hair pulled partially back. Both Aisling and her husband had been deeply affected by Erin's murder and Chris's arrest. After Conor completed his required active service, Aisling returned to Massachusetts, where she moved in with her parents.

In late 2015, Aisling discovered she was pregnant. When the Malakies learned they were having a baby girl, they had no doubt about what they would name her. Erin Malakie was born on June 25, 2016.

"The whole timing of everything, it just felt right,"

Aisling remembered. "As soon as we found out it was a girl, Conor and I were like, 'Let's ask Jon if we can name her Erin.' We never even ran through any other girls' names."

On the witness stand, the new mom spoke about her friendships with both Erin and Chris. Aisling said Chris often disturbed her with dark discussions of death.

"How many times prior to June 28 did you hear the defendant talk about murder?" Daugherty asked.

Raising her eyebrows, Aisling shook her head. "More than I can count."

Shortly before Erin went missing, Aisling remembered Chris contemplating about the best way to dispose of a body. She said she couldn't remember how or why he'd brought it up but that it was strange.

"He had the perfect way to hide a body. He could easily kill someone, then kill a coyote, and dig a hole, put the body in first, cover it with dirt, then put a coyote over it and cover it with dirt," Aisling testified. "So that if they looked for body heat, they would find the coyote first and stop digging."

The day Erin vanished, Aisling feared almost immediately that Chris had killed her.

"I called Nichole and said, 'Where's your husband? There's people here looking for her. Erin's missing,'" Aisling said, choking back tears. "She replied with, 'I don't care what happens to that little bitch.' Then she laughed at me and told me to mind my own business. And then I hung up on her."

Aisling's voice cracked. Thinking about what actually happened to Erin, the statement felt so much crueler.

"To hear her refer to her as 'that little bitch' made me so mad and upset," Aisling said.

"I see you are becoming emotional," Daugherty asked. "Why?"

Aisling put her left hand to her quivering lips and closed her eyes. She took several shaky breaths and paused. "Because I just knew something had happened to Erin at that point. And there was no way she went off on her own."

Following his wife's testimony, Conor Malakie took the stand. For the jury, Conor described how he felt "betrayed" by Chris. Daugherty asked Conor how he felt about testifying against his former best friend.

"It is difficult, but it needs to be done," said Conor, sporting a full beard.

Early on the morning of June 28, Conor was speaking to Chris about his coyote hunting trip when he noticed something in the back of the Jeep.

"I saw a bunch of items covered by a tarp, and I saw a white propane cylinder," Conor said.

"A white propane cylinder?" the prosecutor asked. "Like for a barbecue?"

Conor leaned forward to the microphone. "Correct. Yes."

The prosecutor presented a photo of the propane tank found in the mine with Erin. Conor confirmed it was similar to the one he saw in Chris's Jeep.

"I asked him why it was in there," Conor said. "What he was planning on doing with it."

"What was the defendant's response?" Daugherty asked.

"That he was going to blow up a mine shaft with it," Conor said.

Later that afternoon, Conor texted Chris that he was available to join him on his coyote hunt. Chris responded to meet outside Joshua Tree National Park.

For nearly three hours, Conor drove around the desert trying to find Chris. All calls and texts went unanswered.

Late that afternoon when Chris returned to the apartment, Conor noticed the propane tank was gone. The next morning when he learned Erin was missing, he felt a gnawing apprehension about his friend. Conor confronted Chris, who denied knowing about Erin's whereabouts.

"I believe he had something to do with it," Conor testified. "Because they were having an affair, and Erin had no enemies."

Chapter 37

Dressed in baggy jeans and a brown shirt, Chris's hunting buddy Joseph Hollifield took the stand on October 13. He spoke about his desert trip with Chris on June 22, 2014—less than one week before Erin vanished.

That afternoon, Joseph had snapped dozens of photos of the desert on his phone. Although he didn't know it at the time, those pictures would prove vital to finding Erin's remains. On the stand, Joseph denied having any knowledge about Chris's purpose for visiting the mines. But under questioning, he admitted he still considered Chris and Nichole to be "good friends." From the defense table, Chris smiled and sat a little taller in his chair.

Daugherty confronted Joseph with the text message he had sent his friend on the day Erin disappeared.

"How are the mines?" Joseph had asked in the text.

Joseph claimed ignorance, stating he was unaware Chris planned on returning to the mines that Saturday.

"It was just a random text," Joseph said.

On cross, Kaloyanides seemed to imply Joseph had changed his testimony after speaking with Chris's wife.

"Are you sure you did not discuss your testimony

with Nichole when you talked with her?" Kaloyanides asked.

"I did not." Joseph shook his head.

The next two witnesses were the San Bernardino County sheriff's deputies who had questioned Chris the Sunday after Erin went missing. When Deputy Danny Millan and Corporal Cathy Tabor first approached Chris on the morning of June 29, 2014, he had denied knowing Erin.

"Mr. Lee said they were mere acquaintances, not friends, and he only saw her when she came and left the apartment complex," Tabor said.

When Tabor and Millan learned from the other neighbors that Chris was actually having an affair with the missing woman, they returned to confront him. It was then that Chris changed his story. In a recorded interview in the parking lot of a Vons supermarket, Chris admitted his relationship with Erin was romantic but denied having sex with her, claiming they only kissed.

But Tabor and Millan sensed something a little off about Chris, who didn't seem to want to talk and glossed over many of their questions. The audio recording of the interview was played in court, in which Chris denied having sex with Erin and repeatedly called her a "pathological liar."

Later, Millan and Tabor had searched Chris's Jeep. It was muddy and scratched, as if it had recently driven through rough terrain. Inside, they found ten spent shell casings shot from a .40-caliber rifle.

The final two witnesses that afternoon were two of the men responsible for recovering Erin's body. San Bernardino County Fire Department engineer and paramedic Brenton Baum was the first firefighter to go down into the mine. He told the jury how he had retrieved the propane tank and water jugs strewn around Erin's body.

Sheriff's corporal Robert Whiteside, the program coordinator of the San Bernardino Sheriff's Department's Search and Rescue Unit, testified that crews worked every day for weeks to find Erin.

On August 16, Whiteside explained how searchers came across mine number 108 and discovered something peculiar.

"There was a strong odor of decomposition and gasoline mixed together," Whiteside testified.

The video footage from the homemade bucket cam was shown again in court. On the overhead screen, a shaky, dark image of the inside of the mine appeared. As the camera descended farther down into the murky shaft, the attached floodlight illuminated a few pieces of trash: a soda bottle, a tire, a propane tank. As the camera reached the bottom, Erin's battered body came into view. What remained of her head rested facedown near a tire.

The entire time the video played, Chris never took his eyes off the screen.

Testimony continued on October 17, the second week of the trial, with Paul Anastasia, the San Bernardino County firefighter who was tasked with bringing Erin's remains above ground.

Anastasia testified about the extreme heat and toxic air inside the mine shaft. He had spent about a half an hour gently scooping the corpse into two body bags. Near her body, he also discovered the homemade torch.

Then, Pedro Ligorria from the search-and-rescue crew testified about finding a bullet casing near the mine, which he placed in an evidence bag.

The next witness was a familiar face in the courtroom. Throughout the trial, Detective Jonathan Woods, the case agent, sat alongside the prosecutor to assist with the prosecution.

After Erin's body was recovered, Woods had attended the autopsy and watched as the coroner unstrung the homemade garrote from Erin's neck. He told the jury that Erin's body was so decomposed she had to be identified with dental records.

Woods also spoke about Chris's arrest in Anchorage and the search of his mother's Suburban. Photos taken of the Suburban were displayed on the projector for the jury. The next picture was a close-up of the crudely constructed garrote fashioned from two pieces of plastic rebar, braided paracord, and black electrical tape.

"That was the garrote that was located underneath the front passenger seat," Woods testified.

Following a lunch break, San Bernardino County sheriff's detective Bryan Zierdt was called to the stand to describe a conversation he'd had with Nichole Lee during the search of her apartment.

At first, Nichole claimed her husband's .22-caliber rifle was in the apartment closet, according to Zierdt. Later, she said it was at Isabel Megli's residence at the White Rock Horse Rescue ranch. Zierdt drove Nichole to the rescue and retrieved the rifle.

The final witness of the day was San Bernardino County sheriff's detective Mauricio Hurtado, who testified about the searches conducted of the Lees' and Corwins' apartments, the U-Haul, and the horse rescue. Hurtado also told jurors how crime scene specialists processed the scene surrounding Erin's abandoned car. While initially investigators believed the tire tracks near the Corolla had been made by Chris's Jeep, further examination showed the impressions were not a match to his tires.

Chapter 38

The woman standing in the center of the court-room stared silently at the judge and grinned. She wore a form-fitting black skirt suit with white piping and matching cream pumps, her blond hair cascading across her shoulders. Around her neck, she wore a pair of dog tags etched with her husband's name and birth-day: *Christopher Brandon Lee, 9/12/1989.*

On the fifth day of the trial, Nichole Lee appeared in court for the first time for a witness readiness hear-ing. She spoke to the judge without the presence of the jury, who waited outside to be called in for testimony.

Prior to the trial, the prosecution had served Nich-ole a subpoena in Anchorage to testify as a potential witness. Both the defense and prosecution had consid-ered calling Nichole to prove their case.

"Trials are pretty fluid. So you look where you're at evidence-wise, and you can't tell what's going to happen necessarily," prosecutor Sean Daugherty explained. "I wanted Nichole present in California to call potentially, depending on how the evidence played out."

At the time, the prosecution hadn't yet dismissed the possibility of filing criminal charges against Nich-ole Lee for her possible role in the case, according to Daugherty. Aware of the investigation, Nichole had hired her own attorney, who encouraged her not to testify and instead take the Fifth Amendment, on the grounds that she could inadvertently incriminate herself. But Nichole didn't listen. She wanted nothing more than to tell her story.

"My client wants to testify," her attorney said. "Over my advice."

However, the prosecutor decided not to call Nichole as a witness. Nichole still clearly supported her husband, and her erratic behavior made her volatile.

Judge J. David Mazurek now informed Nichole that Daugherty had since decided not to use her as a witness. However, defense attorney Kaloyanides did want Nichole to testify for the defense, and because of that, she was still under subpoena.

Nichole appeared pleased and smiled again as she passed through the double doors on her way out of the courtroom. She wandered over toward a vestibule that separated the courtroom and hallway, where twelve men and women were lined up against the wall near the other door to the courtroom, waiting for the judge to call them. They each wore yellow buttons with the word *JUROR* emblazoned on them.

One of the female jurors noticed Nichole. "I like your shoes," she said, glancing at Nichole's white pumps. "Where did you get them?"

Nichole approached the juror, and they chatted briefly. Witnesses and potential witnesses are not permitted to talk privately to jurors. It's a severe offense that could potentially result in a mistrial. The bailiff noticed and pulled Nichole aside. "Ma'am, don't talk to the jurors."

Nichole snapped, seemingly indignant. "She was talking to me!"

As she continued to argue with the bailiff, the commotion was so loud that it could be heard from inside the closed courtroom. A few minutes later, the bailiff stepped back inside the courtroom and approached the bench, informing Judge Mazurek what he had witnessed. Upon hearing that Nichole was speaking to a juror, both Daugherty and Kaloyanides appeared dismayed. The attorneys asked the judge to call the juror into the courtroom to find out what the two women were discussing.

When the juror was brought in, Judge Mazurek asked her about the conversation she'd had with the blond woman outside, purposely avoiding using Nichole's name. The juror confessed to complimenting a woman's shoes but said she didn't think she'd done anything wrong. Still, even the defense attorney seemed wary of Nichole.

"This witness is unpredictable, and I'm not sure it was benign," Kaloyanides said.

The judge decided the encounter was irrelevant and called the entire jury back to the courtroom, where the prosecution continued the case.

FBI special agent Kevin Boles was the first witness of the day. He testified that he had examined both Chris's and Erin's cell phone records and was able to pinpoint their approximate locations on the day Erin vanished. Boles told jurors that both phones were headed east toward Joshua Tree National Park early on the morning of June 28. At 7:36 a.m., Chris's phone pinged off a cell tower in the same location where Erin's Corolla was found. The last activity on Erin's phone was at 8:04 a.m., before it was shut off and never used again.

The next witness was Chris's former Marine buddy Andrew Johnson. Since completing active duty in 2016, Andrew had returned to Washington and was working as a shipfitter at Puget Sound Naval Shipyard.

On the stand, Johnson testified how he worked in the same company as Chris and had visited him in June when Chris was working a twenty-four-hour post position. Out of the blue, Chris had started talking about ways to dispose of a dead body and mentioned a chloride plant near Amboy. Andrew saw him making a list of items, including a shovel and chemicals. Weeks later, when Erin went missing, Andrew had been so alarmed that he contacted homicide detectives to relate the story.

Next, San Bernardino County Sheriff's Department crime scene specialist Susan Jaquez told jurors about the evidence she processed for fingerprints and DNA, including the tire, water jugs, propane tank, Sprite bottle, and torch wrapped with white twine. She told the jury that the twine had likely come from the same source as twine found in Chris's Jeep during the search warrant.

Following Jaquez, Detective Woods returned to the stand to discuss the search warrants he had served in Anchorage and the items recovered from the Suburban, including two spools of paracord, knives, and blue climbing rope. That rope was found to be a match to a piece of rope tied around the propane tank inside the mine.

On Wednesday, October 19, Christi Bonar, a criminalist with the San Bernardino County Sheriff's Department's firearms unit, testified about testing Chris's bolt-action .22-caliber rifle. The spent casing found near the opening of the mine shaft was a match to the rifle.

Next, the prosecutor called former Twentynine Palms resident Debbie Valik, who first spotted Erin's abandoned Corolla in the desert near Ranch Road at about 8:30 a.m. on June 28. The photos she snapped on her cell phone appeared on the screen. Two days later, she saw police surrounding the vehicle and learned it belonged to the missing woman.

The final witness before the lunch break was Chris's mother, Karen Lee. The prosecutor didn't ask about Karen's unwavering support for her son or her belief in his innocence. Instead, Daugherty questioned Karen about her Chevy Suburban. Although the vehicle was in Karen's name, Chris and Nichole were the primary drivers after the young couple returned to Anchorage.

"Whenever they needed it, they drove it," Karen said.

It was in the Suburban that detectives found the homemade garrote. When asked about the weapon, Karen said she knew nothing about it and had never seen it before.

After Chris was arrested, their home in Anchorage was searched and photographed. On the stand, Karen was shown one of the pictures from the search taken in the Lees' master bedroom. In the photo was a copy of a magazine—an August 2014 issue of *People* magazine, featuring the military ball picture of Jon and Erin Corwin alongside a head shot of Chris on the cover.

"My husband bought that piece of trash," Karen testified.

When Dennis brought home the magazine, she said, she hid it in her bedroom.

"I didn't want Liberty to see it." Karen frowned. "I was appalled."

During the spring of 2014, Isabel Megli's peaceful charity horse rescue had been the setting of a love triangle between Chris, Nichole, and Erin.

On the witness stand, Isabel told the jury how the drama unfolded. It started in early 2014 when she first noticed Chris flirting with Erin. Soon after, Erin stopped coming with the Lees to the rescue. At first, Nichole didn't explain why she was no longer friends with Erin—but later revealed the details of her husband's affair.

As Isabel spoke, Chris gazed admirably at her from the defense table. At one point, Daugherty paused and pointed out that Chris was smiling at the witness. Isabel avoided looking in his direction and didn't smile back.

Throughout her testimony, the defense objected to many of Daugherty's questions about conversations Isabel had with Chris or Nichole as hearsay.

However, Isabel was able to explain how on the afternoon of June 22, six days before Erin vanished, Chris stopped by the ranch excited by all the "interesting things" he had seen during a desert excursion with his friend Joseph.

"He said there was a mine shaft and that no one would find it," Isabel told the jury.

On the evening before Erin disappeared, Chris and Nichole spent the day at the rescue with their daughter. As Chris was leaving, he'd asked to borrow a propane tank. In court, the prosecutor showed Isabel a picture of the propane tank recovered from the mine shaft. She identified it as the same Blue Rhino brand propane tank she had loaned Chris.

"I asked him if he was going to have a barbecue," Isabel testified. "He said he was going to use it to 'play games.'"

"Did the defendant ever return the propane tank?" Daugherty asked.

"No," she said, shaking her head.

After Erin vanished, Isabel witnessed Nichole fuming at Chris that he was "too dumb to keep his lies straight." Isabel said Nichole also implied that Erin disappeared to frame Chris.

"She said Erin was missing, and that [Nichole] felt she was playing a game," Isabel said. "And that she wished she was dead."

"Did she tell you, 'If there is no body, there is no case'?" Daugherty asked.

"Yes," Isabel replied. "She didn't care if Erin was dead."

The next witness was Detective Dan Hanke. Since the case ended, he had been promoted to sergeant in the San Bernardino County Sheriff's Department. Assisting in solving Erin's homicide had been one of the biggest and most impactful cases of his career.

Hanke was asked about his interview with Chris on July 1, and the first ninety minutes of the recording was played in court. Daugherty pushed Play, and Chris and Hanke appeared on the screen in the narrow interrogation room. He was slumped in a chair against the wall, across from Hanke. In court, Chris sank in his chair at the defense table, mirroring his posture on the screen.

Over the next three days, Hanke would return to the stand three times as the prosecution played the lengthy interrogation.

The third week of the trial began with grim testimony from the chief medical examiner with the San Bernardino County Sheriff Coroner Division, Dr. Frank Sheridan, who had conducted Erin's autopsy.

On October 24, Sheridan explained for the jury the condition of Erin's body. Her skull had been crushed numerous times, but only one of those fractures occurred before her death or slightly after her death, the coroner determined. The break above and behind Erin's left ear appeared to be the result of blunt-force trauma from being hit with a heavy object either while she was still alive or very shortly after she died.

Sheridan also found Erin had suffered postmortem fractures to her left clavicle and left first rib, likely from the fall down the shaft. But, as Sheridan pointed out for the jury, most of the other injuries were masked by the severe decay.

"Because of decomposition, there are just some injuries you're not going to see, especially bruises," Sheridan told jurors.

The decomposition left Erin's uterus in such bad shape that Sheridan could not determine if she was pregnant at the time of her death.

The official cause of death was homicidal violence with evidence of strangulation and with possible blunt-force trauma to the head. The time of her death was unknown, but Sheridan said the condition of her body fit with the timeline of her going missing on June 28, 2014.

On cross-examination, Kaloyanides pressed Sheridan on whether Erin could have been strangled as much as a day before she suffered the skull fractures and other broken bones. Sheridan admitted it was possible.

As the testimony turned gruesome, Lore hung her head and looked away from the screen, shut her eyes tight, and prayed. As she spoke to God, the coroner's words quieted and a sense of calm washed over her. Before the trial began, friends and family had asked if there was anything they could do. "Send prayers," Lore told them. Now, sitting in the courtroom, Lore could feel the love emerging from the hate.

"The peace I felt during the trial could only be from all the prayers," she remembered.

On Wednesday, October 26, San Bernardino County criminalist and DNA specialist Dennis B. Key testified about receiving DNA samples from Chris Lee, Jon Corwin, and Erin Corwin.

The crime lab had tested each item taken from the mine and found Erin's blood and DNA on the garrote, propane tank, and water jugs. Chris's DNA was found on the collar of a green T-shirt used to create the torch.

"There is a one in sixteen billion chance the DNA belonged to someone else," Key told the jury.

"For comparison, how many people are there in the world?" Daugherty asked.

"About seven billion," Key replied.

The mouth of the Sprite bottle contained a mix of DNA for a male and a female that Key determined matched Chris and Erin. Key told the jury there was a 1.4 quadrillionth of a chance that the female DNA was a match to someone else.

"The male contributor belonged to the defendant," Key testified. "There is a one in twenty quadrillion chance it was not Christopher Lee's DNA."

During cross examination, Kaloyanides got Key to acknowledge that Erin's DNA could have been transferred to the items that were next to her during decomposition, but this didn't seem to prove anything in the case.

With the mounting evidence stacked against Chris, the defense's case seemed to be floundering.

That afternoon, Daugherty presented his last piece of evidence. On the projector, the prosecutor showed a photocopy of the letter discovered in Erin's jewelry box after she disappeared. The fingerprint technicians were able to lift a print that belonged to Chris from the piece of paper.

Then the prosecution rested.

After the jury left for the day, Kaloyanides made one more motion asking the judge to throw out the case due to lack of evidence. Motions to dismiss are common legal strategies and are almost never granted.

Upon hearing this motion, the normally jolly judge grew suddenly serious. Mazurek told Kaloyanides that the prosecution had more than proved their case and a reasonable jury could find Chris guilty of first-degree murder. Moreover, there was also plenty of evidence to show that the defendant planned the murder and lured Erin to the desert, meeting the special circumstance of lying in wait.

"In fact, it was a surprise trip for her," the judge said. "But not in the way she thought."

Chapter 39

Chris Lee peered to his left, sneaking a quick glance at the jury. Furrowing his brow, he sank farther into his seat behind the witness stand.

It was Thursday, October 27, and Chris Lee was testifying before the jury. He would be the first and only witness for the defense. Chris wore a crisp white shirt, black slacks, and a contrite expression.

"I need to tell the truth," Chris said sheepishly, leaning into the microphone. "I couldn't live with myself if I kept this a secret any longer."

At the podium in the middle of the courtroom, in a black suit and silver tie, Kaloyanides spoke directly to Chris, guiding him through the summer of 2014.

Calmly, Kaloyanides began by asking questions about Chris's childhood in Alaska, his marriage to Nichole, and his military career. During both his deployments, Chris admitted he never saw any combat or fired his weapon. Still, after his last tour in Afghanistan, he claimed he'd returned depressed. He told the jury part of the reason for his despair was the fact that he hadn't seen any action in Afghanistan and didn't get to shoot anybody.

Once again, Chris blamed his depression and suicidal desires for why he'd started having an affair with Erin. For the first time, Chris publicly admitted that his affair with Erin had been sexual. Chris said he fell in love with Erin and briefly considered leaving Nichole. Even after his wife found out about the affair, Chris confessed he continued to pursue Erin. He now acknowledged to the jury that he had written that love note after their romance had been exposed.

Throughout the spring and early summer of 2014, Chris and Erin continued seeing each other secretly. Then, Erin found out she was pregnant. But according to Chris, Erin was distressed because she didn't know if it was her husband's or lover's baby.

Despite his affection for Erin and her pregnancy, Chris told the jury he still planned on breaking off his romance with Erin and leaving the Marines.

"Did you have any plans after leaving the corps?" Kaloyanides asked.

Chris leaned closer to the microphone. "Yes. Me, Nichole, and Liberty were planning on moving back to Alaska."

"Did you tell Erin this?" the defense attorney asked.

"I did." Chris nodded.

Chris admitted to planning the desert trip with Erin on June 28—the day she disappeared. He said he had been planning a hunting trip for about a week and had invited Erin along so they could talk about their relationship.

"Was it just going to be you and Erin?" Kaloyanides asked.

"No. It wasn't," Chris said, adding he had invited both Skyler and Conor.

"Why were you inviting all these other friends of yours if you wanted to talk to Erin?"

"Because I didn't really want to have a lengthy conversation," Chris said. "So I wanted to be able to hang out with my friends and do some hunting, in case the conversation got too deep or got to the point where I was uncomfortable with it."

But on the morning of June 28, both of Chris's friends had bailed on the hunting trip. So Chris and Erin set off to the park alone. That morning, he conceded, he met Erin in the desert where her Corolla was later found. For the trip, Chris said he borrowed the propane tank, gas cans, and gun because he intended to build a "tire fire" in one of the mines. He also collected a couple of old tires he'd found discarded in the desert.

"Did you tell Erin that you were going to actually go and try and blow up this mine?" the defense attorney asked.

"On the way there," Chris said.

"Do you remember what her reaction was?" Kaloyanides asked.

"She wasn't happy about it. She thought it was stupid, unsafe," Chris replied. "She said she thought this trip was going to be about us talking. And I told her that it was, but I wanted to try to do this, too."

It took nearly two hours on the rugged dirt road to reach the park in Chris's Jeep. When he and Erin arrived at the remote mine outside the northern edge of the park, Chris said he began unloading supplies.

"I took the tires out of my Jeep and tossed them down the mine shaft," Chris testified.

"What was Erin doing during this time?" Kaloyanides asked, leaning casually against the podium.

"She was sitting in the Jeep, listening to music," Chris said. "She didn't want to be near any of this."

"All right, then what did you do next to try and blow the mine?" Kaloyanides asked.

To ignite the tire fire, Chris said he had created a homemade torch out of an old green shirt, a stick, and string.

"I went to the back of the Jeep and took out my torch," Chris said evenly. "And I realized I had not doused it in gasoline."

After unsuccessfully attempting to ignite the mine, Chris grew frustrated and returned to the Jeep. Chris now told the jury how in the weeks leading up to June 28, he had been playing Russian roulette almost every morning.

In the Jeep, Chris grabbed his gun and plopped down in the driver's side. He toyed with the weapon, put it against his temple, and pulled the trigger. It clicked, but didn't fire. There was no bullet in the chamber. Upset that he was acting suicidal, Erin got out of the Jeep and walked away from the vehicle toward one of the mines.

After a few minutes alone in the Jeep, Chris called out for Erin. He got out of his vehicle and chased after Erin.

"We started having a conversation," Chris said.

"About what?" the attorney asked.

"Plans. She wanted to come to Alaska. She wanted to be part of Liberty's life," Chris mumbled. "I told her I didn't want that. I told her, you know, that I decided you can't be part of Liberty's life, and she said that she wanted to, that she loved Liberty. I told her, 'It's not your choice; it's not your daughter. You don't get to love her. She's mine.'"

"What were you thinking at that point?" Kaloyanides asked.

"I was thinking there's no reason for Erin to love Liberty," Chris said. "She's not hers; she shouldn't have any kind of emotional attachment to her."

Chris testified that suddenly a memory had flashed into his head. One night after his wife had given Liberty a bath, Nichole found her daughter's crotch to be red and irritated. Nichole, who at that point did not know about the affair and still allowed Erin to babysit, accused Erin of somehow causing the "suspicious" rash, Chris said.

"She thought maybe Erin had molested Liberty because [Nichole] was uncomfortable with the way she had been around her when she had been watching [Liberty]," Chris said.

"What was your reaction to that?" Kaloyanides tilted his chin sympathetically.

"I felt so safe in my little community that I didn't think it was possible," Chris replied.

"So you didn't believe Nichole?"

"No. Not at the time."

Despite his claim that abuse was suspected, Chris admitted on cross-examination that neither he nor Nichole called the police or a pediatrician. In fact, the family continued to use Erin as a regular babysitter for Liberty.

Standing beside Erin in the desert, Chris said she told him she wanted to be a part of his life because of her love for Liberty. But Chris said there was something alarming about the way Erin talked about his daughter. She seemed way too attached to Liberty.

"When Erin told me that she loved Liberty and that she wanted to be with her, something clicked; it turned a gear in my head," Chris testified. "And I said, 'Why do you care about Liberty so much? Why do you want to be a part of her life?' And Erin told me, 'I just love her.'"

Suddenly, he confronted Erin. "Did you touch Liberty?"

Erin didn't respond. Reeling back, she started stuttering.

"And I stopped her again, and I yelled at her this time, I said, 'Did you molest my daughter?'" Chris said, pausing dramatically between words. "And she said, 'Yes, but' . . . And that was the last thing I ever heard her say."

Chris testified that it felt like a "red-hot knife went through my heart." He told the jury he'd lost control and lunged at Erin in a blind rage.

"It set me off," he said. "I just felt so much hate . . . I wasn't going to let anyone hurt my daughter again."

In the same flat, distant cadence he had in his voice when he talked about Alaska, he now confessed to the horrifying murder in chilling detail.

"I stumbled back, and I sat on the edge of my Jeep and caught myself with my hands. And with my right hand, I felt the metal from the garrote," Chris said. "I grabbed it, and I stood up. And I came up behind her and I put it around her neck. Training took over then. I turned around and just started pulling."

Kaloyanides paused, letting Chris's words resound through the courtroom.

"Every ounce of love I had for her turned into hate," Chris told the court. "I felt justified in a way because of how angry I was . . . Nothing would have stopped me from doing what I was doing."

Kaloyanides asked how Chris felt while strangling Erin. At that moment, Chris admitted he hadn't thought about the repercussions of his actions.

"I told myself while I was doing this, *Never again.* I was never going to let anyone hurt my daughter ever again," Chris said. "I had let her into my daughter's life. It was my fault that my daughter was hurt."

Chris dropped his head and glanced at his hands. He still wore his wedding band.

"I just kept choking her. I pulled and I pulled." His voice wavered as if he were holding back tears. "I don't know how long it was. It might have been five minutes or ten minutes. It felt like forever."

While he appeared to be crying on the witness stand, there were no tears.

"Then the anger, that feeling of disgust and hate, ebbed a little bit, and I let go," Chris testified. "And she dropped to the ground."

Catching his breath, Chris had stopped momentarily, gawking at her body in disbelief. She didn't move; the color had already started draining from her face. Erin Corwin was dead.

"I looked, I didn't see any rise and fall of her chest. I didn't care," Chris said. "I freaked out. I killed her."

On the witness stand, Chris choked out more crying sounds.

"After a few minutes went by, I realized what happened. I knew I killed her," Chris said. "And the garrote was still around her neck. So I grabbed it, and I dragged her to the edge of the mine shaft, and I pushed her in."

Kaloyanides then asked Chris about his actions after Erin vanished, when at first he denied knowing her and insisted she was not with him on June 28.

"Were you trying to hide the facts so you wouldn't get caught?" Kaloyanides asked.

"Yes. I was trying to hide what I did," Chris replied. "I was wrong in what I did and I knew it."

While in jail awaiting trial, he said, he realized he had to tell the truth.

"It eats away at me a little more each day," Chris testified. "Sorry will never be enough."

For two years, Chris had never revealed to anyone he killed Erin. Not his wife, not his mother or father—who were paying for his defense attorney. In the gallery, Karen Lee sat beside her youngest son, Steven. The expression on her face was unreadable. Karen Lee never returned to court after that day.

As the courtroom broke for lunch, Chris hung his head in his hand and appeared to sob. But once again, there were no tears.

Chris Lee's new story portrayed the slaying as a crime of passion by an outraged father protecting his daughter. Though he admitted to killing her, Chris contended he had snapped because Erin supposedly confessed to molesting his daughter. It accounted for all the physical evidence.

Chris's testimony was an attempt to reduce the charges against him. If a jury believed killing Erin wasn't premeditated or planned, they could instead convict him of second-degree murder or even involuntary manslaughter. A first-degree murder conviction carried an automatic life sentence. A manslaughter verdict, however, could allow Chris to walk free in as little as three years.

But it was also a risky proposition. In fact, Chris's own defense attorney worried that accusing the victim of child molestation would turn off the jury. In the end, Kaloyanides had no choice—his client was determined to testify.

"It was what Chris insisted was the truth," Kaloyanides explained.

The explosive allegation of molestation horrified the Heavilin family. When the case entered the justice system, Lore had worried and wondered what the defense would say about her daughter. Now it was clear why Kaloyanides had questioned Lore and Jon about Trisha. Kaloyanides was attempting to show some twisted correlation between Erin's sister's death and her affection for Chris's daughter.

"I knew his attorney would not be able to dig up any dirt on Erin. In the beginning, I said if there was going to be any dirt, it would have to be made up," Lore remarked. "The allegations that Chris claimed were lower than I imagined possible."

No one who knew Erin believed one word, but it was still offensive, painful, and ridiculous, Jon Corwin explained.

"She was nurturing, caring, never did anything elusive or crude or harmful," Jon recalled. "No one who knew Erin, or has ever heard of Erin, would ever believe that."

Even the seasoned homicide detectives were stunned.

"I personally felt disgusted. From all the people we talked to who knew Erin, we didn't think this was even an angle Christopher Lee would play," explained Detective Jonathan Woods. "This came out of left field."

Prosecutor Daugherty was also troubled about the allegation, but not because he worried the jury would believe Chris's story. Rather, he was upset because it meant that Liberty could now be considered a witness in the case. When Chris brought his daughter into his murder defense, he opened Liberty up to the possibility of being forced to testify in trial.

"That was super infuriating, that he brought her into it. It was terrible. Just terrible," Daugherty recalled. "I don't know on what planet that's even conceivable that he would try to sell that to anyone. It was ridiculous. And on top of it, you're bringing your daughter in."

The last thing Daugherty wanted to do was call an eight-year-old to the stand to testify in her father's murder trial. As a prosecutor who often handled juvenile witnesses, he understood how damaging that could be for the girl.

Daugherty knew it was possible that someone may have coached Liberty to lie about her former babysitter.

"All of the sudden, Liberty becomes a potential witness," Daugherty explained. "And frankly, once that became an issue, I had to keep Nichole around because I can have her ordered to bring Liberty in."

The same day that Chris confessed to killing Erin on the stand, Nichole Lee strutted into the courtroom wearing a bright blue dress, white pumps, and a smug expression. In one hand, she clutched a pair of sunglasses and a purse.

Following the lunch break, Judge Mazurek had called Nichole back into the courtroom, outside the presence of the jury, to once again discuss her possible testimony.

The judge told Nichole the defense no longer planned to use her as a witness. The prosecution, however, had renewed interest in calling Nichole in its rebuttal of the case. Nichole informed the judge that her lawyer would be present if she was made to testify for the prosecution.

But now that Chris had accused Erin of molesting Liberty, the judge explained that the prosecution was considering calling the eight-year-old as a witness. As Liberty's guardian, it would be Nichole's responsibility to bring her daughter to court. Mazurek ordered Nichole to make Liberty available if the prosecution decided to call her to testify.

At that, the smile faded from Nichole's face. With a trembling hand, she wiped a tear from her cheek.

The judge dismissed Nichole. Still shaking, Nichole turned and darted out of the courtroom and into the hallway. She threw her purse down; it hit the floor with a loud boom that could be heard inside the courtroom.

Shouting echoed from the hallway. Once the bailiff stepped outside, the commotion grew quiet.

After much consideration, Daugherty ultimately decided not to call either Nichole or Liberty to the witness stand. He just didn't want to put the girl through any of that pain.

Still, it was impossible to fathom that Chris had been willing to paint his own daughter as a sex-abuse victim in a sick attempt to save himself.

Chapter 40

Y ou're the one who killed her?" Prosecutor Sean Daugherty barked at Chris.

"Yes, I am," Chris replied, shifting uncomfortably on the witness stand.

"You're the one who strangled her to death?" Daugherty's voice rose.

"Yes, I did." He nodded ever so slightly.

On October 27, after the lunch break, the prosecutor got his first chance to question Chris. Wearing a blue suit and maroon tie, Daugherty began by establishing Chris's long pattern of lying to detectives.

"You lie when you're ashamed of yourself," he said. "You lie when you're scared."

"Yes," Chris replied.

"Are you scared now?" Daugherty asked.

"Yes," Chris said, his voice flat.

"You're not lying today to protect yourself?"

"No."

Daugherty laid out all of the "coincidences" that happened in the weeks, days, and moments leading to Erin's murder. The same week Erin went missing, Chris had Googled ways to dispose of a body and visited the mining district where Erin's body was dumped. The prosecutor then reminded the jury that Chris had just admitted he knew Erin was pregnant.

"You had a girlfriend who was pregnant, right?" Daugherty questioned.

"Yes," Chris said.

"And you had a wife who was expecting to go back to Alaska in just a few days?" the prosecutor asked.

"I did." Chris glanced at his lap.

Chris, however, maintained he did not kill Erin because he knew she was pregnant with his child. He repeatedly claimed he murdered Erin because she'd confessed to molesting Liberty.

Coolly and methodically, Daugherty confronted Chris with the inconsistent details of his new story. When Nichole found an irritation on Liberty's genitals, neither she nor Chris had called police or taken the girl to a pediatrician. In fact, Erin continued to babysit the girl. And Chris continued to have sex with Erin.

"You heard these accusations from your wife, who you love, right?" Daugherty asked.

"Yes," Chris said.

"So you immediately picked up the phone and called police?"

"No." Chris shook his head.

"Nichole immediately picked up the phone and called the police?"

"No."

"So you're still having sex with the woman who your wife thought was molesting your daughter, right?" Daugherty asked.

Chris leaned forward and matter-of-factly said, "Yes. It wasn't on the forefront of my mind."

Daugherty asked what was on Chris's mind when he killed Erin.

"Just hate, that's all it was. I had loved her, and

every bit of that love that I had was turned to hate," Chris responded.

Pacing back and forth from the prosecution's table, Daugherty paused at the podium.

"You had the choice to tell the truth, right?" The prosecutor's voice rose.

"I did," Chris said.

"You knew Erin had a mother?"

"Yes."

"You knew she had people who loved her?"

"Yes."

"You knew a lot of people were looking for her?"

"Yes, I did."

"And you essentially made the decision to hold them hostage, right?" Daugherty asked.

"Yes," Chris said quietly.

For nearly two months, hundreds of volunteer cavers, investigators, and firefighters had scoured the desert searching for Erin. All the while, Chris knew exactly where she was but refused to tell anyone.

"I was afraid to tell the truth and thinking I could get away with it. I was still really angry at the time, I didn't want anyone to find her then," Chris testified. "I'm not angry anymore, and I'm no longer scared to tell the truth. This is something that I have to do."

Chapter 41

Gripping the handles of the garrote with both hands, Chris Lee twisted the cord around a life-sized cloth dummy and pulled tight. The dummy jerked upward and dangled above the floor of the courtroom as Chris demonstrated exactly for the jury how he murdered Erin.

When Chris first took the stand to testify, Daugherty knew he had a striking way to show the horrors of manual strangulation. The dummy was a tool created by the district attorney's office to use for homicide and assault trials.

"I thought if he's going to say he did it in any way, then I'm going to use some kind of visual demonstration," Daugherty recalled. "A strangulation case takes a long time to kill somebody like that. So I knew I was going to have him demonstrate somehow."

Stepping down from the witness stand, Chris calmly took the garrote and, at Daugherty's instructions, looped it around the dummy's neck. In one swift, horrifying motion, he then spun around so that he was facing the opposite way. He and the dummy were back-to-back. The dummy lurched forward and hung with its legs flopping in the air.

It was such a shocking moment that audible gasps echoed through the courtroom.

Daugherty relayed for the record exactly how Chris had twisted around so he was back-to-back with the dummy.

"And you testified earlier that you pulled 'really, really hard,'" the prosecutor said.

"Yes, sir," Chris said, the doll still on his back.

"You could have stopped there, right?" He pointed at Chris as they stood inches apart, the doll separating them.

"No," Chris replied.

"You already made your decision to kill her, and you were going to follow through on that decision," the prosecutor said.

"Yes," Chris mumbled.

Daugherty's goal was to show how long it took to kill someone in that position. As he questioned Chris, the prosecutor kept one eye on the clock.

"That was about ten seconds in," Daugherty said. "You could have stopped, right?"

Chris was facing the jury, his head hanging down, the dummy on his back. "No."

"Twenty seconds in? You could have stopped," Daugherty said.

"No," Chris muttered.

"Why not?"

"Nothing could have stopped me at this point," Chris said. "I was too angry."

As Chris demonstrated Erin's final, horrifying moments of life, Daugherty noticed the reaction from the jurors. Many of their expressions were pained, some fidgeted in their chairs and looked at the ceiling. One woman was crying.

"It was heavy," the prosecutor recalled. "It was one of the heavier moments I've had in court."

Standing in the middle of the courtroom, as Chris

tugged at the garrote, the seconds seemed to tick by slowly.

"We're about forty seconds in, you are still doing it," the prosecutor noted.

"Yes, sir." Chris remained hunched over in the center of the courtroom, head down.

"Now it's about a minute in. You're still doing it," Daugherty said.

"Yes, sir."

"And your testimony is, you couldn't stop. You couldn't just let go of those handles."

"No."

The doll was suspended in the air for over a minute and a half. Finally, the prosecutor instructed Chris to stop. Chris dropped the garrote, and the doll crumpled to the floor. Returning to the witness stand, Chris let out a deep breath.

"What part of Erin entered the shaft first?" Daugherty asked.

"She went in headfirst," Chris responded without a hint of emotion.

"And then you threw her down a mine shaft."

"I did."

"Like a piece of trash," Daugherty accused.

"I threw her down the mine shaft, yes." Chris remained expressionless.

"Like a piece of trash," the prosecutor repeated.

Staring vacantly at the court, Chris didn't speak.

"Right?" Daugherty's voice rose.

"Is that a question?" Chris asked.

"Yes."

Chris exhaled. "Yes."

On Tuesday, November 1, Chris Lee was back on the stand as the prosecutor continued his cross-examination.

Once again, Daugherty picked apart all of the inconsistencies in Chris's versions of events. If he really intended to go coyote hunting with Conor, why didn't he call him back? If he didn't want to have a "long, drawn-out" conversation with Erin about their future, why was he so persistent in insisting she accompany him to the desert for a surprise?

Daugherty also questioned Chris's claims that he was suicidal and playing Russian roulette every day for a month. Why would Chris try to kill himself if he was so worried about leaving Liberty without a father?

Most significantly, how did Chris happen to have a homemade garrote in his hand when he was suddenly filled with a murderous rage against Erin?

"I made the decision to kill her, I did," Chris testified. "To me, it was an instant and an eternity in the same moment."

Daugherty also asked about what happened to Erin's shoes, purse, cell phone, and car keys—none of which were ever recovered. If the events occurred the way Chris claimed, why weren't those items found in the mine with Erin?

Chris didn't have answers and blamed his fuzziness on the rage. Once he began strangling her, he maintained he was unable to stop.

"I was controlled by the anger. The hate commanded me," Chris said. "The hate I felt that day—it was something I never want to experience again."

Daugherty reminded the jury that Erin was defenseless.

"She had no idea what was coming," Daugherty said.

Daugherty's goal was to show the jury that Chris could not be believed because he was a liar.

"People lie for a reason," Daugherty remarked. "It

was important that I point out that he lies to protect himself."

In one of his final exchanges with Chris, Daugherty accused him of shaping his testimony to fit the evidence and trying to cast blame on Erin. He questioned why it had taken two years for Chris to admit what he had done.

"You chose to do it in front of the jury," Daugherty said. "It's about you. You wanted attention."

"I made the decision to kill her," Chris testified. "The moment I felt the garrote in my hand, it ignited my hatred."

"This is about you," the prosecutor repeated.

Chris, however, maintained he was repentant and ready to accept responsibility.

"I have to tell everyone what I did." Chris paused. "And accept the punishment they give me for it."

On redirect, David Kaloyanides asked about the demonstration with the doll and his perception of the time it took to kill Erin. Chris asserted that when he strangled Erin, time felt "fluid" and he was unable to make any distinction from the moment he realized the garrote was in his hand to the five minutes it took to kill his lover.

Chris stepped down from the witness stand, and Kaloyanides rested his case without calling any other witnesses.

During his rebuttal, Daugherty recalled Detective Woods to reestablish that Erin was not wearing shoes and did not have her car keys, purse, engagement ring, or cell phone when she was discovered in the mine shaft. The prosecution then rested the case.

Chapter 42

Speaking directly to the jury during his closing arguments on November 2, Daugherty talked about a shy young woman who loved horses as Erin Corwin's picture appeared on the screen behind him.

"This case, at its core, is about a young lady from Tennessee." Daugherty gestured to the picture. "The case is about the brutality inflicted upon her."

The perpetrator of that brutality was the defendant, Christopher Brandon Lee, the prosecutor proclaimed. The motive: He was finished with Erin and wanted her out of his life permanently.

"She was a secret who didn't want to be a secret anymore," Daugherty said.

At the defense table, Chris glanced at Erin's picture and blinked hard. Seated just a few feet behind him, Nichole's smile had long since vanished. She was wearing a black skirt suit, platform heels, and a giant cross around her neck, as if she were in mourning.

Pacing in front of the jury, Daugherty reminded them that Chris had invited Erin to the desert for a surprise, arguing that the hunting trip with his friends was a poor attempt at an alibi.

"This was a ruse," Daugherty said. "He was setting it up."

As for Chris's outrageous allegations that Erin molested Liberty, Daugherty reminded the jury that neither parent called the police, visited a pediatrician, or discussed these apparent concerns with military supervisors. He called the accusation "asinine garbage." As for Erin's confession in the desert: "This never happened."

The prosecutor then presented for the jury the events leading up to Erin's murder, from Chris's point of view.

On June 22, 2014, the same day Erin went to the emergency room and confirmed her pregnancy, Chris was exploring the mines in Joshua Tree National Park. By then, he already knew Erin was pregnant and was terrified that his wife would soon learn the truth.

Chris had plotted to get rid of his problem, researching ways to dispose of a body and asking a fellow Marine about a possible dump site. While simultaneously planning a surprise getaway with Erin to celebrate her pregnancy, Chris spoke to two friends about a weekend hunting trip to establish an alibi.

By June 28, he had gathered all the tools needed to commit murder—the propane tank, gasoline, and most disturbing of all, the garrote. Heartbreakingly, Chris used Erin's affections for him against her, luring her to the desert with the promise of romance. He waited until she turned her back before creeping up behind her.

"He strangulated the life out of her," the prosecutor said. "He came up behind her with a weapon of stealth and surprise."

On the screen behind Daugherty, Chris's disheveled mug shot appeared—looming above the now clean-cut defendant.

"If you think the defendant testified to express remorse, ladies and gentlemen, let me say this: The defendant is not remorseful." Daugherty's voice rose dramatically. "He didn't care. He didn't care when search and rescue and homicide and fire departments were putting their lives at risk looking for Erin. He didn't care that he was holding her mother hostage."

Daugherty implored the jury not to believe Chris's latest tale. "Can you trust someone who admits he lies to avoid consequences?"

The prosecutor also reminded jurors that Chris had lied to his own parents for more than two years. "If he lied to his own mother, what do you think he's going to do to you?"

Turning toward Chris, Daugherty wagged his finger. "He didn't care one bit until it came time to talk to you—the people who are going to decide what crime he is guilty of."

Daugherty said Chris's testimony was the lies of a "con man" designed to attempt to get the charges reduced to second-degree murder. "It was scripted, it was rehearsed, it was meant to con you."

Concluding his statements, Daugherty argued that a first-degree murder conviction was the only just verdict for Erin's murder.

"If a man crafts lies to suit his own needs and to everyone important in his life, what do you think he's going to do to you?"

Before Chris had taken the stand, defense attorney David Kaloyanides was given a second opportunity to present an opening statement in the case. Once again, he had declined, instead deciding to let his client speak for himself. Now, he addressed the jury directly for the first and only time to deliver closing arguments.

In a commanding and forceful tone, Kaloyanides argued that Erin's death was a tragic crime of passion, not a premeditated, cold-blooded murder. He claimed that the prosecution had failed to prove its case for first-degree murder with the special circumstance of lying in wait. Instead, a sentence of voluntary manslaughter fit the crime.

"Mr. Lee was provoked," the defense attorney told the jury. "Only you can decide whether that provocation is sufficient to justify the lesser included offense. Not justify the killing, because it wasn't justified."

As evidence, Kaloyanides pointed to the footage the search team had captured on the bucket camera as it was lowered into the mine. In the video, Erin's body was littered with broken rocks, and a tire appeared to cover her head. But the propane tank and Sprite bottle rested near the sides of the mines and didn't conceal Erin's body. Kaloyanides contended that the video proved Chris hurled Erin down the mine shaft only after tossing in all the material to blow up the mine—not as an attempt to incinerate her body.

The defense attorney also reminded the jury that Chris's plot to blow up the mine was reckless and sloppy. While he brought gasoline, he dumped it down the mine before dousing his torch. He hadn't been able to shoot the propane tank and never successfully ignited the blaze.

"How smart is he supposed to be?" Kaloyanides asked the jury. "He forgets to put gas on the torch . . . that's a smart con man?"

While the prosecutor described Chris as an icy, ruthless killer, Kaloyanides painted Chris as a careless, scared young man. Why else would Chris leave items with his DNA in the mine with her body?

"If he's so smart, why is he so stupid when it comes to a cover-up?" Kaloyanides said.

Such a chaotic crime scene proved that Chris never planned to kill Erin, the defense attorney contended.

Instead, it proved that Chris was a concerned father who simply snapped.

"You have to decide," he told jurors. "Was he provoked?"

Finally, Kaloyanides asked the jury to carefully weigh the evidence when deciding Chris's fate.

"Was it murder? Was it deliberate, willful, premeditated, lying-in-wait murder?" Kaloyanides pointed emphatically at the jury. "Or was it a tragic killing that shouldn't have happened?"

Daugherty had the last word in the form of his rebuttal.

He used the moment to challenge the defense's claim that the video showed a tire covering Erin's head. During the coroner's testimony, Dr. Frank Sheridan had told the jury that he believed one of the fractures to Erin's skull had happened while her heart was still beating. The cause of that wound was a blunt-force object to the head, not as a result of her body crashing into the floor of the mine.

Now, Daugherty suggested to the jury that wound was perhaps caused when Chris hurled the tire into the mine shaft in an attempt to incinerate Erin's body.

The prosecutor also equated Kaloyanides's last-minute plea to the jury to something out of the movie *The Wizard of Oz*.

Daugherty told the jurors, "Pay no attention to the man behind the curtain."

Jurors had sat through ten days of disturbing testimony from nearly two dozen witnesses. On November 2, the twelve men and women entered the jury room to decide Chris Lee's fate. Because it was already late in the afternoon, they had just enough time to elect a foreperson and set a schedule before adjourning for the day.

As the jurors filed out of the courtroom, Sean Daugherty couldn't help but worry. While he was confident that he had presented the strongest case possible, there was always a chance that even one juror could see things differently.

"You're always nervous. You lose years off your life from the time the jury leaves to the moment the verdict is read," Daugherty explained. "The best you can do as a prosecutor is present the truth."

The next morning, November 3, the jurors arrived at 10:00 a.m. and filed back into the jury room, conferring until the lunch break. Then, a few minutes after 1:00 p.m., word broke: A verdict had been reached. The jurors had only met for an hour and a half. Anxious, Lore returned to the courtroom and sat down in the gallery, surrounded by detectives, crime scene investigators, and a gaggle of search-and-rescue volunteers.

Chris appeared unruffled and nodded casually at Kaloyanides when the attorney joined him at the defense table. As the jurors funneled into the jury box, Chris glanced back at Nichole.

The courtroom fell silent as the jury foreman read the verdict.

"We the jury find the defendant, Christopher Brandon Lee, guilty of first-degree murder." The foreperson paused. "The defendant intentionally killed the victim by means of lying in wait."

Squeals of joy came from the gallery. At the defense table, Chris dropped his shoulders slightly and sighed but otherwise appeared unaffected. The sentence would be inevitable: State law required a sentence of life imprisonment without parole for homicides involving special circumstances.

Emotionally and physically exhausted, Lore Heavilin shuffled out of the courtroom. For more than two years, she had carried with her the heavy burden of grief.

"I could barely walk because it was so hard to lift my feet," Lore recalled.

Speaking with reporters, Lore told them that the verdict brought the family closer to closure. "[Erin] was taken away from us in a cruel manner," she said. "I feel like justice was done for my daughter."

For Jon Corwin, the verdict meant stepping out of the shadows of a murder suspect. He had been proven innocent.

"It was like taking a breath of fresh air," Jon explained.

As he left the courtroom, Daugherty turned to the cameras and said he was thankful that the jury had seen the truth.

"I'm glad the victim's family was able to get some sense of peace," Daugherty said. "I think the defendant's cold-blooded actions here were just devastating to that family."

That night, when Daugherty returned home to Victorville, he hugged his kids a little tighter than usual. Even though he'd won his case, he knew there weren't any real winners—just loss.

"Everything that Erin missed in life. All the beautiful things she could have seen and done in her life," Daugherty reflected. "It's just so sad."

For Sergeant Trevis Newport and the detectives who worked so hard to solve Erin's murder, the verdict was satisfying. But everyone seemed keenly aware of the enormity of the tragedy.

"Erin was a kid. She had her whole life ahead of her," Newport remarked. "She just didn't know that, in my opinion, she was dealing with the devil."

Following the verdict, the San Bernardino County district attorney sent out a press release.

"This was a terrible crime that showed absolutely no regard for the value of human life," District Attorney Mike Ramos wrote. "Erin Corwin was just a young girl with her entire life ahead of her. And now, all that's left is her memory. While justice was served today, it can only be a small consolation to her family and friends who will have to suffer a lifetime of pain knowing she died such a senseless death."

Chapter 43

While the jury had conferred for nearly two hours, deliberations lasted just fifteen minutes.

For ten days, retired California schoolteacher Donna Walker had sat in the front row of the jury box, taking copious notes. She'd always had an interest in the justice system. Over the years, she had intently watched several trials broadcast on television. In 2013, she and her husband had even driven down to Arizona to attend a day of testimony in the high-profile trial of Jodi Arias, an aspiring photographer who was convicted of slaughtering Travis Alexander, her ex-boyfriend.

Still, she said nothing could prepare her for the twisted testimony and ghastly evidence in Erin's case. By the time the jury began deliberations, Walker had already made up her mind that Chris was guilty.

"The evidence was overwhelming," Walker explained. "It became apparent that Chris had thought about and planned killing Erin for quite some time. I believe it was months. Even if that were not the case, it was obvious that he had the intention of killing her on the day he did it."

When court adjourned on the last day of testimony, however, Walker worried the other jurors hadn't seen it her way. The next morning when the jurors returned for deliberations, the foreperson realized there was just one copy of instructions from the judge and had to wait for the bailiff to make more copies. Once the instructions were handed out, each juror scanned the pages.

There were two main issues the jury had to tackle: Did Chris kill Erin, and was he "lying in wait" when he did it? For Walker, Chris's own testimony proved the prosecution's case.

"He had surprised us all by testifying and admitting the killing. When he demonstrated how it happened, I remember thinking, *Case closed,*" Walker recalled. "Because Erin was facing away from Chris when he attacked, he was lying in wait. Since he attacked from behind, it was already decided."

At least one juror, however, was not convinced Chris had planned to kill Erin before June 28. For a moment, Walker's heart sank. Then the juror explained that he did believe Chris intended to kill Erin once they had gotten to the desert, and Walker breathed a sigh of relief. They all agreed he was guilty. The jurors took just one vote, and it was unanimous.

But by the time they had received copies of the instructions, it was nearly noon. They decided to break for one last lunch together before telling the bailiff they had reached a verdict.

"We never looked at any evidence," Walker remarked. "There was no need."

Following the verdict, a victim's advocate escorted Lore and a small group of Erin's loved ones downstairs to where the jury would exit the courtroom. Lore carried a stack of twelve thank-you cards she had handwritten to each member of the jury. The cards read, "No matter what the verdict is, I want to thank you for giving up so much of your time for this."

"I had written them thank-you cards because I

wasn't sure if we would be allowed to tell them thank you," Lore recalled. "I just wanted God to shine through all this."

Surrounded by a gaggle of reporters and cameras on the main floor of the courthouse, Lore waited for the jurors.

"I just wanted to tell them thank you," Lore told the media. "I'm looking forward to not having to deal with this every week."

Out of the corner of her eye, Lore saw Nichole Lee sitting several yards away on a bench beside her brother, who was fiddling on his phone. Suddenly, the man rushed toward Lore, cell phone in hand, thrusting the screen toward her face. On it was a picture of Liberty.

"She remembers everything that was done to her," Nichole's brother sneered.

Lore was completely taken aback.

"We just turned around away from them," Lore recalled. "We weren't going to engage in that."

Moments later, Nichole sprang out of her seat, charging toward the group.

"She remembers every touch, every tickle!" Nichole shrieked. "She remembers everything!"

"Then Nichole starts screaming at the top of her lungs," Lore remembered. "We just kind of all looked around at each other. One of us said, 'Where in the world is this coming from?'"

Their blank expressions seemed to outrage Nichole. "Quit laughing!" she screeched. "Stop it!"

Lore glanced at her friend and back to Nichole. No one was laughing.

"OK," Lore said, stunned. "We weren't laughing, but that's fine."

The commotion had attracted the attention of one

of the security guards. The guard pulled Nichole aside and told her she needed to leave the courthouse. Stomping angrily past the media, Nichole shouted at reporters. "He's an ex-Marine. Put that camera down!"

Nichole and her brother were escorted from the courthouse a few moments before the jurors arrived. Lore was able to say thank you in person and deliver the cards personally. Several of the jurors had tears in their eyes as they hugged Erin's loved ones.

Chapter 44

L ore sat in the front row of the courtroom surrounded by her daughter, Kristy, and daughter-in-law, DeeAnna. United with the Heavilin family were Jon Corwin and his parents. Among the spectators in the gallery were a handful of the jurors, who all wore purple in honor of Erin.

It was Tuesday, November 29. Erin's family and friends had returned to San Bernardino one more time for Chris Lee's sentencing.

Each person in Erin's life had been impacted differently by her horrifying murder. For the first time, they were given the opportunity to explain that suffering to the court and to Chris. In the jury box, seated beside his attorney, Chris wore a blue jailhouse jumpsuit and the scruff of a beard. For more than an hour, as Erin's loved ones took turns reading heartrending statements, Chris sat wordlessly, staring straight ahead. Occasionally, he glanced at the person at the podium.

Jon gave a short statement, thanking the prosecutor, jurors, and investigators who helped bring Chris to justice. Older sister Kristy lamented the fact that her children would not get to grow up knowing their aunt.

"I feel I should've been able to protect Erin somehow," Kristy told the judge.

Sister Taylor was unable to attend the sentencing hearing. But in her victim impact statement, she wrote about the day she'd had to explain Erin's murder to her son.

"My shattered heart broke into a million pieces," Taylor wrote. "I became indifferent to God."

In their victim impact statements, family members implored the judge to sentence Chris to life without the possibility of parole. Taylor said they hoped Chris would use that time in prison to reflect on his crime and make amends to God.

"He has to be held accountable for his actions, whether in this life or the next," Taylor told the judge.

Sister-in-law DeeAnna Heavilin spoke emotionally about the effect that Erin's slaying had had on the family.

"Erin's murder has pushed and stretched and broken us in ways that no family should endure," DeeAnna said through tears. "When a family loses someone so senselessly, every little thing takes on a new meaning . . . I'll never be able to hear the words *strangle, propane, rebar,* or *mine* without being brought back into the hell that we've been thrust into for the past two years."

When it was Lore Heavilin's turn to speak, the courtroom fell silent.

"When Chris chose to plan and go through with the murder of Erin, my daughter, who is one of the most important people in my life, he took so much from me and many others," Lore told the court. "He took my breath of fresh air, my shy, loving, nurturing, trusting, naïve animal whisperer."

Since Erin's murder, Lore told the court she had been diagnosed with depression, panic attacks, anxiety, and post-traumatic stress disorder. Every day she felt the loss, most recently when quilting a blanket for her newest grandson.

"I realized I will never make a quilt for Erin's children," Lore said sadly. "That was an incredibly tough realization. The memories that we will never make with Erin because they have been stolen from us are too numerous to even think about beginning to list."

Before Erin left for Twentynine Palms, Lore told the court how she had tried counseling her daughter to prepare her for life as a Marine wife. One of the reasons Erin had married Jon when she did was so that she could live in the safe confines of the base.

"Little did we know that she would be living by a predator that wouldn't hesitate to take advantage of a trusting, naïve young lady that happened to move in beside him," Lore said.

Lore also acknowledged that her daughter had made a mistake in engaging in the affair.

"I'm not saying it was right for Erin to have an affair with Chris. That was so out of character for Erin that I still struggle to wrap my brain around it," Lore said. "Even if she made a conscious decision to have an affair with Chris, that does not justify a very planned-out murder."

With great empathy and compassion, Lore recognized that her family wasn't the only one suffering.

"My heart aches for his mom," Lore said. "I imagine her holding Chris after he was born and how excited she must have been. The dreams she had for him. How proud she must have been when he played sports and joined the Marines."

Finally, Lore expressed disbelief at the senselessness of it all. All Chris had to do was move to Alaska and change his number. Instead, he murdered Erin in an unbelievably cruel fashion.

"One of the things that haunts me to this day is wondering what she was thinking when he wrapped that garrote around her neck when she was out there with somebody that she trusted," Lore told the court. "Somebody that she thought loved her. What was going through her mind?"

With a stony expression, Chris rose from the jury box and briefly addressed the court.

"I cannot forgive myself," he said, insisting he understood the weight of his crime.

As he had in his testimony, Chris denied planning to kill Erin and said he was "truly sorry."

"I took the stand to tell the truth." Chris glanced at the gallery where Lore was seated. "I did this knowing that, because I took your daughter in an act of rage."

Chris said he had confessed to Erin's killing in an attempt to "save his humanity."

"I will accept punishment for the crime I committed, but I cannot, and will not, admit to crimes I did not commit," Chris said. "I did not want to kill Erin, and I did not plan to kill Erin."

The sentence of life without parole was already inevitable. Chris would spend the rest of his life in prison. But before delivering the sentence, the judge took a moment to address Erin's family. Through the trial, Mazurek said, he had gotten to know Erin as a young woman just starting her life.

"I'm sorry I can't give you true justice in this case, which is returning Erin to you," Mazurek said. "I'm sorry I can't return that vibrant person to you."

The crash of the gavel resonated through the courtroom, and just like that, it was over. Chris was transferred to a prison cell in the Richard J. Donovan Correctional Facility in San Diego, where he'll be known as inmate number BB8171.

Erin's killer had been brought to justice. Still, somehow the verdict felt hollow. It didn't change anything. Erin was still dead.

"It was kind of anticlimactic after what we had been through," Lore recalled.

For years, whenever Lore had thought about Erin's murder, she hated Chris. But being angry had only fueled further grief and wreaked havoc on her soul. With the strength of God, Lore did something remarkable: She forgave her daughter's killer. Forgiveness was a way to move on from Chris.

"I decided I refused to be bitter and angry. It wasn't hurting him, it was hurting me," Lore recalled. "I decided, he's already taken enough from me. If I'm bitter and angry, he's taking my mind, my soul, and my heart. And I'm not giving him that."

Abandoning that hate brought more peace. The darkness recessed, and glimmers of light shone through the tragedy. So many people had helped search for Erin—dedicated Marines, volunteer cavers, law enforcement officers, and firefighters had all fought tirelessly to find Erin. It was truly inspirational how much everyone cared.

"I feel like everyone involved in this case was taking it personally," Lore explained. "The rescue people were acting like it was their daughter, their sister, their niece, their aunt. It was that important to them to find her."

At home in Oak Ridge, that support continued as emails, cards, and gifts came from across the globe. Erin's story had touched so many strangers, who reached out to the Heavilins through email and Facebook. Intermixed with the messages of support were letters from desperate, grief-stricken parents struggling with the sudden death of a child. They had questions for Lore about living with loss. And through her own horrible experience, Lore was able to share some words of comfort.

"I believe God challenges you to go through things so you can be there for other people when they are going through it," Lore explained. "People helped me through it, so now it's my chance to help other people."

The Heavilins no longer think much about Chris Lee. Forgiving Erin's killer allowed them to forget about the disgraced former Marine.

Instead, they remember Erin as the girl who adored horses, dogs, cats, gerbils, and rabbits. To those who loved her, Erin Corwin will forever be just nineteen years old—on the cusp of becoming both a woman and a mother.

Afterword

O n the top of a lonely high-desert hillock, wildflowers bloom in a garden bordered by painted
purple boulders. Mauve-colored cacti sprout near a pile
of turquoise stones collected from the nearby mines.
A small concrete bench proclaims to visitors that they
have arrived at *Erin's Garden,* about twenty miles
southeast of Twentynine Palms.

The garden grows in Erin's memory in the same
desolate place where she took her last breath. After her
body was recovered from the unnamed mine, caver
Doug Billings built the garden on a hill five miles adjacent to the mine as a memorial. Periodically, he stops
by to water the flowers, tend the grounds, and send pictures to Lore in Tennessee.

While in town for the trial, Billings personally escorted Lore, Jessie Trentham, and a few of Erin's
friends to the garden. Sitting on the engraved bench,
Lore looked toward the mountain and could just make
out a landmark identifying the mine that had served
as Erin's tomb for eight weeks.

Tears blurred her vision. She closed her eyes and
blinked hard. This was the very last view her daughter had seen before she died.

Beneath the bench, shielded from the sun, was a

black book in a waterproof can. Flipping through the notebook, Lore saw page after page was filled with messages addressed to Erin and her family. Billings had left the registry for people touched by Erin's story to leave messages and condolences.

Scribbled on one page: "Saw your story on the news, and my heart went out to your family. I was very much praying for you." On another: "It's a beautiful garden for a beautiful soul taken way too soon." And on yet another: "Erin—we got him! Sentenced to life . . . I know you are resting in peace since you are with the Lord."

Since the trial, hundreds of locals and dozens of the volunteers and detectives who helped solve her murder have hiked to the garden to leave gifts of purple garden windmills and sculptures of horses. One person donated a plaque with the words: "And with your final heartbeat, kiss the world good-bye. Then go in peace and laugh on Glory's side."

Seeing all the trinkets and reading the messages was touching for Lore. Releasing a deep breath, she felt remarkably serene.

"The garden is beautiful, just like my girl," Lore remarked. "It's a peaceful place. I have a peace that can't be explained."

On the dirt floor of an abandoned mine shaft, the lifeless body of a pregnant Marine wife baked in the summer heat for eight long weeks in 2014. Miles from civilization, 140 feet below the earth's surface, Erin Corwin was never supposed to be found.

If not for colossal search efforts, Erin would have remained at the bottom of the mine until she was nothing but bones, the smell of decay dissipating on the desert winds. The case would have gone cold, and Erin's disappearance would have remained a mystery.

For her family, it would have been hell. Immersed indefinitely in a pit of agony, never knowing exactly where she was, clinging to the desperate hope she was still alive. Any parent who has ever lost a child knows the pain is excruciating. But it's the parents of the missing who experience permanent purgatory.

Meanwhile, Chris might have gone to college in Anchorage, made something of his life, and likely would have gotten away with murder.

The Heavilins thank God that never happened. To the family, the remarkable series of events that led to the recovery of Erin's body is nothing short of miraculous. The factors that came together on the last day of the search were both inexplicable and profound. In an interview following the verdict, even the prosecutor expressed a sense of wonder.

"I don't really have another explanation for it," Sean Daugherty reflected with a sigh. "Things just really fell into place."

The compassion and dedication of law enforcement, volunteers, firefighters, and Marines was awe-inspiring and erases some of the bitter bile spilled over Twentynine Palms that summer.

The Heavilins believed that God was with the rescuers in the desert on the very last day of the search. They just never realized that, in the confines of the Marine base, their daughter would encounter evil.

I did not want to write this book.

When I first heard about the missing Marine wife, it was the summer of 2014—just days into the search for Erin Corwin. In Phoenix, on the other edge of the Mojave, I lived just a few hours from Twentynine

Palms. At the time, I was finishing my third book and was emotionally spent from the brutalities of crime writing. I wasn't thinking as a journalist; I was just following news updates on the investigation, hoping she'd be found alive. Eight weeks later, when her corpse was recovered from the mine shaft, I knew I definitely did not want to write this book. It was just so horrific and sad.

But months passed, and I couldn't forget about Erin. There was something about her photo—that demure smile, the gentle blue eyes. She looked so young, so innocent. As her mom had feared when she moved to Twentynine Palms, Erin made mistakes. And her biggest mistake cost her her life. While young people often make bad choices while navigating their way into adulthood, most have the chance to learn, grow, and become the people they were meant to be. When Chris stole Erin's life, he robbed her of that chance.

So while I initially didn't want to write the book, something kept telling me I should. I had become a writer to tell people's stories and tended to gravitate toward impactful ones. Something about this story seemed very meaningful. I pitched the book to my publisher in the spring of 2016, months before the trial. With Lore Heavilin's blessing, I set out to tell Erin's story, pouring my heart into it like I do with all my books.

I wanted to tell the story of Erin's life. She was so much more than a murder victim. She was a daughter, a wife, a friend, a pet parent, and a beautiful soul. Erin had such potential, and her entire life in front of her. But then she met Chris Lee.

In Twentynine Palms, Chris Lee masqueraded as an honorable, valiant Marine. But the fatigues and dress blues were just a costume, camouflaging a beastly brute of a man. Chris used his overseas deployment as an excuse for wicked behavior back on base. He led a platoon, reported for duty, and saluted the American flag, all while plotting to strangle the life out of the woman who loved him.

After more than fifteen years of war with Afghanistan, there is little doubt the horrors of battle have had a lasting impact on the mental health of thousands of veterans. So many military members genuinely suffer from depression and post-traumatic stress disorder. Tragically, more than twenty veterans take their own lives each day.

Following his second tour of duty in Afghanistan, I do believe Chris Lee returned disturbed—but for a truly disturbing reason.

By his own admission, Chris didn't witness so much bloodshed overseas that he returned from war gravely despondent. In both his tours of duty, he never saw a single day of combat or fired his weapon at a threat. By his own admission, he didn't even miss his wife and daughter all that much while in Afghanistan. His biggest disappointment—and the reason he wanted to return to war—was because he had never gotten the chance to kill. There was a black spot on Chris's soul that wanted to know what it felt like to take a life.

Coupled with his dark obsession with death, Chris seemed to believe he had missed out on something during his time at war. As he grew disenchanted with his mundane, pedestrian life, he sought out the affections of his attractive teenage neighbor. I'd like to believe that at one point, Chris really did love Erin. The thought is somehow more comforting than the notion that Erin was just a fantasy he planned on snuffing out before he returned to Anchorage.

When he was caught cheating, Chris cowardly used depression and suicide threats as a shield to deflect blame. And he did it again on the witness stand, spewing stories of his own depression in a twisted bid for sympathy. Even after Nichole threatened divorce, Chris continued pursuing Erin.

Then she got pregnant. In early June 2014, when she told Chris she was having his baby, Erin unwittingly became a threat. Like a trained sniper, Chris targeted Erin in his scope.

It's a chilling and rarely cited statistic: The leading cause of death in expectant mothers is murder. While data is limited, recent studies found 20 percent of women who die while pregnant are murder victims. Most are killed by their domestic partners—husbands, boyfriends, and lovers.

Most famously in California, eight-month-pregnant Laci Peterson disappeared from her Modesto home on Christmas Eve 2002; her headless torso was later recovered from the San Francisco Bay. Two years later, her husband, Scott Peterson, was convicted of double homicide and sentenced to death.

It's only in recent years that the murder of pregnant women and their fetuses has been legally addressed, with the 2004 Unborn Victims of Violence Act classifying fetal deaths as murder if death occurred during the commission of the crime. Thirty-eight states, including California, have gone further, enacting even harsher penalties when a murder victim is pregnant. Because Erin's autopsy was inconclusive, there wasn't enough proof of her pregnancy to charge Chris with double homicide. But that doesn't mean Erin wasn't killed because of her unborn baby.

To keep Erin quiet about the pregnancy, Chris acted delighted to hear he'd be a father again. In one of the most unsettling facts I learned reporting the story, Chris had even been talking about baby names with Erin.

As a Marine, Chris had been trained that death was part of war—a necessary evil required to protect the lives, values, and ideals of Americans. Chris seemed to deeply internalize that message, justifying Erin's murder if it meant keeping his family together. He treated the murder as if it were a mission. On the witness stand, he even testified that when he killed Erin, "training kicked in," as if the military prepares Marines to strangle teenage girls to death.

But if he was trying to protect his family, Chris failed miserably. For in his attempt to spare Liberty from a broken home, Chris did something much wickeder: He betrayed every woman who ever loved him.

One stunning aspect of this case was how much truth was intermixed with Chris's lies. In his police interrogation and on the witness stand, Chris was remarkably honest about many of the facts of the murder. The lies were blended so seamlessly with the truth, it was as if Chris were cleverly toying with detectives.

But Chris was not clever. He practically led law enforcement to the mines, drawing a map of his route into the desert. To his fellow Marines, he gleefully dissected the best ways to dump a body like he was discussing a science fair project. To concoct an alibi, he invited friends on an inexplicable summer morning coyote hunting trip, while telling Erin the ruse was intended to fool his wife. Scoping out the battlefield, Chris even traveled to the mining district just six days before the murder. Then he assembled his weapons: fashioning a homemade garrote, borrowing a propane tank, collecting tires, and filling water jugs from the base with gasoline.

The most powerful weapon he used against Erin was her love for him, luring her to the desert with the promise of romance. Once at the mines, Chris had a rifle and could have ended Erin's life with a bullet. Instead, he killed her with his bare hands and brute force. Stealthily, he waited for Erin to turn her back and then pounced, wrapping the garrote around her neck, flipping himself around so they were back-to-back, and strangling her for five minutes before letting her body crumple to the desert floor. Dragging the corpse with the handles of the garrote, Chris tossed Erin headfirst down the shaft, then chucked in the tire and propane tank, poured in the gasoline, and ineptly attempted to incinerate the mine.

Foolishly, he didn't douse the torch with gasoline; because of the slope of the mine shaft, he was unable to shoot the propane tank. Instead, he departed the desert, leaving Erin's body to decompose, assuming the mine was so remote that no one would ever find it. Returning to the apartment, Chris took a nap with his wife and watched cartoons with his daughter, devoid of any guilt or remorse. While he thought he could get away with it, he had no idea his sinister scheming had left a trail of evidence leading detectives directly to Erin's open grave.

Was Chris so self-destructive that he wanted to get caught? Maybe he was "too dumb" to keep his lies straight, as Nichole told Isabel Megli. But I have come to believe Chris was so perilously arrogant he thought he'd get away with it. After all, Erin was never meant to be found.

After he was arrested, Chris stewed in prison for two years before finally confessing in court, in what he claimed was an attempt to "save his humanity." But that was another pathetic lie. His claims of a sudden passion slaying were just another effort to save his own life. In the vilest, sickest twist of all, I believe he used his own daughter in an outrageous attempt to portray Erin as a child molester. It was offensive and so preposterous that not one juror seemed to give it a second of consideration, arriving at a guilty verdict in fifteen minutes.

Since the verdict, Chris has doubled down on those abominable allegations. In his first appeal, he claimed through his new attorney that the judge made an error by not properly instructing the jurors to consider his "heat of passion" defense. If even one juror understood that Erin had provoked Chris and he'd simply snapped, then he would have only been convicted of manslaughter, he argued. It's just more proof Chris has no remorse; any humanity he may have once possessed has long since vanished. In August 2018, that appeal was denied.

While at first I didn't want to write this book, after deciding to share the story, I knew I didn't want the focus to be on Chris. Still, as a journalist, I reached out to him in prison through letters and his attorney. He declined to speak, citing his upcoming appeal.

I wasn't disappointed. Really, what is there left to say? Give another excuse for murdering Erin? Lay the blame at someone else's feet? Or spew more lies about the woman he so brutally murdered?

He'd already told his story in his police interrogation and in courtroom testimony—which I used to present his sides of the story in this book. Beyond that, I doubt I'd glean any valuable insight into Chris. For when Chris admitted to strangling Erin, he told the world all it ever needed to know about the dishonorable dullard who killed his pregnant lover.

From the beginning, it was obvious to me and the

jury that Chris killed Erin to rid himself of her pregnancy. The enduring mystery for me is Nichole. Both the homicide detectives and the prosecutor once considered her a person of interest, although cell phone records indicated she never left base that day. Still, her cold, cruel behavior following Erin's disappearance led detectives to believe she may have known more than she revealed. While she was never charged with any wrongdoing, the prosecutor has not ruled out the possibility of charging Nichole with something in the future, if further evidence warrants it. I also reached out to Nichole through her attorney, but she never responded.

But even if Nichole didn't know then that Chris killed Erin, she knows now and has chosen to remain married to a convicted murderer. She's traded in her lonely life as a Marine wife for the bleak existence of a prison wife.

Chris Lee got exactly what he deserves. Savage beasts belong in cages.

Unlike some cunning killers who cause deep public fascination, Chris is too basic and dumb to be fascinating. He's a cruel thug who cares about no one but himself.

Locked away in a six-by-eight-foot cell for the rest of his life, Chris will grow older, but he won't really ever move beyond the summer he ruined his family. As he appeals the verdict, Chris will live perpetually in 2014, retelling his stories to judges, lawyers, and corrections officers.

I don't know what will happen to Chris and Nichole as a couple. For a while, I suppose she will continue with phone calls, letters, and occasional visits. She may never divorce Chris, clinging to thirty-minute phone calls with nothing but her husband's cold steel dog tags for support. And Liberty won't grow up with a father figure to help her with her homework, celebrate her birthdays, and one day walk her down the aisle.

Perhaps Chris is selfish enough to wish such a sad fate upon his own family. But I pray her father's twisted lies don't haunt Liberty. I hope she doesn't grow up questioning whether or not she was a victim of sexual abuse. Most of all, I pray she never encounters anyone who treats her with the same cruelty as her father treated Erin.

There should not be any more suffering from Erin's death. Nobody wants that sort of vengeance. Not the police, not the prosecutor, not the Heavilin family, and not me.

Like the desert garden, those left in the hellish aftermath of Erin's murder have grown some beauty from this tragedy.

Jon has since remarried. Months after returning to Oak Ridge, he met his wife. He has since completed training and is working as a welder in Oak Ridge. Still, when he thinks of Erin, he is heartbroken.

"I sure wish I could have been there for her more," Jon said wistfully. "I tried my hardest, but it wasn't enough."

Lore and the Heavilin family take comfort in all the humanity that arose from the tragedy. As she told me, "God touched people's lives through Erin, and He is continuing to do so."

Lore still keeps in contact with Detective Dan Hanke and many of the rescuers, jurors, and several of Erin's friends. In retirement, she and Bill spend their time visiting their children and grandchildren.

Meanwhile, many of the San Bernardino County Sheriff's detectives who worked on Erin's case continue to serve in the department. Trevis Newport is now a lieutenant with the department's Bureau of Administration. Jonathan Woods still works in homicide and has been promoted. Dan Hanke is now a sergeant in the homicide division. And just in case Chris Lee is curious, Hanke completed his detective career with a perfect clearance rating of always recovering the missing person he was searching for.

I only realized how much I didn't want to write this book after I started writing it. I spent most of 2017 researching the story in a chaotic year consumed by partisan divide, deadly natural disasters, and mass shootings. I avoided my laptop, asked for two extensions, and genuinely questioned why I ever wanted to write the book. There were many sleepless nights and lots of tears.

But as I dug deeper, I found an inspirational tale of humanity buried under all the loss. One evil man extinguished Erin's life, but hundreds of good people sacrificed so much to bring her family justice. I realized that's the story I wanted to tell—one of homicide detectives sleeping in their cars outside Joshua Tree. Of firefighters staving off bee attacks and dehydration in the middle of the Mojave. And of brave volunteers plunging down pitch-black mine shafts during the scorching summer of 2014.

Finally, there was one more story I wanted to tell: that of a heroic adventurer who has served his final rescue mission.

August 3, 2017

The rapids flowed fiercely, spilling high onto the rocky banks of the Kings River in south-central California. Tethering his climbing rope to a boulder,

Luca Chiarabini waded into the water, wearing a helmet, wetsuit, and fins. But no life jacket.

One of California's most prolific canyoneers, Chiarabini was among the seasoned volunteers with the San Bernardino County Cave and Technical Rescue team, with which he had assisted in dozens of searches, including the recovery of Erin Corwin nearly three years prior. But on August 3, 2017, it was Chiarabini who needed rescuing.

The previous morning, he and two fellow adventurers had hiked down to the riverbank in the Yucca Point area, northeast of Hume Lake. Crossing the river, they camped overnight on the north shore. The next morning, the trio began to cross back to the south shore. The plan was for one person to swim across the river with a rope to help the others cross.

As was typical for Chiarabini, he was the first to volunteer. Wading into the water, he was more than two-thirds across the river when he lost his footing and the current swept him downstream. He signaled for his partners on shore to yank him back. But the rope pooled in a tangled heap. His teammates could not pull the slack quick enough, and Chiarabini was swept farther down the river.

The line went tight. Chiarabini was trapped. One of his buddies made a split-second decision to cut the rope. But the rope caught on the rocks, dragging Chiarabini's body underwater. His teammates activated his emergency beacon, equipped with inReach Satellite Technology, which notified the Fresno County Sheriff's Office to respond. But it was too late. That afternoon, a sheriff's helicopter spotted Chiarabini's body downriver. It took a full day before he could be brought to shore.

While they were experienced adventurers who

were typically prepared, Chiarabini and his team were unaware the water in Kings River was flowing at a faster pace than in years past. The summer had been unseasonably warm; for eight days in June, temperatures from Fresno to Bakersfield exceeded one hundred degrees. Thousands of feet above the Kings River, in the Sierra Nevada, the heat surge melted California's historic snowpack. The melting snow poured in at an overwhelming rate from the reservoir into the Kings River.

At forty-seven, Luca Chiarabini was pronounced dead. He was remembered by his fellow rescuers for his passion for adventure and exploration. And for being the very first to volunteer to descend into the fume-filled mine shaft on August 16, 2014, to recover the body of Erin Renae Corwin.

Author's Note

This book is a journalistic account of a true story. The quotes used to compile this book were obtained from interviews with sources, trial testimony, court documents, television programs, and newspaper articles. Conversations portrayed in the book have been reconstructed using trial testimony, extensive research, interviews, and press accounts.

All of the names, dates, and locations mentioned throughout the book are factual. The only names changed were Tiffany and David Peterson.

Although Christopher Lee has been convicted by a jury of his peers of first-degree murder, he has since filed an appeal of the verdict, which was denied.

Acknowledgments

As I typed the final words of the afterword for this book, I wept, overcome by emotions. My fingertips went numb, my mouth went dry. I couldn't swallow, could barely type.

My fourth true-crime book is the saddest story I've ever written. While every homicide case is awful, this one affected me deeply because of the sheer loss of life and potential. But while Chris was a selfish, evil killer, I met so many wonderful people through this story.

First, I'd like to thank Lore Heavilin for working closely with me on this book. For more than a year, she spent countless hours helping me with both the details of her daughter's life and her personal struggle as the mother of a murder victim. Her strength and dignity in the face of horrifying circumstances was inspirational.

True-crime writers have to go where the interviews take them. Grief affects people in different ways, and I always try to be respectful traipsing through people's lives. Not everyone in Erin's family wanted to speak to me, which I respected. Regardless, I've gained tremendous respect for the entire Heavilin family—good people who never deserved such enormous pain.

As a wrongfully accused murder suspect, Jon Corwin endured more suspicion than anyone should. I developed great admiration for the fortitude he showed throughout the last few years. He really, truly loved Erin. But they were just both so young.

My heart also went out to Jessie Trentham. As Erin's best friend and the protector of her secrets, the murder was particularly agonizing. She'd never spoken to the media before, and I'd like to thank her sincerely for speaking exclusively with me for this book. I hope I did her story justice. To Aisling Malakie, who also shared her story for the first time, thank you. Raising the baby girl she named Erin, she thinks of her lost friend almost every day.

To Trevis Newport, Daniel Hanke, Jonathan Woods, and the hundreds of law enforcement officials—it was a true honor to watch your passionate fight for justice. As Sean Daugherty told me, "The sheriff's team were such badasses." It was true—there was never any doubt they'd find Erin. Special gratitude to Mr. Daugherty for interviewing with me and helping me navigate some of the legal aspects of this case.

I was particularly inspired by the bravery of the volunteer search-and-rescue teams who scoured the desert for Erin. In particular, I'd like to thank Doug Billings and John Norman, who set up interviews with the rescuers, including with the late Luca Chiarabini, who died just three months after I first interviewed him. I was shocked and saddened by his death and decided to include his story in this book as a tribute to his memory. I will be donating a percentage of my personal royalties from this book to the brave volunteers of the San Bernardino County Cave and Technical Rescue team.

Personally, I'd like to thank my former journalism professor turned friend, Christia Gibbons, for her editing expertise and for being my very first reader. I've learned so much from you, and your friendship is one of the most meaningful relationships in my life.

I also owe special gratitude to my literary agent, Sharlene Martin, for her continual support of my career. Additionally, thank you to my superb editors at St. Martin's Press: Sarah Grill and Charles Spicer.

To my entire family—namely, my aunts Teri Hooper and Elaine Flowers, as well as my grandmother Carol "Mimi" Hogan—I love and appreciate all your continued support. Also thank you to my mom, Debbie Hogan, the kindest, strongest woman in my life.

Most importantly, I would like to thank my best friend and husband, Matt LaRussa, for always being there for me. Matt is a Navy veteran who served from 1992 to 1996. Throughout the writing process on four books, he supported and encouraged me, comforted me when I was miserable, and never let me give up. I wouldn't have achieved what I have in my career without him. Thank you, Matt, for being the love of my life.